EMOTIONS, ETHICS, AND CINEMATIC EXPERIENCE

# Emotions, Ethics, and Cinematic Experience

New Phenomenological and Cognitivist Perspectives

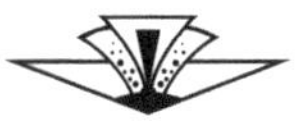

*Edited by*
*Robert Sinnerbrink*

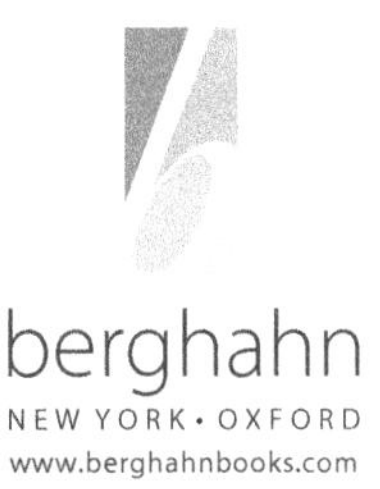

berghahn
NEW YORK · OXFORD
www.berghahnbooks.com

Published in 2021 by
Berghahn Books
www.berghahnbooks.com



Originally published as a special issue of *Projections*,
Volume 13, issue 2 (2019).



**Library of Congress Cataloging-in-Publication Data**

Control Number: 2021937635

**British Library Cataloguing in Publication Data**

A catalogue record for this book is available from the British Library

ISBN 978-1-80073-144-8 hardback
ISBN 978-1-80073-145-5 paperback
ISBN 978-1-80073-146-2 ebook

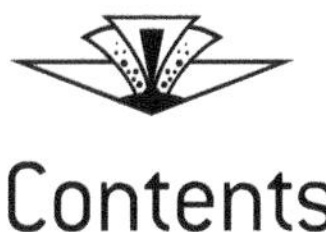

# Contents

# Illustrations

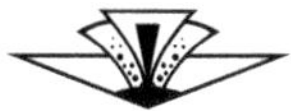

# Preface

**Robert Sinnerbrink**

In recent years, a debate has emerged over the question of film theory and the humanities, and the relationship between philosophy of film and empirical research/ scientific modes of theorization. Murray Smith (2018), for example, has called for a naturalised aesthetics of film, arguing for a pluralistic naturalism that would supplement and support, rather than renounce or replace, humanistic modes of inquiry concerning cinema. D.N. Rodowick (2007, 2015), by contrast, has criticised analytic-cognitivist approaches for being reductivist and ethically deficient, and pleaded for a humanistic film-philosophy that foregrounds our ethical commitments while remaining independent of reductive 'scientism'. At bottom, this debate turns on whether we take naturalistic and humanistic approaches to be compatible and complementary, or else opposed and incommensurable. Linked to this is the question of how best to acknowledge the ethical and ideological dimensions of film (and our ways of theorizing it): does a commitment to naturalism, for example, entail an indifference towards, or inability to acknowledge, these ethical and ideological dimensions? Alternatively, does a commitment to 'humanistic' modes of inquiry—whether understood in hermeneutic, descriptive, critical, constructivist, or speculative terms—demand a dismissal or empirical research or intellectual indifference towards causal-explanatory accounts of phenomena?

The wager of this book—and of the Special Journal Issue of *Projections* from which it derives—is twofold. First, that we need not accept such false dilemmas pitting naturalism against humanism, hermeneutic against explanatory accounts, cognitivist film theory as opposed to film-philosophy, and so on. Second, that a pluralist or compatibilist approach will enhance, rather than enervate, philosophical, aesthetic, and ethical inquiry into film. Indeed, this book treats the debates outlined above in an exploratory and experimental spirit. Instead of adopting a fixed *a priori* position 'for or against' either side, participants were invited to explore the crossovers, compatibilities, and productive possibilities of interdisciplinary inquiry, with the aim of bringing phenomenological and cognitivist perspectives on contemporary cinema into productive dialogue and inventive exchange. The focus, in particular, was on the multifaceted relationship between emotion, ethics, and cinematic experience, broadly construed, exploring the ways in which both cognitivist and phenomenological approaches might work together to enhance our understanding of important philosophical and ethical issues in contemporary film theory/philosophy of film. Instead of arcane metaphilosophical discussions about the ethical/epistemic virtues and vices of particular approaches, or general arguments concerning the 'theoretical correctness' of one's preferred paradigm, the contributors to this volume take a pragmatic and exploratory approach, testing their theoretical perspectives in a variety of contexts and in response to a wide range of problems, debates, and audiovisual works.

The result is a stimulating, productive, and innovative series of chapters spanning a rich and exciting array of topics. These include cognitivist aesthetic analyses of the 'fascist affect' in Zack Snyder's *300*; a phenomenological aesthetics exploring perception, touch, and our relationship with animality in Laurie Anderson's *Heart of a Dog*; and a phenomenological account of 'elemental imagination' and its important ecocritical and ethical significance. There is a hybrid model of 'distributed affectivity' offered that is applied to films dealing with experiences of trauma and historical dislocation; philosophical and ethical reflections on objectivity in observational documentary; and a descriptive-conceptual mapping of 'synthetic beings' in new digital media, including the need to develop a 'synthespian ethics' in response to the challenges raised by virtual digital entities. The authors, who encompass a range of theoretical and philosophical backgrounds, thereby demonstrate how a pluralistic approach, spanning the 'naturalistic/phenomenological' divide, can yield rich results, enhancing our understanding of the complex nexus between ethics, emotion, and cinematic experience. Indeed, this focus on the relationship between emotional engagement, aesthetic experience, and ethical reflection requires a pluralistic approach, one capable of describing and explaining, analysing and evaluating, criticizing and exploring the many dimensions of cinematic experience understood in a holistic manner and as an object of interdisciplinary inquiry. Despite the lively debate concerning the future of philosophical film theory in the academy, and its complex relations with both humanistic and naturalistic traditions, reports of the death of (film) theory have been greatly exaggerated—as I hope the contents of this book will make clear.

Finally, I would like to thank our authors for their excellent contributions, for their co-operation and diligence, and for showing by example how a pluralistic approach to philosophical film theory might work. I would also like to thank my editors at Berghahn for inviting us to publish the *Projections* Special Issue in book form, and for all their patient, helpful, and timely assistance along the way, especially during these difficult pandemic times.

## References

Rodowick, D. N. 2007. 'An Elegy for Theory'. *October* 122 (Fall): 91–109.
Rodowick, D. N. 2015. *Philosophy's Artful Conversation*. Cambridge, MA. and London: Harvard University Press.
Smith, Murray. 2018. *Film, Art, and the Third Culture: A Naturalized Aesthetics of Film*. Oxford: Oxford University Press.

# Introduction
## Phenomenology Encounters Cognitivism

**Robert Sinnerbrink**

Contemporary philosophical and theoretical inquiry into cinema has become increasingly interdisciplinary. With the rise of influential phenomenological and cognitivist approaches focusing on cinematic experience and aesthetic inquiry, the possibility of a productive synthesis of these hitherto opposed approaches has now emerged as a growing trend in contemporary research (see D'Aloia 2012, 2015; D'Aloia and Eugeni 2014; Ingram 2014; Rhym 2018; G. Smith 2014; M. Smith 2018; Stadler 2008, 2011, 2016, 2018; and Yacavone 2015). Despite the welcome work of individual theorists, and the increasing pluralism evident in leading film journals, the two approaches still remain frequently estranged from each other. Or where there is no theoretical conflict, they can remain confined within well-defined disciplinary and institutional boundaries, thus rendering the possibility of a synthetic or pluralistic approach more of a promissory note than a live possibility.

This special volume is therefore dedicated to exploring the ways in which phenomenological and cognitivist approaches offer complementary and overlapping ways of theorizing our experience of film.

The central focus is on the relationship between emotion, ethics, and cinematic experience, drawing on phenomenological and cognitivist perspectives, and showing how theoretical reflection on cinematic experience works hand-in-hand with close analysis of particular films. This volume features authors noted for their work on cognitivist as well as phenomenological approaches, and aims to show the rich theoretical possibilities opened up once we regard these as having open borders rather than fixed boundaries. The chapters featured here tend to emphasize one or another of these approaches but also show how they might be brought together in innovative ways. They focus on a range of related topics and diverse film examples in order to illuminate different aspects of cinematic spectatorship. These include topics such as the workings of affect, emotion, and mood; exploring new ways of theorizing subjectivity and objectivity in film; the ethical implications of new digital technologies; and the practical significance of imaginative aesthetic engagement with both narrative and nonfictional works. They also suggest ways in which we might enrich our investigation of contemporary cinema by drawing on what both theoretical methodologies have to offer while remaining committed to analyzing key aesthetic and contextual features of complex cinematic works.

In what follows, I outline the shared theoretical *problématique* defining the encounter between phenomenology and cognitivism, and argue for a more pluralistic and synthetic approach to film inquiry. What I call a "dialectical synthetic" approach offers the possibility of combining "thick" phenomenological description of cinematic works and aesthetic experience with empirically grounded, cognitivist explanatory accounts of the causal processes behind such phenomena. There is a productive and exciting space of interdisciplinary inquiry opening up where the attention to subjective experience, aesthetic engagement, and the close analysis of form intersects with theoretical models of explanation grounded in empirical research. In this way, we can do justice to both the experiential and aesthetic richness and complexity of cinema and offer explanatory models that promise to make a modest but important contribution to explaining how these works achieve their powerful aesthetic and ethical effects.

### Cinematic Ethics: Phenomenology and Cognitivism

One of the areas of contemporary theoretical inquiry in which a synthetic approach is not only desirable but necessary is what I have elsewhere called "cinematic ethics" (Sinnerbrink 2016): the idea of cinema as a medium of ethical experience, where the power of film to elicit affective, emotional, and cognitive responses to moral situations contributes to the generation of complex forms of ethical experience prompting critical reflection. Although there has been much work on spectatorship, on the one hand, and ethical aspects of film production and reception, on the other, the manner in which particular kinds of cinematic experience can be ethically significant, whether in evoking different kinds of subjective or social experience, challenging our habitual beliefs or settled convictions, or prompting empathic/sympathetic engagement with sociocultural perspectives differing from one's own, is now finally receiving the theoretical attention that it deserves (see Grønstad 2016; Plantinga 2009, 2018; Sinnerbrink 2016; and Stadler 2008). Drawing out the ethical significance or socially transformative effects of film experience requires a combination of both phenomenological theory and cognitive theory along with contributions from other empirically as well as socially and historically grounded approaches. From this point of view, cinematic ethics is one important way in which phenomenological and cognitivist approaches might be brought together in order to better theorize emotional engagement and moral understanding evoked via cinematic means.

Indeed, there are already impressive attempts to explore, from phenomenological, cognitive, and philosophical perspectives, the ethical significance of our aesthetic experience of cinema (see Grønstad 2016; Hanich 2010; Plantinga 2018; and Stadler 2008). Such approaches place an emphasis on the "subjective" phenomena of affect, emotion, and mood, but also on more "objective" cognitive processes of critical reflection, questioning, and moral evaluation. Together, we can arrive at a more descriptively rich but also more explanatorily powerful ways of thinking about various aspects of cinematic experience, questions of ontology and aesthetics, and aesthetic features of the medium. To do this, however, phenomenology and cognitivist theory should work together: we need both phenomenologically "thick" descriptive as well as cognitive explanatory accounts complementing and mutually informing each other in order to do justice to the complexity of cinematic experience. We might call this a "dialectical" intellectual encounter or transformative philosophical exchange, one that synthesizes relevant elements of both approaches in order to better articulate the whole.

Why has there hitherto been much misunderstanding or mutual suspicion between these approaches? At one level, this is no doubt due to the background dispute between traditions of film or screen theory influenced by European "Continental" philosophical traditions and those more recent developments rejecting this paradigm, which draw instead on analytic aesthetics and empirically grounded forms of cognitivist theory (see Nannicelli and Taberham 2014; and Sinnerbrink 2011). Although the polemical character of this dispute has largely dissipated, the lack of familiarity across the so-called "divide" still breeds suspicion, if not contempt, in some quarters. Deleuzians, film phenomenologists, and "affect" theorists sometimes accuse cognitivists of a dogmatic scientific "imperialism" that ignores culture, history, and politics, whereas cognitivists and analytic philosophers of film criticize the former in turn for impressionistic and associative approaches to theorization, a dogmatic deference to "master thinkers," and overestimation of film interpretation as equivalent to film theory (see Sinnerbrink 2011). Yet there is much common ground between both approaches, despite differences in background traditions, theoretical commitments, and epistemic attitudes toward the relationship between the sciences and the humanities. As Murray Smith argues (2018), a pluralistic rapprochement between these traditions is needed; C.P. Snow's "Two Cultures" problem still persists in film theory / philosophy of film, which means that efforts to address and overcome this opposition are as important as ever. Indeed, Smith's own conception of the need for a "triangulation" of aesthetic experience—recognizing the interplay of phenomenological, psychological, and neurophysiological dimensions of our experience of art—is a good example of the synthetic approach that I have in mind.

One area that presents obvious overlap and affinities (and that reveals underlying theoretical differences) is theoretical inquiry into affect and emotion in cinema. Both phenomenologists and cognitivists agree on the importance of embodied experience, contextualized or "embedded" in sociocultural niches, mediated via technological prosthetic devices (extended), and with an emphasis on activity, interactivity, and modes of communicative and pragmatic exchange (enactive). Cinema itself can be understood in relation to the idea of the extended mind, with scholars now exploring the ways in which 4E (embodied, embedded, extended, and enacted) theories of cognition open up new paths of inquiry into diverse aspects of cinematic experience (see Coëgnarts and Kravanja 2015). On the other hand, the tendency of phenomenology to privilege the "primacy of perception" (as per Merleau-Ponty), often reverting to first-person experiential perspectives as evidence for theoretical claims, can come into tension with cognitivists' emphasis on empirically grounded explanatory models that attempt to articulate the underlying causal processes and neurological, perceptual, and cognitive operations that make such phenomenological experience possible. In many ways, however, this represents something of a false or misleading dichotomy, since it is precisely in the interaction between phenomenological and cognitive perspectives that we are able to develop theoretical models that can do justice to both subjective and objective dimensions of cinematic experience. Were Merleau-Ponty alive today, he would doubtless be drawing on 4E cognitive theory as much as embodied phenomenological approaches (many of which are inspired by his work).

Another common source of theoretical confusion and misunderstanding concerns the different methodologies that film phenomenologists and cinematic cognitivists draw upon. We could roughly describe these as descriptive/experiential versus empirical/explanatory approaches. The role of heuristic strategies or reasoning protocols, which can include the use of cognitive shortcuts, illuminating ideas, synthetic concepts, or suggestive metaphors, differ widely in these two approaches. By theoretical heuristics, I mean exploratory ideas or theoretical framing perspectives that can enable us to "see" or articulate a phenomenon more clearly, make theoretical or conceptual connections, draw productive parallels, test theoretical or empirical claims, compare competing perspectives, or develop theories creatively and critically. The idea of the mind/brain as an information-processing device (computer) or of cinema as a "film-body" are two influential theoretical heuristics in philosophical film theory that have enabled productive inquiry but that have also generated certain theoretical confusions. For every productive connection or insight gained thanks to a suggestive parallel or analogy, there are also misleading inferences and important disanalogies that are not to be gainsaid.

This means that we need to be methodologically reflective or self-critical in our use of theoretical heuristics, being mindful of the temptation to take them to designate empirical realities or provide theoretical evidence (neither of which they necessarily do). The mind/brain differs in many ways from a computer (computers are neither embodied nor socially, culturally, and historically embedded, for example, a point that both phenomenologists and 4E cognitive theorists take very seriously), whereas the "film-body," like our own bodies, is also embedded within a relational world articulated through practical engagements and shaped by shared horizons of meaning—an aspect curiously omitted in most haptic or "embodied" modes of phenomenological film theory, which assume something of a worldless "body in a vat" approach to their descriptions of cinematic engagement.

Both phenomenological and cognitivist approaches use heuristics that are productive and useful for practices of film theorization, but they would also benefit from further critical self-reflection on the methodological and epistemic benefits and drawbacks of using such devices as ways of bootstrapping the construction of theories. We should remain mindful of the methodological need to combine "thick" description of phenomena with empirical explanatory accounts of the causal processes underlying these phenomena. In short, it is important to acknowledge the productive role of theoretical heuristics and heuristic perspectives, but also not to confuse heuristic approaches or devices with descriptive or explanatory approaches as such.

### Phenomenological Approaches to Film

As Christian Ferencz-Flatz and Julian Hanich remark, providing a coherent overview of film phenomenology is no easy task; it requires surveying a large and sprawling field, "the contours of which seem to be as vague as the foggy landscapes in an Antonioni or Angelopoulos film" (2016, 11).

One of the key challenges is simply defining what we mean by "phenomenology": if the definition is overly broad (referring to any approach that focuses on subjective experience), then the term becomes so inclusive that even structuralist approaches can count as having a "phenomenological" dimension; if the definition is too narrow or strict (as in Husserl's foundational descriptive science dedicated to articulating universal, invariant structures of consciousness via the phenomenological *epoché* and detached contemplation of "essences" (*Wesensanchauung*)), then almost no film theory would count as properly phenomenological in any robust sense (Ferencz-Flatz and Hanich 2016). Here, I strike a middle course. I acknowledge, on the one hand, that film phenomenology refers to a pluralistic set of theoretical approaches foregrounding subjective embodied experience, and that it is an essentially descriptive approach focusing on detailed or "thick" description, interpretation, and analysis of relevant aspects of cinematic experience. And on the other, I recognize that if phenomenology is to mean more than merely cataloguing one's personal or idiosyncratic impressions of a film, it ought to aim at shared structures or common features of our embodied engagement with cinema, providing a descriptively rich interpretation and analysis of subjective phenomena that in turn can provide the basis for further (explanatory or contextualizing) theorization.

The relationship between phenomenology and film theory has, historically speaking, been rather halting and interrupted. With the exception of Merleau-Ponty's occasional essays and remarks dealing with film, "classical" and existential phenomenologists have generally ignored or dismissed it (e.g., Husserl and Heidegger). French phenomenology (drawing on Husserl and Heidegger but largely shaped by Merleau-Ponty and Sartre) was brought to bear on film by theorists such as Amédée Ayfre, Henri Agel, and Jean-Pierre Meunier, as well as by individuals working within the interdisciplinary model of the *filmologie* movement (Ferencz-Flatz and Hanich 2016; Hanich and Fairfax 2019). In the Anglophone world, however, it was not until the 1990s that phenomenology was properly introduced, thanks to the groundbreaking work of Vivian Sobchack (1992, 2004) (with a contribution from Allan Casebier). Sobchack's approach, adopted by many of her followers, has always been eclectic, drawing on elements of Husserl but largely drawing on concepts from Merleau-Ponty. It also combined concepts and approaches from both Merleau-Ponty's earlier (primacy of perception) and later (chiasmus and "the flesh") phases of philosophical inquiry. This eclecticism has become a hallmark of contemporary film phenomenology, including the addition of Deleuzian as well as cognitivist elements with the rise of "affect theory" and embodied approaches to cinematic experience (Barker 2009; Marks 2000, 2002; Massumi 2015; Pisters 2012).

Within this eclecticism, it is worth noting two difficulties. The first is the risk of conflating everyday and technical senses of "phenomenology"—that is, a broad conception of subjective experiential processes versus hermeneutic interpretation and formal analysis of particular aspects of consciousness or our "being-in-the-world" (Heidegger). The eclectic approach also runs the risk of offering first-person experiential "evidence" as though this would suffice for phenomenological demonstration. It is worth recalling, however, that "classical" phenomenology always aimed at invariant, *universal* features of consciousness; in film phenomenology, by contrast, there is typically a particularist focus on "the body," affect, emotion, spectatorship, interpretation, and evaluation coupled with "symptomatic" readings of film as reflecting these "particularist" theoretical emphases. Whatever its theoretical provenance, phenomenology has always emphasized the importance of a descriptive account of situated experience of embodied spectators always already embedded within a meaningful social and historical world. It also focuses on corporeal, affective, aesthetic, and ethical aspects of film experience from a "bottom-up" rather than a "top-down" point of view.

The second difficulty is the tendency to cite theoretical descriptions or accounts of experience as though this were to do phenomenology: quoting Merleau-Ponty on perception or "the flesh," however, is not the same as thick phenomenological description or interpretative analysis of cinematic experience. Contemporary film phenomenology is defined by diverse (and sometimes incoherent) strands: Merleau-Ponty, Husserl, and Heidegger; affect theory (Deleuzian); theories of corporeality; embodied spectatorship; aesthetics of "touch" (hapticity); gender and queer theories; and intersectional approaches. Whatever one's particular theoretical or practical commitments, however, it is worth noting that "applying" theory is *not* the same as practicing phenomenology in the proper sense. If nothing else, phenomenology maintains a commitment to some kind of theoretical "bracketing" or suspension of presupposed theoretical concepts or frameworks in order to deal descriptively with phenomena or "the things themselves" while remaining mindful of the partial and contextual (i.e., hermeneutic) conditions of possibility defining any kind of phenomenological investigation.

### Phenomenology: Two Problems of Subjectivism

The "classic" difficulty facing phenomenological approaches, whether in pure or applied terms, is that of *subjectivism*: the privileging of first-person perspectives raises the question of the warrant or justification for the theoretical claims made on the basis of a descriptive account of such perspectives. Phenomenological approaches are essentially descriptive but include both interpretation and analysis of descriptive accounts of subjective phenomena, aiming to reveal their shared structures and communicable meanings. This suggests that phenomenology is particularly suited to illuminating our aesthetic experience of film but that it is not necessarily methodologically suited to providing explanatory accounts of the causal processes underlying such experience.

There are two related issues that are typically raised as criticisms of phenomenological approaches to cinematic experience. The first is the charge of *aesthetic subjectivism*, the argument that to provide a personal, first-person subjective (aesthetic) response is to provide evidence supporting interpretative and even theoretical claims. We do of course experience cinema from a first-person perspective, but one's own idiosyncratic responses do not, of themselves, provide adequate evidence to support stronger theoretical claims. The second is *epistemic subjectivism*, the use of anecdotal ("just so" / ad hoc) evidence to support theoretical claims without offering adequate conceptual argumentation or theoretical justification. In some cases, this can be compounded by a dogmatic reliance on presupposed theoretical or conceptual frameworks, which clearly violates one of the cardinal precepts of phenomenological inquiry (Husserl's motto, "to the things themselves!"). Because phenomenology is focused on a descriptive account of subjectivity, it inevitably courts the risk of subjectivism, whether aesthetic or epistemic. Phenomenological descriptive theory provides the basis for all sorts of theorization, but it does not constitute an explanatory account in its own right.

Indeed, as a corollary to these twin charges of subjectivism, there is the related risk of reverting to speculative theory, which arises when one makes "theoretical" claims based on phenomenological evidence. As I remarked above, the use of heuristics and conceptual-metaphorical models ("cinema as brain," "skin of the film") can guide theoretical practice in an illuminating way, but such practices do not themselves constitute theoretical claims supported by empirical evidence. Rather, the heuristic use of guiding metaphors/concepts for the purpose of generating, developing, and transforming theoretical problems and debates soon become speculative and ungrounded if taken as part of a theoretical model with explanatory aims.

**Two Responses to Subjectivism: Projection and Distribution**

Film theorists influenced by phenomenology implicitly recognize the problem of subjectivism, but generally reject the classical phenomenological response of focusing on the disclosure of shared "structures of consciousness." Instead, alternative strategies have emerged in order to deal with this problem, what we could call the *projection* and *distribution* responses. We can "desubjectify" affects—lived bodily responses to the affordances of our world—by "projecting" them onto nonhuman objects, events, or environmental states of affairs. Deleuzian affect theory, for example, drawing on a distinctive conception of affect deriving from Spinoza, Bergson, and Nietzsche (where affect is defined in relation to bodily capacities to be affected and to express such affection through transformations of the body via action and thought), projects affect beyond the "subjective" sphere such that objects, landscapes, and nature itself can be described as expressing "affect" in this corporeal-relational sense (Deleuze's "pure qualities") (Del Rio 2008; Shaviro 2010).

In a similar manner, we can also distribute these affective states across a plurality of related objects, creating a "distributed" or pluralized affective state encompassing a relationally defined composite body. Accordingly, shared affects are no longer primarily "subjective" but dispersed or distributed across a range of different bodies forming a relational composite whole. On this account, affects are no longer defined primarily in relation to the experiencing human subject but as "desubjectified," free-floating intensities attributable to the "assemblages" formed by human and nonhuman bodies, artifacts, things, objects, and natural environments (Brinkema 2014; Massumi 2015; Shaviro 2010). This projective-distributive approach attributes affective states encompassing a plurality of related objects and bodies, creating "shared" affects that are distributed across different bodies and escaping subjectivism via collective affective expression.

Recent versions of this approach echo the idea of distributed cognition, positing an embodied response to moving images that is also projected/distributed so as to incorporate the film itself (the idea of a cinematic body or film-body, the "skin of the film," or disembodied affects constituted by and expressed as cinematic form) (Brinkema 2014; Del Rio 2008; Marks 2000, 2002). The difficulty is that, however suggestive and illuminating these theoretical approaches may be, they are heuristic forms of theorization that draw on phenomenology and conceptual models in order to propose productive theoretical frameworks and to help us rethink how we conceptualize cinematic experience. They do not constitute, however, either a "phenomenological" descriptive account of subjective experience (since they are applying presupposed theoretical ideas) or a theoretical explanatory account of the processes underlying such experience (since they purport to reconceptualize such experience), however much theorists may imply that they do.

**Cognitivism and Cinema**

The broad field of "cognitivist" approaches to cinema, which spans many theoretical perspectives, can be defined by its theoretical and methodological commitment to naturalistic theorization and "piecemeal" modes of inquiry (see Carroll 2008; Nannicelli and Taberham 2014; and Plantinga 2018). It emerged as an alternative to the prevailing paradigms of film or screen theory—so-called "Grand Theory"—that synthesized, often in an eclectic manner, semiotic, psychoanalytic, and structuralist/poststructuralist theory and philosophy while remaining committed to a critical (ethico-political) perspective on ideological structures rather than empirical or explanatory approaches to theorizing cinematic experience (Sinnerbrink 2011). Earlier generations of cognitivist theory were influenced by computational theories of mind as well as by work on AI systems and empirical-experimental models (drawing on cognitive psychology and the neurosciences). This research program has now broadened out to include evolutionary perspectives; bioculturalist models; multimodal, network, and distributed models, as well as 4E theories of cognition (see Coëgnarts and Kravanja 2015; and Nannicelli and Taberham 2014). As a naturalistic approach to theory—namely, that all relevant processes pertaining to cinematic experience can be explained in terms of natural causal processes as analyzed within empirically grounded theories—cognitivism remains committed to providing explanatory (rather than descriptive or hermeneutic) forms of theory. In keeping with this commitment, cognitivists thus endeavor to produce causally explanatory theories of perception, cognition, and emotional engagement with film, venturing also into questions concerning the aesthetics and ethics of cinema.

Contemporary cognitivists, however, reject the traditional dualism between reason and emotion, embodied versus mentalistic responses, exploring instead the interaction and dependency of these processes in our complex affective, emotional, and cognitive engagement with moving images (Nannicelli and Taberham 2014). They not only focus on the role of "top down" or higher-order cognitive processes (reflection, inference-making, hypothesizing, practical reasoning) but on the important "bottom-up" or lower-order embodied and affective processes involved in cognition that occur at sub-personal, automatic, or minimally conscious levels of awareness (physiological, corporeal, affective, and emotional-cognitive "priming" effects). Together these theories seek to provide explanatory accounts—drawing on empirical theory and research—to explain the causal processes, mechanisms, and experiential components making up our complex experience of cinematic engagement. More recent work ventures into film aesthetics and ethics of film in order to bring the insights of cognitive theory to account for the aesthetic effects of cinematic form and style as well as the moral significance of such forms in our cognitive engagement with audio-visual media (D'Aloia and Eugeni 2014; Nannicelli and Taberham 2014; Plantinga 2018; Shimamura 2013; M. Smith 2018).

Two critical objections to cognitivist approaches have appeared in recent years, which both focus on topics that were a focus for the psychoanalytic-semiotic-poststructuralist paradigm of film theory (Sinnerbrink 2010). First, can cognitivist approaches provide robust forms of critical interpretation / aesthetic evaluation of nonmainstream forms of cinema? (the aesthetic or "what about art film?" objection). And second, can cognitivist approaches account for the ideological-political effects of (popular) cinema? (the symptomatic or "what about ideology?" objection). To take the first, cognitivist theories, from David Bordwell and Noël Carroll to Murray Smith and Torben Grodal, have offered powerful explanatory theories that deal well with canonical forms of popular narrative cinema. But how well do they deal with art cinema that eschews, for example, "erotetic" (question and answer), cognitive puzzle-solving, or PECMA (perception-emotion-cognition-motor action) flow models of narrative engagement defining popular cinema? Cognitivist models of narrative theory may work convincingly for genre films like *Love Actually* (Richard Curtis, 2003) or *Transformers: The Last Knight* (Michael Bay, 2017), critics may claim, but they work less well for "art films" like *Le Quattro Volte* (Michelangelo Frammartino, 2010) and *The Turin Horse* (Béla Tarr and Ágnes Hranitzky, 2012).

The second (the symptomatic) objection focuses on the question of cinema and ideology, asking whether cognitivist approaches, due to their commitments to scientific naturalism and empirical research, are adequately equipped to grapple with the ideological dimensions of film. Much of the work in so-called "Grand Theory"—particularly feminist film theory and Marxist critical theory approaches—has focused on the ideological structures shaping our engagement with (popular) cinema and the manner in which it can serve as a powerful vehicle of ideological influence, especially with regard to key aspects of personal identity (e.g., gender, race, and class). Can cognitivist theories engage with these ideological dimensions of cinematic experience without risking some version of the "naturalistic fallacy"? It is important to explain the causal processes shaping general features of our affective, emotional, and cognitive engagement with film, but we also need to address the question of how cinema contributes to the ideological context of contemporary cultural and sociopolitical institutions.

To these two objections, the aesthetic and the ideological, we can respond by saying that they remain inconclusive and are increasingly countered by new work focusing precisely on film aesthetics and ethico-political questions (ideology). To be sure, there are important issues pertaining to how "art films" work and how their particular aesthetic strategies thwart "standard" models of cognitive engagement. And there are important questions concerning the ideological dimensions of cinema that film theorists, whether cognitivist or phenomenological, would do well to consider more explicitly. Here, however, we can point to various attempts by cognitivist theorists to address both "art film" and ideology using the resources of cognitive theory. A number of theorists deal explicitly with nonstandard forms of narrative cinema, including experimental cinema, from cognitivist, neuroaesthetic, and even evolutionary biocultural perspectives (Grodal 2012; Shimamura 2013; M. Smith 2018). Their work shows how such approaches can provide us with the conceptual tools we need to undertake sophisticated and illuminating critical interpretations and aesthetic evaluations of challenging cinematic works. There are also attempts to tackle the ethicopolitical question of ideology in contemporary cinema drawing on the work of cognitive theory and phenomenology (Plantinga 2018; Stadler 2008). Such work seeks to account for how popular narrative film effectively captures audience attention and solicits moral-ideological allegiance via affective-emotional as well as cognitive-evaluative means. Carl Plantinga's essay on Zack Snyder's *300* in this volume is a compelling case in point. In short, both phenomenological and cognitivist approaches can be brought to bear on complex narratives and aesthetically challenging works, and they can examine the mechanisms and effects that make possible the uptake of ideological meanings in our sociocultural engagement with contemporary media.

### The "Reductionism" Objection

Both of these objections reduce, so to speak, to versions of the "standard" objection to cognitivist approaches, which is what we could call the *reductionism* objection—that cognitivist approaches, again due to their naturalistic commitments, risk offering "reductive" accounts of relevant aesthetic elements pertinent to cinematic experience (the role of affect and mood, aesthetic experience, and noncognitive forms of engagement). This rather broad and vague claim—it is not difficult to charge any theory with "reductionism" given that most (piecemeal) theories target discrete phenomena or processes—can be broken down into two more specific claims. First, there is the claim that cognitivism ignores "noncognitive" affective processes that are central to cinematic experience, and so is reductive in being "too mentalistic" in its explanatory focus on "higher-order" aspects of engaging with film. And second, there is the claim that there are phenomena relevant to cinematic experience that just resist cognitivist (naturalistic-explanatory) theorization (the psychoanalytic conception of the unconscious, for example, or the above-mentioned projective/distributive forms of affect), and so cognitivism is simply "too rationalistic." Such phenomena are often taken to be central to accounting for our experience of "art cinema."

In response, we can say that the first objection, once again, is readily countered by the rise of "antimentalist" accounts of affect, emotion, and cognition. Although earlier forms of cognitivist theory tended to focus on higher-order "top-down" forms of cognition, more recent approaches emphasize "bottom-up" processes in order to provide a richer, more adequate account of affective-cognitive engagement (see Coplan 2006; Plantinga 2018; and Stadler 2008). The recent emphasis on embodied cognition and on situated accounts of cognitive experience—acknowledging the essential role of social interaction, sociocultural learning, intersubjective communication, sociocultural "scripts," and enactive engagement with others in the world—brings cognitivist theory more into line with phenomenological perspectives (see Coëgnarts and Kravanja 2015). The second objection depends on the validity of the claims made concerning such phenomena as the Freudian/Lacanian unconscious, psychoanalytic accounts of repression, fantasy, and the "perverse" character of cinematic spectatorship. Once again, the danger here is that of conflating heuristic concepts with empirical phenomena, treating "the unconscious" not as a heuristically useful notion but as designating some putative entity in the human psyche, and arguing that theories that fail to take this into account fail to adequately describe, hence theorize, their object.

In short, both versions of the "reductionism" objection (the too mentalistic / too rationalistic objections) are better understood as claims concerning the need to provide rich and complex phenomenological descriptive accounts of our objects of theoretical reflection. I would contend further that the charge of "reductionism" is actually a claim about the need for an adequate phenomenology of the objects of cognitive theorization: before we proceed with higher-order cognitive (naturalistic and explanatory) theory, we should ensure that we have adequately prepared the ground for such theorization by ensuring that we have an adequate phenomenological description of our object in order to better track our object. This claim calls for some further elaboration because it means that phenomenology and cognitivism can, and indeed should, be brought together in a complementary, even synthetic manner. In this way, we can do justice to the complexity of the phenomena in question when theorizing cinematic experience.

**A Dialectical Tracking Model**

Here, I would like to sketch a brief outline of how this kind of complementary or synthetic approach might work, which I will call (with a nod to both Hegel and Carroll) "a dialectical tracking model." As I remarked above, phenomenology provides rich descriptive accounts of relevant phenomena pertinent to understanding cinematic experience, but such descriptive accounts stand to benefit from supplementation or elaboration by cognitivist theories in order to account for these phenomena in a causal manner. And, as I also remarked above, cognitivism provides rich explanatory theories of relevant aspects of cinematic experience, but these stand to benefit from supplementation by phenomenological descriptive accounts in order to track more accurately the phenomena that they are attempting to explain. Early cognitivist film theory lacked an adequate phenomenology, for example, of the overlapping relations between affect, emotion, and mood, and hence tended to focus on cognitively discrete emotions at the expense of affect and mood, offering theories that risked being overly mentalistic or rationalistic (a deficiency that has recently been corrected) (see Plantinga 2012; and Sinnerbrink 2012). Phenomenologically oriented "affect" theories, on the other hand, attempted to avoid the charge of subjectivism via strategies of projecting and distributing affect across bodies and milieux, but such approaches risk becoming overly speculative by conflating heuristic, descriptive, hermeneutic, and explanatory modes of film theorization concerning related aesthetic and ethical aspects of cinematic experience.

What all of this suggests is the need to develop adequate descriptive and explanatory accounts of cinematic experience if we are to do justice to its complex character. A dialectical approach—identifying limitations or inadequacies in existing theoretical models and supplementing or correcting these by way of synthetic theory construction—offers one way to combine phenomenological and cognitivist approaches in order to better describe and track, interpret and analyze, conceptualize and explain diverse but related dimensions of cinematic experience. This would enable us to develop descriptively rich and empirically grounded explanatory models of the relevant aesthetic and ethical aspects of cinematic engagement, and it would also allow us to track more accurately their phenomenological complexities. To do this, however, would require theoretical reflection on the methodological characteristics and theoretical specificities of heuristic, descriptive, and explanatory roles or modes of theory. It also demands theoretical vigilance to avoid conflating levels or types of theoretical inquiry, to avoid theoretical reductionism, and to avoid the temptations of speculative "pseudo-theory." This kind of methodological self-reflection would also provide a more robust basis for exploring the essential contextual dimensions of cinematic experience (i.e., the role of social institutions, cultural practices, historical horizons of meaning, and ideological and political forces), without which the phenomena of subjective experiential encounters with film, not to mention our aesthetic and ethical experience of it, would make little sense.

• • •

The chapters in this volume all contribute, in diverse ways, to furthering the interaction between phenomenological and cognitivist approaches to theorizing emotion, ethics, and cinematic experience. The authors draw on both theoretical perspectives and offer a range of methodological approaches combining theoretical conceptualization, descriptive analysis, critical reflection, and film interpretation. Carl Plantinga brings a cognitivist approach to the question of the "fascist affect" in Zack Snyder's *300* (2007). He argues that a close analysis reveals the cinematic strategies designed to elicit affective-emotional engagement; such an analysis can be used to explain the film's unsettling proximity to "fascist aesthetics" and controversial ideological messaging. Drawing on cognitivist accounts of affect, emotion, and mood, Plantinga examines what makes a film like *300* attractive and appealing to many audience members, examining "the moods and emotions *300* attempts to elicit through the viewing of the film, and in support of the fascist ideology it exhibits."

Saige Walton, by contrast, focuses on a nonmainstream art film, Laurie Anderson's experimental essay film, *Heart of a Dog* (2015), a lyrical eulogy to her beloved companion animal, Lolabelle. Drawing on

Merleau-Ponty's phenomenology of embodied experience, in particular the aesthetic experience of depth in relation to visual art, Walton examines Anderson's film as an exploration of interspecies communication, affective bonding, and the experience of loss. Merleau-Ponty's phenomenological insights into the relationships between depth and movement, body–world relationships, and the imaginative aesthetic encounter with elements and surfaces allows the film to explore loss in a manner that avoids the heaviness of grief in favor of a lyrical affirmation of shared experiential encounters. The film's experimental aesthetic style is itself a mode of ethical engagement with forms of experience that are both familiar and unfamiliar, probing the boundary between human and non-human animality.

Ludo de Roo continues the phenomenological and ethical exploration of novel forms of cinematic aesthetics in his examination of elemental imagination and film experience in the urgent context of climate change. De Roo's film-philosophical inquiry takes a phenomenological approach to what he calls the "elemental imagination" (elemental in that it is oriented toward the elements of our natural environment but also elemental in the sense of primary or fundamental for our experience of the world). It combines this with an ecocritical perspective on the ethical potential of immersive cinematic experience to resensitize us to the importance of the natural world and the ordinarily backgrounded natural elements that provide the "ground" of our existence. By close analysis of the aims and limitations of ecologically oriented documentary works and fictional films, we can raise ecological awareness via the experience of cinematic immersion. The latter has the potential to give us access to the ordinarily concealed dimension of the natural elements, de Roo argues, upon which human and nonhuman life on our threatened planet depends.

Brigid Martin brings an intercultural comparative aesthetics perspective to bear on both cognitivist and phenomenological approaches to cinematic experience, focusing on the remarkable rendering of (personal as well as sociocultural) trauma in the Korean film *Aimless Bullet* (Yu Hyun-mok, 1961). As Martin argues, contemporary theories of affect, combining phenomenological and cognitivist approaches, tend to focus on sympathy and moral allegiance, which means that "complex affects that problematize empathy and moral judgments" tend to be ignored. The role of complex affective experience in revealing facets of a broader social and historical milieu requires an account of "how *affective-aesthetic affordances* establish distributed spaces for dynamic affective engagement." Martin develops this approach by drawing on theories of scaffolded mind, classical Indian *rasa* aesthetics, and phenomenological aesthetics, a pluralistic mode of theorizing that enables us to understand more clearly "the ethical significance of complex affective situations" in cinematic works.

Documentary film is often overlooked in contemporary debates over the relationship between cinema and ethics; philosophical engagement with the ethical and aesthetic issues raised by the documentary form is even less well addressed. Mathew Abbott responds to this neglect by focusing on the controversial yet fascinating case of the Maysles brothers' *Grey Gardens* (1976) and the ethics of observational documentary. Following recent attempts to defend the film for its candidly "subjective" (rather than "objective") depiction of the reclusive Bouvier Beale sisters, Abbott revisits arguments over the claim of *vérité* and observational documentarians being able to capture truth and objectivity in their work, and explores the now orthodox skeptical rejection of such claims so memorably formulated by Emile de Antonio ("As soon as you point a camera, objectivity is romantic hype"). Against both critics citing problematic claims to objectivity and recent defenders of the "subjectivity" of *Grey Gardens*, Abbott analyzes the questionable philosophical assumption underpinning both positions—namely, an uncritical commitment to scientistic conceptions of objectivity akin to Thomas Nagel's critique of the "view from nowhere" account of knowledge—arguing "that the film's objective treatment of its subjects is part of its aesthetic and ethical achievement." Far from claiming an untenable "view from nowhere" or celebrating the irreducibility of subjectivity that such views often entail, Abbott argues that "objectivity" in observational documentary is as much an ethical as an aesthetic attitude. As he concludes, it does not mean taking a purely dispassionate stance toward one's subjects but rather "treating them without prejudice or moralism and letting them reveal themselves."

Finally, Jane Stadler turns to some of the perplexing aesthetic and ethical issues raised by the advent of virtual/synthetic performers ("synthespians") thanks to digital, CGI, postproduction, and virtual reality technology. Stadler examines the manner in which contemporary cinema and audiovisual media both explore and reflect upon the technological and ethical challenges posed by biological as well as by media technology. Cinema is not only a space of imaginative reflection enabling us to track technological developments, but it also allows us to extrapolate and project their possible social, cultural, moral, and political consequences. Indeed, cinema is the way that contemporary "technological and ethical concerns surrounding synthespians, representations of replicants, and manifestations of synthetic biology" are made vividly manifest. Films like *Blade Runner 2049* (Denis Villeneuve, 2017) not only examine the ethics of "digital embodiment technologies and cybernetics" but open up ethical questions that require collaboration between the sciences and the humanities. This will enable us to understand more precisely the challenges to embodiment raised by contemporary technologies and ethically challenging developments in audiovisual media "such as the creation of virtual humans and 'deepfake' digital doubles in screen media."

All of these contributions to the aesthetic and ethical aspects of cinematic experience demonstrate the benefits of an interdisciplinary approach to theorizing film. They also show the manner in which phenomenological and cognitivist perspectives can work together to enhance our theoretical understanding of emotion, ethics, and cinematic experience. Our hope is that these chapters will serve as an invitation to further interdisciplinary and pluralistic investigation of the complex nexus between emotional engagement, ethical evaluation, and cinematic experience.

**Acknowledgments**

Some of the contributions in this volume were originally presented at the "Cinematic Ethics 2: Emotion, Ethics, and Cinematic Experience" symposium held at Macquarie University, Sydney, 15–16 December 2016. I would like to thank all the participants involved in that event for their generous cooperation and commitment to developing their work for publication. This symposium was part of my Australian Research Council (ARC) Future Fellowship project, "Cinematic Ethics: Exploring Ethical Experience through Film" [FT FT130100334], and I would like to acknowledge the funding support provided by the ARC to hold this event. I would also like to thank Ted Nannicelli for his editorial acumen and for his enthusiastic support of both that symposium and this volume.

---

**Robert Sinnerbrink** is Associate Professor in Philosophy at Macquarie University, Sydney. He is the author of *Terrence Malick: Filmmaker and Philosopher* (Bloomsbury, 2019), *Cinematic Ethics: Exploring Ethical Experience through Film* (Routledge, 2016), *New Philosophies of Film: Thinking Images* (Bloomsbury, 2011), and *Understanding Hegelianism* (Acumen, 2007/Routledge 2014). He is a member of the editorial boards of *Film-Philosophy*, *Film and Philosophy*, and *Projections*. He has published numerous articles on film and philosophy in journals such as *Australasian Philosophical Review*, *Angelaki*, *Conversations: The Journal of Cavellian Studies*, *Film-Philosophy*, *NECSUS: European Journal of Media Studies*, *Projections*, *Post-Script*, *Screen*, *Screening the Past*, and *SubStance*. Email: robert.sinnerbrink@mq.edu.au

# References

Barker, Jennifer M. 2009. *The Tactile Eye: Touch and the Cinematic Experience*. Berkeley: University of California Press.

Brinkema, Eugenie. 2014. *The Forms of the Affects*. Durham, NC: Duke University Press.

Carroll, Noël. 2008. *The Philosophy of Motion Pictures*. Malden, MA.: Blackwell Publishing.

Coëgnarts, Maarten, and Peter Kravanja. 2015. "Film as an Exemplar of Bodily Meaning-Making." In *Embodied Cognition and Cinema*, ed. Maarten Coëgnarts and Peter Kravanja, 17–42. Leuven: Leuven University Press.

Coplan, Amy. 2006. "Catching Characters' Emotions: Emotional Contagion Responses to Narrative Film." *Film Studies: An International Review* 8 (1): 26–38. doi:10.7227/FS.8.5.

D'Aloia, Adriano. 2015. "The Character's Body and the Viewer: Cinematic Empathy and Embodied Simulation in the Film Experience." In *Embodied Cognition and Cinema*, ed. Maarten Coëgnarts and Peter Kravanja, 187–201. Leuven: Leuven University Press.

D'Aloia, Adriano. 2012. "The Intangible Ground—A Neurophenomenology of the Film Experience." *NECSUS: European Journal of Media Studies* 1 (2): 219–239. doi:10.5117/NECSUS2012.2.DALO.

D'Aloia, Adriano, and Ruggero Eugeni. 2014. "Neurophenomenology: An Introduction." *Cinéma & Cie* 14 (22–23): 9–26. https://www.researchgate.net/publication/297045397 _Neurofilmology_An_Introduction.

Del Rio, Elena. 2008. *Deleuze and the Cinemas of Performance: The Powers of Affection*. Edinburgh: Edinburgh University Press.

Ferencz-Flatz, Christian, and Julian Hanich. 2016. "Editors' Introduction: What Is Film Phenomenology?" *Studia Phaenomenologica* 16: 11–61. doi:10.5840/studphaen2016161.

Grodal, Torben. 2012. "Frozen Style and Strong Emotions of Panic and Separation: Trier's Prologues to *Antichrist* and *Melancholia*." *Journal of Scandinavian Cinema* 2 (1): 47–53. doi:10.1386/jsca.2.1.47_1.

Grønstad, Asbjørn. 2016. *Film and the Ethical Imagination*. London: Palgrave Macmillan.

Hanich, Julian. 2010. *Cinematic Emotions in Horror Films and Thrillers: The Aesthetic Paradox of Pleasurable Fear*. London: Routledge.

Hanich, Julian, and Daniel Fairfax, eds. 2019. *The Structures of Film Experience: Historical Assessments and Phenomenological Expansions*. Amsterdam: University of Amsterdam Press.

Ingram, David. 2014. "Emotion and Affect in Eco-Films: Cognitivist and Phenomenological Approaches." In *Moving Environments: Affects, Emotion, Ecology, and Film*, ed. Alexa Weik von Mossner, 23–39. Waterloo: Wilfried Laurier University Press.

Marks, Laura U. 2000. *The Skin of the Film: Intercultural Cinema, Embodiment, and the Sense*. Durham, NC: Duke University Press.

Marks, Laura U. 2002. *Touch: Sensuous Theory and Multisensory Media*. Minneapolis: University of Minnesota Press.

Massumi, Brian. 2015. *Politics of Affect*. London: Polity Press.

Nannicelli, Ted, and Paul Taberham, eds. 2014. "Introduction: Contemporary Cognitive Media Theory." In *Cognitive Media Theory*, ed. Ted Nannicelli and Paul Taberham, 1–23. New York: Routledge.

Pisters, Patricia. 2012. *The Neuro-Image: A Deleuzian Film-Philosophy of Digital Screen Culture*. Stanford, CA: Stanford University Press.

Plantinga, Carl. 2009. *Moving Viewers: American Film and the Spectator's Experience*. Berkeley: University of California Press.

Plantinga, Carl. 2012. "Art Moods and Human Moods in Narrative Cinema." *New Literary History* 43 (3): 455–475. doi:10.1353/nlh.2012.0025.

Plantinga, Carl. 2018. *Screen Stories: Emotion and the Ethics of Engagement*. Oxford: Oxford University Press.

Rhym, John. 2018. "Historicizing Perception: Film Theory, Neuroscience, and the Philosophy of Mind." *Discourse* 40 (1): 83–109. https://www.jstor.org/stable/10.13110.

Shaviro, Steven. 2010. *Post-Cinematic Affect*. London: Zero Books.

Shimamura, Arthur. 2013. *Psychocinematics: Exploring Cognition at the Movies*. Oxford: Oxford University Press.

Sinnerbrink, Robert. 2010. "Cognitivism Goes to the Movies: *The Routledge Companion to Philosophy and Film*; *Moving Viewers: American Film and the Spectator's Experience*; *Embodied Visions: Evolution, Emotion, Culture, and Film*" (Review Article). *Projections* 4 (1): 83–98. doi:10.3167/proj.2010.040106.

Sinnerbrink, Robert. 2011. *New Philosophies of Film: Thinking Images*. London: Continuum.

Sinnerbrink, Robert. 2012. "*Stimmung*: Exploring the Aesthetics of Mood." *Screen* 53 (2): 148–163. doi:10.1093/screen/hjs007.

Sinnerbrink, Robert. 2016. *Cinematic Ethics: Exploring Ethical Experience through Film*. New York: Routledge.

Smith, Greg M. 2014. "Coming Out of the Corner: The Challenges of a Broader Media Cognitivism." In *Cognitive Media Theory*, ed. Ted Nannicelli and Paul Taberham, 285–302. New York: Routledge.

Smith, Murray. 2018. *Film, Art, and the Third Culture: A Naturalized Aesthetics of Film*. Oxford: Oxford University Press.

Sobchack, Vivian. 1992. *The Address of the Eye: A Phenomenology of Film Experience*. Princeton, NJ: Princeton University Press.

Sobchack, Vivian. 2004. *Carnal Thoughts: Embodiment and Moving Image Culture*. Berkeley: University of California Press.

Stadler, Jane. 2008. *Pulling Focus: Intersubjective Experience, Narrative Film, and Ethics*. London: Continuum.

Stadler, Jane. 2011. "Phenomenology Goes to the Movies." *Projections* 5 (1): 87–101. doi:10.3167/proj.2011.050107.

Stadler, Jane. 2016. "Experiential Realism and Motion Pictures: A Neurophenomenological Approach." *Studia Phaenomenologica* 16: 439–465. doi:10.5840/studphaen20161616.

Stadler, Jane. 2018. "Mind the Gap: Between Movies and Mind, Affective Neuroscience, and the Philosophy of Film." *Projections* 12 (2): 86–94. doi:10:3167/proj.2018.120211.

Yacavone, Daniel. 2015. *Film Worlds: A Philosophical Aesthetics of Cinema*. New York: Columbia University Press.

*Chapter 1*

# Fascist Affect in *300*

**Carl Plantinga**

The word "fascist" appears all too frequently in today's political climate. It is often used loosely, so one had better take care when using the term. And yet in relation to the epic action film *300* (2007), the word fits well. Adapted from the 1998 comic series created by Frank Miller and Lynn Varley, *300* tells the story of 300 courageous Spartan soldiers who, led by their ferocious King Leonidas (Gerard Butler), valiantly battle the threatening Persian army of 300,000 men until, after being betrayed by a hunchbacked Spartan outcast, they all are slaughtered. Their defeat, however, alerts the rest of the Greeks to the significance of the Persian threat, and promises future victory as the entire Greek nation rises up to battle the Persians. The story is loosely based on the Battle of Thermopylae during the Persian Wars of the fifth century BCE. Considerations of the film as history, however, are ultimately less interesting than analyses of the film's political function in its contemporary context. *300* can certainly be seen as a political allegory that embodies tensions resulting from the Iraq War and conceptions of Iran as a node of the "axis of evil." This chapter will instead discuss the film's incipient fascism, a broad threat that resonates more powerfully today, given the events of the past few years.

*300* is a highly stylized fantasy film shot almost entirely on blue-screen soundstages with digital backgrounds added in postproduction.

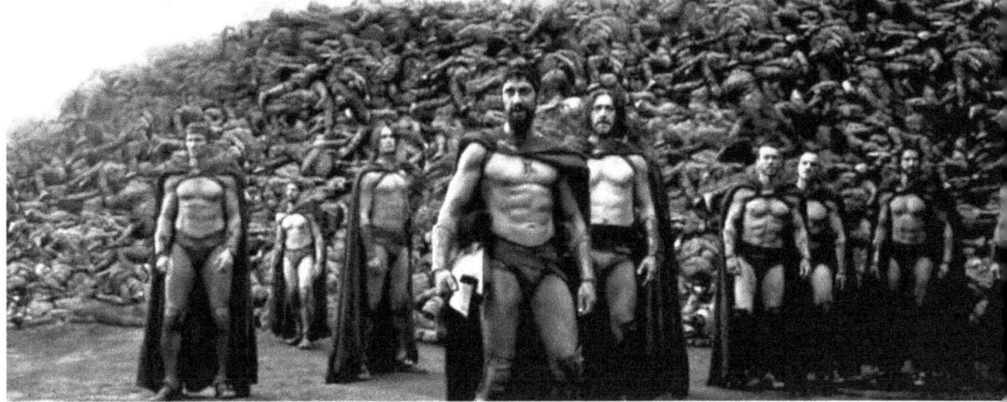

*300* is notable for its striking visual style, for its idealization of the courageous Greeks (all handsome men who sport muscular physiques and wear only tight leather "short shorts" and capes), and for its vulgarization of the invading Persians (represented as monstrous and/or effeminate).

Many scenes feature the preparation and training for combat, fierce chanting ("A-whoo, A-whoo!"), and forcefully intoned epithets ("We are Spartans!" and "No prisoners! No mercy!). Female characters get in on the slogans as well, for example, when Queen Gorgo (Lena Headey) sends her husband-king off to battle by telling him to come back "with his shield or on it." The film's centerpiece, however, is the fighting itself, which is represented graphically, often in slow motion, with fountains of spurting blood, decapitations, impalements, deep base choir intonations to suggest the powerful maleness of it all, and rhythmic drumming as underscoring. After the Greeks are slaughtered, the last scenes serve as a eulogy for the fallen heroes, with music and *mise-en-scène* suggesting the mythic significance of their mission and sacrifice. We see the dead Leonidas on his back, his body pierced by arrows, his arms splayed to the sides in an obvious reference to the sacrifice of Jesus Christ on the cross. The film did very well at the box office, with a lifetime gross revenue of over $450 million, which led to a sequel, *Rise of an Empire* (Noam Murro, 2014).

Director Zack Snyder's wife and production partner, Deborah Snyder, described *300* as a "ballet of death" (Daly 2007). Perhaps it is this, in conjunction with the film's implicit fascist ideology, that caused audiences at the Berlin Film Festival to walk out and to boo the film. *300* also provoked intense criticism in the Middle East for its portrayal of the Persians as monsters and deviants, with the Iranian Academy of the Arts lodging an official complaint against the film with UNESCO, calling it an attack on the historical identity of Iran. *300* has been called homophobic, racist, antidisability, tribalist, and militaristic. It is the film's incipient fascism, however, that unites these tendencies within a unified ideology. *300* has been called "the ur-text of the alt-right," "*Hamilton* for neo-fascists," and "our *Birth of a Nation*" (Breihan 2017). *New York Post* critic Kyle Smith (2007) writes that the film would have pleased "Adolph's boys," while *Slate*'s Dana Stevens (2008) compares the film to the Nazi racist screed, *The Eternal Jew* (Fritz Hippler, 1940).

Are these charges of fascism fair? And should we take the socio-political and ethical experience offered by such an action/adventure fantasy seriously? This chapter will argue in the affirmative for both questions. Yet these charges of fascism are easily made, and this chapter goes beyond that to attempt to understand some of what makes fascist ideology, in a story format, attractive to many audiences. To do this, I will first discuss fascist art generally, then I will examine the moods and emotions that *300* attempts to elicit through the viewing of the film and in support of the fascist ideology that it exhibits. I call this "fascist affect."

## Fascist Art

Fascism is a political ideology with a constellation of associated social and ethical commitments (Hayes 1973; Payne 1980). This constellation of commitments has existed since the rise of fascism in Italy in 1922, and is a consistent threat to reemerge now and in the future. Fascism is historically associated with the political formations in Germany, Italy, and Japan before and during World War II, and to some extent in Spain until the fall of Francoism in 1975. As a political ideology, fascism is above all nationalist, elitist, and antiliberal. It is a form of extreme nationalism that attempts to unite a favored people (the "folk"), sometimes with an appeal to a mythic and glorious past, under a strong leader figure who is acceded complete control. Walter Laquer writes that fascist movements were "headed by a leader who had virtually unlimited power, was adulated by his followers, and was the focus of a quasi-religious cult" (1996: 14). Japan had Emperor Hirohito, Germany had Adolf Hitler, and Italy had Benito Mussolini. Italian fascism looked to the Roman era for its inspiration for the rebirth of a muscular Italy for the present.

Fascism evinces an ethos of ethnic and national purity, favoring the strong, healthy, and pure over what is thought to be weak, diseased, and impure or inauthentic. Fascism believes not in political democracy and cultural liberalism, but in the "natural" social hierarchy and the rule of the elites. Fascism is, as Yuval Noah Harari argues, a form of "evolutionary humanism" (as opposed to liberal or socialist humanism) that considers humans to be a mutable species that might evolve into superhumans or devolve into a degenerate species. Thus, all social policy must be designed to protect humankind from this degeneration and to promote evolution into superhumans (Harari 2011, 258–263). This ethos led to the Holocaust during World War II, during which the Nazis murdered millions of Jews, homosexuals, political dissidents, and anyone thought not to contribute to the development of a strong and pure Aryan people under the leadership of Adolf Hitler.

Fascism is also imperialistic in that it promotes the right of the "naturally superior" to colonize, exploit, and even kill the inferior and "defective." Fascism celebrates militarism and physical power, and often sentimentalizes "glorious death" for the good of the people. One sees this in the chilling images of regimented military might highlighted in Leni Riefenstahl's *Triumph of the Will* (1935), and in the employment of suicide attacks by Japanese fighter planes on American forces during World War II. It foregrounds a sense of discontent, crisis, and/or impending danger, thus making nationalism and militarism seemingly necessary (Laquer 1996). In sum, fascism is about total stability, control, and homogeneity under the headship of an idealized leader. It appeals to a mythic and idealized nation and points to a glorious rebirth. As Benito Mussolini put it: "We have created our myth. Our myth is a faith, it is a passion, in our myth is the nation, and to this myth, to this grandeur we subordinate all the rest" (quoted in Laquer 1996, 25).

Our idea of fascist art has been influenced most by documentarian, photographer, and Nazi propagandist Leni Riefenstahl by way of Susan Sontag's famous essay, "Fascinating Fascism." Of course, Riefenstahl was already famous for her documentaries made during the Nazi era, including *Triumph of the Will* (1935) and *Olympia* (1938). The former film celebrates both militarism and uniformity with scenes featuring massive formations of military personnel marching in lockstep. It also features the emotional adulation of Adolph Hitler, as he first descends from the skies in his plane, like some kind of god sent to save Germany, and later addresses the 1934 Nazi Party rally to thunderous applause. Of fascist dramaturgy, Sontag writes that it "centers on orgiastic transactions between mighty forces and their puppets, uniformly shown in ever-swelling numbers. Its choreography alternates between ceaseless motion and congealed, static, 'virile' posing" (1981: 91).

*Olympia* is less political, but it puts the Olympic Games into a kind of mythic context by emphasizing their roots in the ancient world and a devotion to the beauty of the athletic human body. The Sontag essay was a meditation on Riefenstahl's 1973 book, *The Last of the Nuba*, a book of photographs of the men of Nuba, an African tribe. As Sontag writes, fascist art "displays a utopian aesthetics—that of physical perfection." "Painters and sculptors under the Nazis," she goes on, "often depicted the nude, but they were forbidden to show any bodily imperfections. Their nudes look like pictures in physique magazines: pinups which are both sanctimoniously asexual and (in a technical sense) pornographic, for they have the perfection of a fantasy" (1981, 92). Fascist art celebrates "the ideal of life as art, the cult of beauty, the fetishism of courage, the dissolution of alienation in ecstatic feelings of community; the repudiation of the intellect, the family of man (under the parenthood of leaders)" (1981, 96).

When one looks at *300*, one sees clear examples of these and other aspects of what various scholars have called "fascist aesthetics." Fascism attempts to build on the supposed cultural achievements of former cultures thought to evince the heroic qualities toward which contemporary society ought to return and to provide models for regeneration. Thus

Mussolini and Italian fascism looked to and idealized ancient Rome, to an era when Rome dominated the world. The Nazi architect, Albert Speer, developed a "theory of ruin value" for buildings of the Third Reich, as Mark Antliff writes, "to ensure that they would resemble Greek and Roman models after centuries or even thousands of years had passed (1998, 28). Zach Snyder's *300*, of course, looks back to ancient Greece, to the Spartans who ostensibly modeled heroic masculinity, courage, and sacrifice in significant quantities.

We have seen that fascist aesthetics values representations of the ideal male body rooted in works of Greek sculpture. We see this, of course, in the representations of the Spartans in *300*, who are all represented with traits that the film takes to be bodily perfection: muscular physiques, shining blue eyes, and full manes of hair. It is interesting that although actual Spartans would have worn full armor when engaging in battle, these cinematic Spartans are nearly nude aside from their helmets, capes, and tight shorts. Thus *300* partakes of the aestheticized body characteristic of fascist art, and has clear affinities with Leni Riefenstahl's *The Last of the Nuba* and *Olympia*. As the boy Leonidas kills a wolf, the voiceover narrator intones that his hands are steady and "his form perfect" as he kills the outmatched animal.

The romantic inspiration drawn from an idealized past and an interest in the perfection of human form are both important elements of the fascist aesthetic. My primary interest in this chapter, however, is what I call "fascist affect" in *300*. What do I mean by this? By affect here, I am primarily interested in mood and emotion, both examples of affect that I will examine in more detail below. No types of moods or emotions are fascist in themselves. Anger in itself is not fascist, any more than a mood of earnest seriousness is. It is only affects in relation to their rhetorical uses that can properly be so called. But moods and emotions can be marshaled in the context of a narrative to assist in highlighting the appeal of the fascist imagined order. Fascist moods and emotions are affects that are used to sell the fascist program. Certain moods and emotions, though not fascist in themselves, tend to recur in fascist art and storytelling. When they occur in combination, and when they occur in support of fascist ideas, then we can call them "fascist affects."

What the remainder of this chapter does is identify a constellation of moods and emotions at work in *300* and describes the use of mood and emotion in providing an experience of fascist ideology as it is played out on the screen.

### Mood in *300*

Moods and emotions are both examples of human affects, but emotion is thought to have a stronger cognitive component (Plantinga 2009), as I will briefly explain in the next section. Moods, as human affects, are a bit trickier. My sad mood in real life may not stem from any particular incident. I may simply be sad for some unknown reason. But a sad mood in a screen story is different. When a person has a mood, it is a mental state. When a screen story has a mood, it must be something else, quite obviously. Whatever that something else is, it is likely to have a fittingness or affinity with human moods; but unlike a human mood, it cannot itself be a mental state.

Moods in screen stories, as I have argued elsewhere, have two essential components. Such a mood is (1) the affective character or tone of a scene or entire screen story (2) that serves as an expression of the perspective of a character or group within the story and/or the expression of the perspective of the narration as a whole on the story (Plantinga 2018; Sinnerbrink 2012). Mood depends in part on the sort of events that are depicted. Obviously, the mood of an auto accident scene will tend to differ from that of a birthday party, as the affective character of a funeral scene will differ from that of a wedding scene. Filmmakers are not typically satisfied to let the represented event signal mood by itself. The mood of a screen story is also developed through the manifold registers of style and technique in the rich medium of moving images: cinematography and videography, special effects, music and other sound, editing, production design, editing, acting, and much else. These elements are orchestrated and/or designed to effect a mood that serves certain ends. A sad mood or tone, for example, is typically designed to suggest that the events depicted are sad or that a certain character is sad. Thus moods embody and/or help develop the cognitive orientation of the narration toward the events depicted (Plantinga 2018).

How does this play out in *300*? The film presents some extreme perspectives and behaviors undertaken by the Spartans, for whom viewers are meant to have allegiance. Yet the eugenics practiced by the Spartans, for example, would be considered to be reprehensible to most viewers. Spartan baby boys are examined at birth, and if found to be small, puny, sickly, or "misshapen," are discarded and killed. When engaged in battle, the Spartans chant "No mercy! No prisoners!" We see the Spartans, after a successful fight against the Persian hordes, piercing wounded enemy soldiers with swords, casually killing them as they engage in lighthearted post-battle banter. The 300 Spartans who eventually face a massive Persian force in the film's climactic action expect only to be able to slow the Persians down and to demonstrate the ferocity with which the Greek nation will face them if they pursue their invasion further. But the 300 all expect to die, to sacrifice their lives for the sake of their nation.

The mood established by the film is designed to justify all of this, to make it seem appropriate and fitting. Filmic moods are often difficult to describe in language; their qualitative feel is often beyond linguistic expression. To be best understood, they must be experienced. Yet moods have a strong effect on the rhetoric of a film and may encourage cognitive biasing (Carroll 2003). Thus, moods have implications for an ethics of spectatorship. The mood of *300* can be described, however imprecisely, as a kind of fierce, melancholic foreboding in the face of urgent crisis and threat. The extreme militarism, aggression, cruelty, and violence of the Spartans are played against a background established and justified by mood.

The film's mood is in part established by the narrative events the film depicts and by what the viewers *are shown*. The characters, settings, and events as represented have an affective character. Among the most striking images that we see are geysers of blood, decapitations, impalements, deformities, monsters, and grotesque creatures. It is a dangerous and unsettling world indeed, quite a far cry from *The Sound of Music* (Robert Wise, 1965). After the opening title, the first image shown is that of a pile of skulls. This is a film in which the specter of death is ever-present. Sparta and all of Greece are threatened by the gigantic Persian army, consisting not merely of hundreds of thousands of very ugly soldiers, but by elephants, rhinoceri, a giant with bad teeth who resembles Jaws (Richard Kiel) in *Moonraker* (Lewis Gilbert, 1979), and an assortment of hideous monsters. Early in the film, we are introduced to the training of Spartan boys, and we see Leonidas, as a child, forced to fend for himself in the wilderness, where he is attacked by and then kills a vicious wolf. We later see a Greek village that has been destroyed by the Persian forces, in which the dead villagers have been impaled on tree limbs. We see a defensive wall constructed by the Spartans for which they used their enemies' dead bodies as "mortar." We see that all of the enemies of the Greeks are hideously deformed or else effeminate (as is Xerxes). We see constant fighting, yelling, and bodily injury. Even back in Sparta, the world is an excessively dangerous place. Queen Gorgo must deal with the duplicitous Theron (Dominic West), a corrupt Spartan politician who lures Gorgo into having sex with him by promising in return his fealty to

*Illustration 1.2. Spartan newborn boys are either kept or killed after a close inspection. (300, Warner Bros., 2007).*

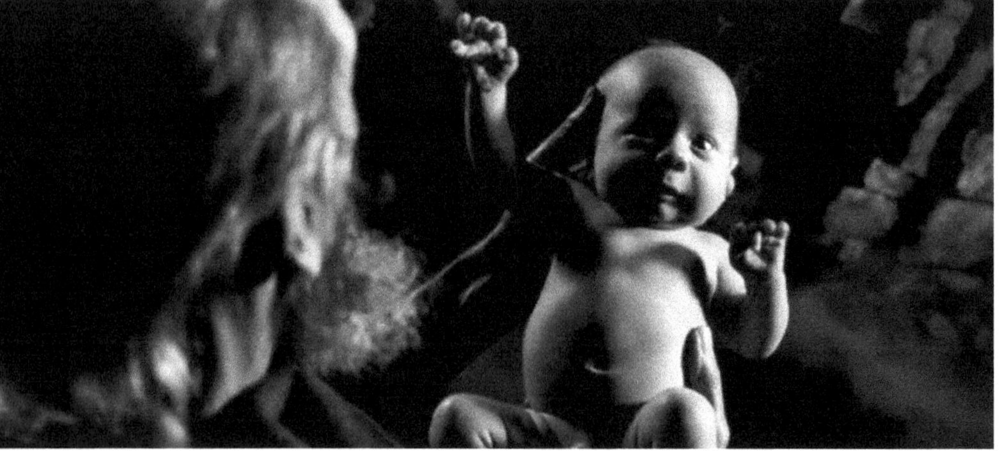

her husband, but then betrays her (for which she plunges a blade into his body).

It is important to remember that the eugenics practiced by the Spartans is represented as a cultural convention not tied to any particular war or invasion. Sparta is represented as in a constant state of threat. As the specter of the advancing Persian army is introduced, the voiceover narrator links this to the wolf-killing scene: "Now, as then, a beast approaches." Eugenics is related to the military training that all Spartan boys must undergo, as all boys must become killing machines "baptized in the fire of combat." As the voiceover narrator intones, in Sparta there is "no place for weakness. Only the hard and strong may call themselves Spartans." As if to drive home the point, the narrative repeats slowly: "Only the hard, the strong." Killing imperfect babies and Persian messengers is justified by the frightening nature of the world, by a worldview. This is just the way the Spartans do it, because the Spartans experience the world as one of never-ending threat. It is as though Sparta is permanently under siege, and that threat and crisis must be always emphasized to justify such outrageous practices.

All of the elements of film style are marshaled to contribute to this mood of melancholic foreboding and determination in the face of threat. Filmed with a chroma-key technique, the visual design of the film replicates the look of the Frank Miller comic series on which the film is based. Much of the film is muted in blues and greys, and other scenes in nostalgic sepia tones, with few bright or saturated colors save for the deep reds of the blood that freely splatters and flows throughout. Many of the exterior scenes are played out against a backdrop of austere natural beauty as a mythical backdrop. Day scenes invariably occur under clouds, often with shafts of light beaming through the cloud cover to suggest the fierce beauty of the deadly Spartan mission. In one scene, Leonidas stands at the window of his bedchamber, the moon unnaturally large in the sky to lend a cosmic significance to his impending sacrifice. This all suggests the eternal, destiny, and large concepts. (In this, it also relates to the godlike physiques of the Greek soldiers). Night scenes are often decidedly low key, often lit with flames that suggest the dramatic weight of the present and the conflagrations to come at daybreak. And the blood—my goodness. The blood spurts and splashes almost as freely as the severed limbs and heads of the combatants, becoming an integral design element of the *mise-en-scène.* So much blood, such a bloody world, such a dangerous world.

The soundtrack is also important in creating the film's mood. The voiceovers and dialogue never fail to remind the viewer of the majesty of Spartan power and the weight of responsibility. Delios, the voiceover narrator, provides the Spartan perspective and an account of the battles in hushed tones and with an ardent sense of mission: "Spartans never retreat; Spartans never surrender." Queen Gorgo is also granted lines that espouse the essential seriousness of life and the Spartan mission, in this case echoing contemporary bumper stickers: "Freedom isn't free at all," she says, "it comes at a high cost, at the cost of blood." The dialogue helps to effect a mood of urgent crisis, and so do the music and sound effects. The mood of a film's first scenes tell us much about the narrative perspective; over the shots of dozens of infant skulls in the film's first images, we hear foreboding music and the rumble of thunder. The score for the film, composed by Tyler Bates, contains much percussive battle music, low-base windy sounds, male voices chanting and harumpfing, heroic choral music, and heavy rock themes with electric guitar riffs for some of the energetic battle scenes. Bates describes the score as "beautiful themes" tempered with "extreme heaviness," adding that the score has a lot of "weight and intensity in the low end of the percussion," which Snyder found fitting for the film (Epstein 2005).

It should be noted that the battle scenes are sometimes infused with a mood of good cheer, as though fighting and killing are the Spartan *telos*, the glorious expression of their very being. It is only during the many fighting scenes that the melancholy of approaching death takes a momentary hiatus: it is replaced by good-natured male camaraderie and energetic guitar rock. Tellingly, this is when the filmmakers employ slow motion, which is here designed to slow down the action so that it can be emphasized, so that the viewer can better see the swinging and thrusting of the blade, the piercing of the flesh, and, most importantly, the splattering of blood. It is also a way to slow down the images in the name of comic book graphics. Slowed down like this, they better resemble the frames and pages of the comics, with their stylized virile posing and capacity to capture the high moments of the action. It also highlights and emphasizes the fighting, further amplifying its supposed magnificence and its relationship to glorious death (a concept that I will examine in the next section).

Moods, as Greg M. Smith (2003) writes, pervade a film at the global level and provide a kind of affective framework from which films elicit more local emotions. This is certainly true in the case of *300*, where a mood of melancholic foreboding, punctuated by scenes of furious and energetic hand-to-hand combat, provides a context for the emotions that I describe in the following section. The mood suggests that life is a constant struggle undertaken under permanent threat. It seems fitting here to consider this excerpt from a chapter entitled "The Laws of Nature and Mankind" in a 1942 German biology textbook: "The battle for existence is hard and unforgiving, but it is the only way to maintain life. This struggle eliminates everything that is unfit for life, and selects everything that is able to survive.... The meaning of life is struggle. Woe to him who sins against these laws" (quoted in Harari 2011, 262).

**Fascist Emotion in *300***

As concern-based construals, emotions have an "aboutness" to them; emotions have objects. Emotions are concern-based construals. For example, when I become angry at characters in a film, my anger is directed toward the characters and/or their actions (the object), and it expresses a perspective about those actions (a construal) in relation to my concerns. If the antagonist hurts a beloved protagonist, my construal is that the antagonist behaved badly; my concern is for the well-being of the protagonist. My anger is not just a feeling. Even if it is elicited largely unconsciously and immediately as a kind of intuition, it is also an expression of an attitude or perspective on the events. Thus, it has a strong cognitive component. Presumably, the makers of screen stories elicit emotions intentionally, and those intended emotions are also expressions of a point of view—a perspective on a character, event, or theme. If one denies the cognitive component of emotion, one must also deny the aboutness of emotion—the idea that an emotion expresses a perspective on the world (Plantinga 2009).

In this regard, the remainder of this chapter will focus on five ideas that *300* embodies, and the emotions (and moods) that the film elicits to support them: (1) an extreme tribalism; (2) disdain for the "other" and the outsider; (3) militarism; (4) suppression of "soft" emotions traditionally thought to be feminine; and (5) a fascination with glorious and honorable death. Together with the mood described above, these emotions comprise the fascist affect and aesthetic of *300*.

### Tribalism

Fascism is widely thought to be intensely tribal, emphasizing the goodness, idealness, and superiority of its tribe (whether racial or ethnic) under the absolute rule and authority of a leader who is granted complete authority. This devotion to tribe and tribal leader takes on a quasi-religious aspect, becoming a powerful force of inspiration and direction. In *300*, the attractiveness of tribal emotions is typically promoted through developed allegiances with sympathetic characters that supposedly represent the authentic qualities of the tribe, and by the idealized representation of a leader character (King Leonidas). The emotions celebrated here are tribal pride, patriotism, loyalty, reverence, and vainglory, which are combined with admiration for and submission to a great tribal leader.

Emotions like reverence, loyalty, and devotion to both Sparta and its king run rampant through the sympathetic Spartan characters in *300*. The film's dialogue and voiceover narration are peppered with phrases proudly declaring what it means to be a Spartan and declaring that Spartan values are worth dying for. I have quoted many of these lines above. The figurehead of the tribe is blue-eyed King Leonidas, who is treated as a great man and a sacrificial hero. It is Leonidas who, as a boy, is shown undergoing rigorous Spartan training and killing a savage wolf. And the king is singled out several times for special veneration. When the Spartans watch a failed landing of Persian ships, in which many are dashed onto the rocky coast, the narrator intones: "Only one among us keeps his reserve; only he; only our king." It is Leonidas who refuses to kneel before the "holy" Persian King Xerxes and whose sacrificial death at the film's end is treated as a Christ-like sacrifice. As the Spartans die, the narrator speaks: "The old ones say we Spartans are descended from Hercules himself. Bold Leonidas gives testament to our bloodline. His roar is long and loud."

It is important to recognize that character and viewer emotions may differ significantly. Although the characters evince devotion and patriotism to the point of death, the viewer is intended to have different emotions. The viewer may not feel any patriotism for Sparta or any loyalty to Leonidas. What the viewer may feel is admiration for the Spartans and their king, or even elevation. Elevation refers to a positive emotion resulting from witnessing what is taken to be another's act of moral goodness. In this case, the sacrificial deaths of the Spartan heroes may elicit elevation.

### Disdain

The danger of tribalism is the vilification of the enemy, or even of anyone who does not happen to belong to the tribe. In this case, "vilification" becomes literally the making vile or loathsome of the enemy. It is expected that the Persians would be represented in stark terms as morally evil. *300* goes beyond this to represent them as biologically disgusting as well. As in many other conflict scenarios, the outward physical attributes of the enemy are signs of their inner corruption, thus promoting the harmful association of physical ugliness or deformity with evil, while physical

*Illustration 1.3. A hideous Persian giant roars like a beast before attacking the Spartans (300, Warner Bros., 2007)*

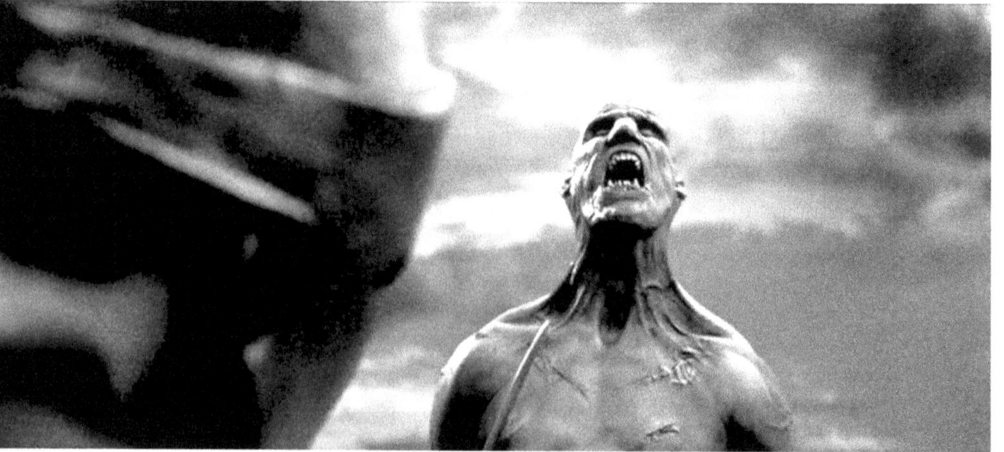

beauty and perfection signify the morally good. Thus the devotion to purity, beauty, and the threat of pollution are not only elements of the fascist aesthetic, but also serve to mark tribal differences between the good Spartans and the bad Persians.

Both race and sexuality work into this stark differentiation as well, as purity is designated to the white heterosexual male. The Persians are dark-skinned while the Spartans are light-skinned, and the Persians are marked as homosexual and Persian men are shown as either effeminate or monstrously ugly, while the Spartans are full-blooded, well-formed Caucasian heterosexuals with bulging arms and six-pack abs. Thus Xerxes, the Persian god-king, though a man with a beautiful face, also apparently wears lipstick and eyeliner, his face covered with jewelry and piercings, all of which suggests effeminacy. One of the most effective ways of vilifying others in moving image media is by eliciting disgust toward them (Plantinga 2009). The rank and file Persians, as the pustule-faced Ephors (mystics), are often depicted as visually revolting, some of them monsters of huge stature, often with scars, deformities, putrid and decaying flesh, horrifying teeth, and vocalizations usually heard only by carnivorous beasts in cartoons. One particularly loathsome monster has large blades in place of his arms, and it is not clear whether these are biological or mechanical appendages grafted onto his body. His role is to execute those who displease Xerxes by chopping off their heads.

The threat of pollution from the disgusting "other" is nowhere more apparent than in the figure of Ephialtes, the hunchbacked and variously deformed Spartan-in-exile. His mother had taken him away from Sparta as a baby to escape the infanticide meted out to deformed children, and he approaches Leonidas to ask to join forces with the Spartans. Leonidas rejects his help as a soldier because Ephialtes cannot lift his shield high enough to fit into the Spartan defensive formations. The enraged

*Illustration 1.4. Ephialtes the hunchback, who was born a Spartan, had years ago escaped the Spartan eugenics practice, but betrays the Spartans and thus justifies the practice (300, Warner Bros., 2007)*

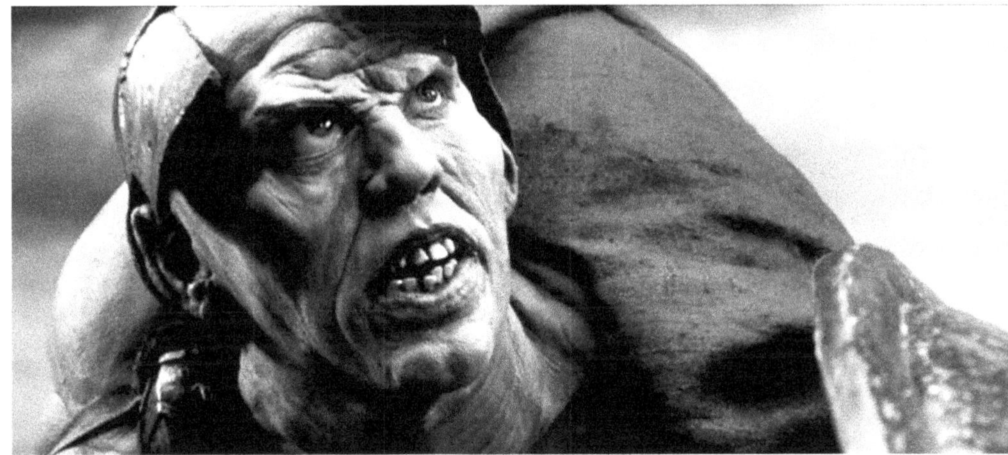

man visits the Persian king in whose tent we see writhing female bodies apparently engaged in an orgy. The camera lingers on two women kissing each other, again to associate the Persians and lesbianism with a threat to purity and authentic heterosexual Spartanism. Xerxes offers unlimited pleasures in return for Ephialtes's help, and as Ephialtes accepts this devil's bargain, the women move toward Ephialtes, suggesting the impure and disgusting thought of young female bodies consorting with this hideous creature. (Such "impure" relationships had earlier been suggested during the scene in which the "diseased, rotten, corrupt" Ephors consult the oracle, a young and beautiful Greek female with whom, it is implied, they also have sex). Thus in tried-and-true fashion, the physically disgusting and repulsive are mapped onto moral offensiveness; they are threats to Spartan purity, beauty, and authenticity. This was also accomplished during the Nazi decades in Germany, when Jews were associated with rats as a means of dehumanizing them and rendering them disgusting to the German populace.

The promotion of the strong over the weak is everywhere apparent in the film, as the virtues of manhood are associated strictly with excellence in battle. Thus, even the Athenians, who are Spartan allies, are implied to be weak and soft in comparison with the buff Spartans. Their help in battle is accepted though not highly regarded, and the only identifiable Athenian among them continually expresses fear and doubt, where the authentic Spartans express only fierce resolve. The "poets," "potters," and "blacksmiths" of the Athenian army, it is implied, are not genuine warriors because they have not devoted their lives solely to the arts of battle. They have not sufficiently realized that all of nature, and all of life, is a deadly struggle.

The Spartans are strong, beautiful, heterosexual, and white, while the Persians are dark-skinned, homosexual or effeminate, ugly, putrid,

*Illustration 1.5. The effeminate Xerxes (notice his eyeliner and painted fingernails) puts his hands on King Leonidas, eliciting homophobic disgust (300, Warner Bros., 2007)*

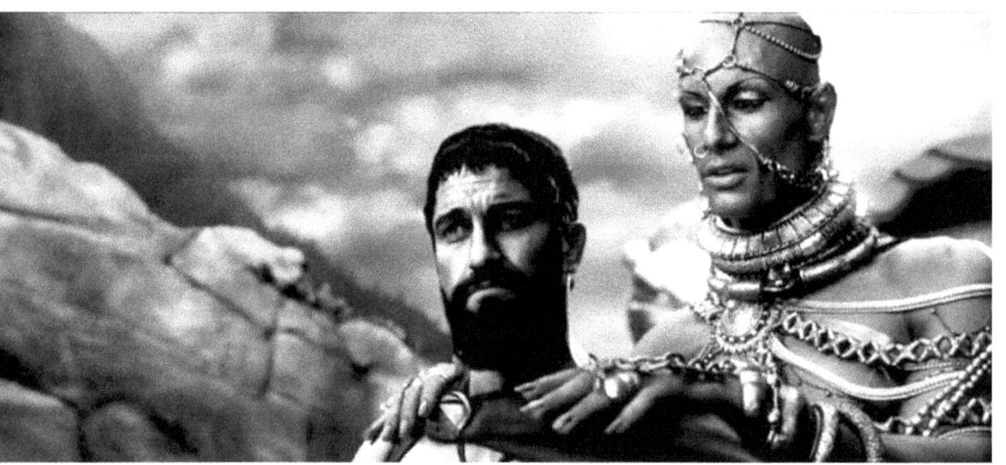

and/or deformed. This simplistic and exaggerated portrait of the "other," which is designed to elicit disgust, is an obvious feature of the promotion of tribalism at the heart of the fascist aesthetic.

### Militarism

We have seen so far that *300* creates a mood of urgent crisis, idealizes the tribe and its leader, and portrays the enemy—and in fact nearly anyone who is not a member of the tribe—as either monstrous or effeminate. In such a dangerous world, and a world in which good and evil are so easily determined, it might be thought perfectly natural that violent combat be romanticized, military training valorized, and the combatants themselves idealized. And of course, bloody combat scenes and the glorification of the Spartan combatants comprise the heart of *300*. Spartan boys are "baptized" in the fire of combat to create the "finest soldiers the world has ever known." The film's early stages suggest the austere beauty and necessity of the boys' military training, suggesting that to be a Spartan is a fine thing indeed—worthy of adulation and admiration.

In the film, the Spartans like to think that they preserve freedom, reason, and justice in the face of mysticism and emotion. The Ephors, for example, are "diseased old mystics" and remnants of a senseless tradition. Leonidas, according to Spartan law, must consult with them to his great distaste. But Spartan "honor culture" is an "imagined order" just as fascism or mysticism is. A lesson in honor and respect is granted the viewer early on, when several dark-skinned Persian emissaries visit Leonidas and the Spartans to bring a message demanding submission to Xerxes. Feeling the winds of Spartan beauty and tradition, Leonidas instead kills the Persian king's representatives by having them thrown down a bottomless pit. Later in the film, the effeminate Xerxes demands that Leonidas submit by kneeling before him. Instead, Xerxes is nearly impaled by Leonidas's spear, which grazes and cuts his face. Spartan militarism, it seems, is driven by a fierce sense of honor, such that any submission to the outsider becomes a loathsome, despicable act. Those who bring such a message to the Spartan king are worthy of death itself because, well, reason demands it! Yet Sparta itself was a helot-owning culture, so presumably it was fine to demand the submission of the people of conquered tribes (even the citizens of other Greek city-states). It is only the special favors tribalism grants to its own tribe that make submission to the outsider such a mark of shame.

At this point, one might object that the valorization of militarism in the film is wholly justified in that the Spartans actually did face a significant threat from the invading Persian forces. This really *was* a dangerous time that demanded a strong military response. The reader should ask why *300* needed to be retold at this particular time and in this particular way. The purpose is not a history lesson; the film is replete with historical errors and besides, historical accuracy is not really the point. The important question to ask is what role the telling of the story plays in our culture today. Of course, the makers intended to entertain and to fascinate. But we can also see the film as a restaging of a paradigm scenario that rehearses certain kinds of desires and responses, that elicits various supporting emotions and moods, and that uses these to support views about violence, masculinity, and tribalism. The popular success of the film implies that incipient fascist perspectives are potentialities that await only the right cultural context to be fully released.

### *Suppression of Feminine Emotion*

Occasionally, the Spartan men gather for group chanting. When building up their resolve, or celebrating their great leader, they sometimes chant "A-whoo, A-whoo!" and sound a bit like fans at a sports match. At other points, we hear exclamations such as this: "No prisoners! No mercy!" From the beginning, we learn that for Spartans mercy and compassion are rejected ideals. Mercy is a sign of weakness and a failure to recognize the cruel and dangerous nature of the world. While a softhearted liberal or a woman might administer mercy and compassion, the Spartan men reject it outright. Post-battle, as we have seen, this allows the Spartans to casually kill wounded Persians while engaging in lighthearted banter about something else altogether. This is the Spartan way. Neither do the Spartans want mercy and compassion for themselves. We learn that Spartans never retreat and never surrender, and that they expect no mercy from their enemy. Just before the apocalyptic final battle, Captain Artemis (Vincent Regan), who has lost his eldest son to the Persian sword, tells the king: "I have filled my heart with hate." "Good," Leonidas replies.

For Leonidas (and the other Spartans), controlled hatred and anger are fine, but the "soft" emotions must be avoided at all costs. When his son dies, Captain Artemis experiences uncontrollable grief and anger as he breaks formation to wildly swing his sword at the Persian hordes. We are reminded that keeping one's reserve in the face of outrageous events is the hallmark of King Leonidas, who had witnessed the destruction of the Persian navy with a stoic demeanor. We must remember that "only the hard and the strong may call themselves Spartans." Emotional control in all cases must be a maintained, and the "soft" or "effeminate" emotions must be quelled altogether.

Mercy and compassion would seem to call into question much that these fictional Spartans stand for: eugenics, rigorous and dangerous combat training, the dehumanization of other tribes, the killing of Persian wounded and even messengers, and, in general, a rejection of human consideration beyond the narrow confines of family and tribe. And like the mood of urgent crisis that seemingly makes the Spartans' hard violence necessary, the elimination of compassion and mercy make certain Spartan practices more acceptable.

### Fascination with Death

This attitude toward mercy and compassion, then, does leave an interesting question. Typically the death of a hero is met with a certain amount of sentiment: sadness, compassion, mourning, grieving. After viewers of *300* are repeatedly taught that mercy and compassion are weak, how are viewers cued to experience the deaths of King Leonidas and his men? The short answer is this: the death of Leonidas and his cohorts is a fulfillment of their destiny and of their very identity as Spartans. It is not a cause for mourning, but for glorification, remembrance, and even celebration.

Susan Sontag, in her essay on fascist aesthetics, writes that fascist art "glamorizes death" (1981, 91). It promotes mass obeisance to the hero through immortalizing him and the doctrines that he represents. In *300*, it is the deaths of Leonidas and his men that are designed to cement their legacy and to glorify what they stand for. If death in the service of race or ethnicity is the ultimate glory, then there is little to be sentimental about when the hero dies. Early in the film, we learn that Spartan boys are taught that "death on the battlefield in honor of Sparta is the greatest achievement." As we see Leonidas embarking on his mission to save all of Greece, the voiceover narrator intones that Leonidas's "only regret is that he has so few to sacrifice."

As the Spartans view the Persian hordes from above, one Spartan soldier smiles as he considers that among this mass of Persian soldiers there may be one man "capable of granting him a beautiful death." (An Arcadian who overhears this shakes his head in disdain, but what would an Arcadian know? They are merely blacksmiths, poets, and potters.) As Leonidas prepares his troops for battle, he tells them: "Spartans, prepare for glory!" and "A new age has begun." After the climactic battle had ended, all of the Spartan 300 are dead, Leonidas's body splayed with

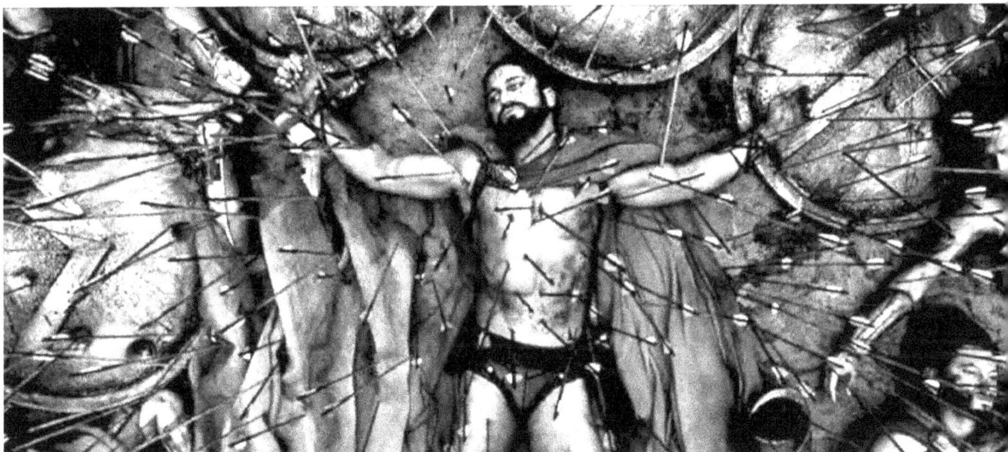

*Illustration 1.6. Leonidas as Christ, having gloriously sacrificed himself for the Spartan nation (300, Warner Bros., 2007)*

arms to his sides and his body pierced, an obvious Christ reference. The ritual celebration of these sacrificial deaths plays down sadness and grief, but emphasizes the glorification and the representation of death on the battlefield as the highest achievement available to a Spartan hero. The spectator is meant to feel subdued pathos but full-scale admiration and elevation. Delios says: "Remember us. Remember why we died."

### Conclusion

Fascist art and stories are dangerous art. Fascist art helps disseminate fascist ideas and a fascist "emotional regime" even (and perhaps especially) among those who have no historical framework, who have no idea what fascism is or why it is a threat. As I argue in *Screen Stories* (2018), mass stories on screens have the potential to significantly influence both individuals and cultures. The affective character of *300* seems designed to make extreme tribalism, nationalism, militarism, leader-worship, disgust for the "other," and heroic death seem very attractive if not absolutely necessary in a world of urgent crisis and threat.

Madeleine Albright, in her recent book, *Fascism: A Warning* (2018), notes that Donald Trump is the first antidemocratic president in US history. The forces that he threatens to unleash have connections with fascism—authoritarian, xenophobic nationalism and a seeming contempt for liberal democracy. The threat of fascist resurgence is real. To think that the mass narratives that populate Western culture could have no influence in inculcating the sorts of affects and perspectives that contribute to fascism would be naïve.

---

**Carl Plantinga** is Arthur H. DeKruyter Chair of Communication at Calvin University. His most recent books are *Alternate Realities* (2021) and *Screen Stories: Emotion and the Ethics of Engagement* (2018). Plantinga is currently Principal Investigator for a grant from the Templeton Religion Trust, entitled "Screen Stories and Moral Understanding".
Email: cplantin@calvin.edu

## References

Antliff, Mark. 1998. "Aestheticized Politics." In *Encyclopedia of Aesthetics* Vol. 4, ed. Michael Kelly, 26–29. Oxford: Oxford University Press.

Breihan, Tom. 2017. "Zack Snyder's *300* Presaged the Howling Fascism of the Alt-Right." *AV/Film*, August 11, 2017. https://film.avclub.com/zack-snyder-s-300-presaged-the-howling-fascism-of-the-a-1798265082.

Carroll, Noël. 2003. "Art and Mood: Preliminary Notes and Conjectures." *The Monist* 86 (4): 521–555. doi.org/10.5840/monist200386426.

Daly, Steve. 2007. "Double-Edged Sword: How *300* Was Positioned To Be a Box Office Hit." *Entertainment Weekly*, March 11, 2017. http://ew.com/article/2007/03/11/how-300-was-positioned-be-box-office-hit/.

Epstein, Daniel Robert. 2005. "Exclusive Interview with Tyler Bates, Score Composer for *The Devil's Rejects*." *UGO Entertainment*, July 16, 2005. http://www.gerardbutler.net/news/Print.php?NewsID=1112.

Harari, Yuval Noah. 2011. *Sapiens: A Brief History of Humankind*. London: Penguin.

Hayes, Paul M. 1973. *Fascism*. New York: Free Press.

Laquer, Walter. 1996. *Fascism: Past, Present, Future*. Oxford: Oxford University Press.

Payne, Stanley G. 1980. *Fascism: Comparison and Definition*. Madison: University of Wisconsin Press.

Plantinga, Carl. 2009. *Moving Viewers: American Film and the Spectator's Experience*. Berkeley: University of California Press.

Plantinga, Carl. 2018. *Screen Stories: Emotion and the Ethics of Engagement*. New York: Oxford University Press.

Sinnerbrink, Robert. 2012. "*Stimmung*: Exploring the Aesthetics of Mood." *Screen* 53 (2): 148–163. doi:10.1093/screen/hjs007.

Smith, Greg M. 2003. *Film Structure and the Emotion System*. Cambridge: Cambridge University Press.

Smith, Kyle. 2007. "Persian Shrug." *New York Post*, March 9, 2007. https://nypost.com/2007/03/09/persian-shrug/.

Sontag, Susan. 1981. *Under the Sign of Saturn*. New York: Vintage Books.

Stevens, Dana. 2008. "A Movie Only a Spartan Could Love." *Slate*, March 8, 2007. http://www.slate.com/articles/arts/movies/2007/03/a_movie_only_a_spartan_could_love.html.

# Chapter 2

# Other Sides
## Loving and Grieving with *Heart of a Dog* and Merleau-Ponty's Depth

**Saige Walton**

*"Wouldn't it be great to have a second brain or a reserve heart that would just … drop down into place when the first one breaks?"*
*— Laurie Anderson*

Can the loss of a loved one ever be measured? Bridging documentary, the film essay, and experimental film practices, Laurie Anderson's film Heart of a Dog (2015) is explicitly concerned with death and the emotions that accompany it (love, grief, guilt, and loss). First commissioned by the Franco-German company Arte TV to create a "philosophy of life" project, the American performance artist, sound artist, and musician made her feature following the 2011 death of a beloved family member, a small rat terrier dog named Lolabelle. The result is a powerful testament to the interspecies bonds that we share with animals and to animal grievability. It is also a heartfelt portrait of Lolabelle herself, which is filtered through the stories, sounds, memories, and imagined perspectives of Anderson, her human owner.

Watching Heart of a Dog for the first time, I found myself deeply and profoundly moved by Anderson's attempts to translate the gift of

Lolabelle's animal companionship to the screen, her free-floating meditations, the film's aqueous images and sounds, and its unexpected transitions. Thinking about the passing of my own furry sidekick and of others filled me with feelings of sadness and loss.[1] And yet, despite its elegiac subject matter, the film still managed to convey an overall sense of lightness, lyricism, and fluidity. In this chapter, I look to the philosopher Maurice Merleau-Ponty's later writing on depth in order to approach but not try to measure Anderson's film and its poetic evocations of loss. Drawing on Merleau-Ponty's "Eye and Mind" and other relevant texts, I examine *Heart of a Dog* as one instance of what we might call "depthful" cinema, focusing on its aesthetic and implicitly ethical effects.

In his later writing (1959–1961), Merleau-Ponty connects depth to movement, the debordering of body–world relations, properties of the imagination, nonmimetic style, surfaces, and the elements (e.g., air, water). Bringing *Heart of a Dog* into a dialogue with depth, the film essay, and the lyrical film tradition, I hold that Anderson's film refuses the emotional weight of grief through its dispersals of the "eye/I" and its experimental aesthetic. Through its deployments of the liquid and the lyrical, its foregrounding of surfaces, its dispersals of the self, and its readiness to embrace multiple perspectives (including that of the nonhuman), Anderson's film lends poignant, cinematic form to Merleau-Ponty's depth as an elemental opening onto the world and onto others. As an opening onto the artistic imagination, also, Merleau-Ponty's depth is befitting of Anderson's efforts to capture the loving heart of a dog.

**The Depth of the Visible**

In "Eye and Mind" (the last text published during his lifetime), Merleau-Ponty mobilizes painting and the figure of the painter to illustrate the "enigma … of visibility" and its connections with depth (2004, 297). As is typical of the philosopher's later thought, the enigma of which he speaks is bound up with a reversibility of subject/object positions.[2] Writing of vision, he asserts: "That which looks at all things can also look at itself and recognize, in what it sees, the 'other side' of its power of looking" (2004, 294). This looking from the "other side" can also be extended to art. It is "the mountain itself … from out there" that "makes itself seen by the painter," he writes, just as it is by "lending his body to the world that the artist changes the world into paintings" (2004, 298; 294).

As phenomenological scholar Mauro Carbone (2015) observes, it is through painting that Merleau-Ponty figures his later, mobile conception of vision. Whereas the *"representative* model of the window" and the techniques of Renaissance art "made us believe that we could *fix* the visible 'in its place,'" Merleau-Ponty's visible (including the visible of painting) cannot be fixed (2015, 3, emphasis in original). For Merleau-Ponty, images are not to be conceived of as a "tracing, a copy, a second thing" (2004, 296). The embodied, imaginative contact that the painter makes with the world complicates any easy divisions between the "outer" perceptions of the eye and the "inner" movements of the mind. For the viewer, too, painting encourages an imaginative coming-to of visibility. It "makes us see a *space*" or an object "where there is none" (2004, 304, emphasis in original).

Rather than beginning in the "real" world, Anderson opens her memorial to Lolabelle on the page. As instrumental strains of music begin, the camera pans across a pinkish surface, revealing black hatchings, scrawled words, and the image of two small black dogs. These are some of Anderson's own monochromatic ink-and-line drawings, which are included in the film. One drawing features a dog that has its head slightly tilted, capturing the canine gesture of a quizzical look. The upside-down lettering of words suggests a tumultuous, unstable space. The profile of another dog comes into view, its snout and ears peeking through upward-sweeping brushstrokes. To the left of this dog, two human figures rise and fall with their arms outstretched. Surrounded by thick, flowing black lines and the outlines of raindrops, these figures are drawn as if they were caught up in heavy gusts of wind and water. Later, we will discover that these are some of Anderson's drawings of the now deceased Lolabelle, who is imagined in the bardo of the Tibetan afterlife (a metaphysical state in between death and rebirth). In *Heart of a Dog*'s rendition, the bardo is populated by human and animal (dog) souls, and it is wracked by wild storms.

Whereas the window model of art and vision is associated with fixity, distance, and mimesis, "Eye and Mind" presents us with an alternative in which images radiate, "filling our perception as well as our imaginary" (2015, 4). Consider Merleau-Ponty's account of France's Lascaux Cave. The ancient animals that are painted there are not felt *in situ* like the cave's limestone walls are, but nor could we say that they are "elsewhere." Instead, Merleau-Ponty insists that the animals "radiate about the wall without ever breaking their elusive moorings" (1994, 126, emphasis added). Before I return to *Heart of a Dog*'s own radiating depictions of the animal, it is worth lingering on this passage further in order to grasp Merleau-Ponty's animate, mobile, and multidirectional account of painting. Contemplating the walls of Lascaux, he writes:

> *I would be at great pains to say where is the painting I am looking at. For I do not look at it as one looks at a thing; I do not fix it in its place. My gaze wanders in it as in the halos of Being. It is more accurate to say that I see according to it, or with it, than that I see it. (2004, 296, emphasis in original)*

Spatially and affectively, the painted animals (or any image for that matter) cannot be fixed in place by art's material foundations.[3] They irradiate and they spread, commingling the cave's solid mass with lively impressions of movement, the "quasi presence and imminent visibility which make-up ... the imaginary" (2004, 296).

In his book *The Flesh of Images: Merleau-Ponty between Painting and Cinema*, Carbone (2015) has also picked up on the significance that "Eye and Mind" holds for film. More particularly, he proposes that Merleau-Ponty advances a screen-based model of vision, reflecting his lifelong interest in the medium of cinema.[4] Citing the philosopher's description of Lascaux, Carbone maintains that cinema is another medium that we "see according to, or with," without mistaking its screen-mediated vision for one's own (Carbone 2015, 3; Merleau-Ponty 1994, 126). Given that "Eye and Mind" contains a brief reference to the cinema—indeed, an important aqueous reference that I will return to below—the philosopher may well have been thinking of film alongside the art of painting. Missing from Carbone's discussion, however, is how Merleau-Ponty's concept of depth figures in this scenario, and how the aesthetics of depth manifests on-screen.

While depth is grouped alongside other formal characteristics such as color and light, it is important to note that Merleau-Ponty's depth is not visible. As Sue L. Cataldi affirms: "Depth 'as such' or 'in itself' is neither completely perceived nor completely perceptible" (1993, 77). Similarly, when Merleau-Ponty invokes depth in art, he is not referring to the depth effects of linear perspective. Throughout "Eye and Mind," the philosopher is at pains to extricate depth from its commonplace association with spatiality or depth perception. If depth is not space, then what exactly is depth? At various points, Merleau-Ponty refers to depth as the third, the first, or the missing dimension, contrasting it with "height and width" (2004, 304). Whereas height and width are typically juxtaposed, depth is the means by which these might be seen from yet another angle. Unlike height and width, depth is not something that can be empirically measured. Inasmuch as it registers and reveals something "more" to the lifeworld (including art), depth is what opens up an alternative angle and another point of view on things.

Following our first glimpses of Lolabelle in the *bardo*, an animated self-portrait of Anderson appears:

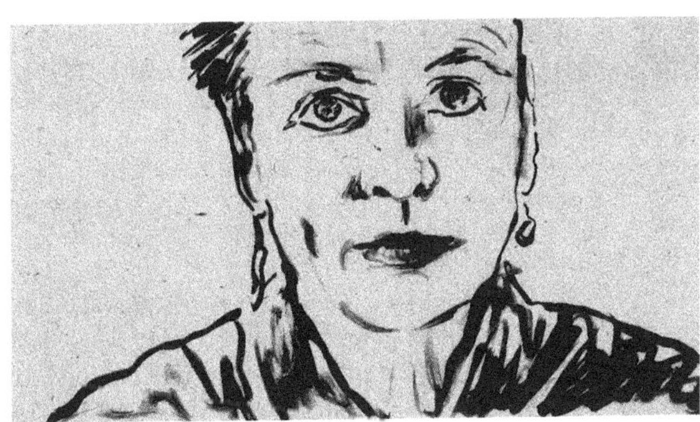

*Illustration 2.1. Laurie Anderson's self-portrait (*Heart of a Dog*, Arte TV/HBO, 2015).*

She proceeds to recount a dream in which she is lying in a hospital bed about to give birth to her own full-grown dog. "Hello little bonehead," she tells Lolabelle, who is all bundled up like a newborn: "I will love you forever." Interspecies love, care, and bonding are crucial concerns in this film—no one in the hospital scene diminishes Anderson's outpouring of affection for an animal. At the same time, she recounts that Lolabelle barks and struggles against the doctors, the nurses, and the wishes of her owner. As the animated Anderson explains, she had "arranged" to have the dog sewn into her stomach so that she could "give birth to her" (a situation that even the animated Lolabelle resists). Contra Anderson's voiceover, the drawings that precede Lolabelle's birth suggest that this was not the way "things had to be." Like the film's sweeping depictions of the *bardo*, these lines are in the process of forming nascent shapes and swirling, emergent figures.

In a later section of "Eye and Mind," Merleau-Ponty posits that depth is not really a dimension at all but that it is instead "the experience of the reversibility of dimensions" (2004, 311). Depth is what allows us to see and imagine from the "other side." It is thanks to depth, he surmises, that artists so often include depictions of themselves in their work—imaginatively layering what "things saw of them" into their metamorphoses of the visible (2004, 300). By way of her drawings of Lolabelle and her own animated self-portrait, Anderson indicates the importance of imagined and occluded perspectives for *Heart of a Dog* from the outset. Had the point of view of the hospital scene been attached to Lolabelle, for example, the power of the line could have been walked (or drawn) in another direction. Had Lolabelle's barking been listened to or had it been given as much precedence as Anderson's voice, this opening "story" might have been told differently.[5]

### Depth as Dispersal

Held together by Anderson's distinctive voice and her especially composed score, *Heart of a Dog* deploys a "structurally liquid" style that refuses linear narration and chronology (Chang 2015). Except in animated form, the artist's adult self rarely appears on-screen. Live action footage of Lolabelle (filmed at various stages in her life) is interwoven with 8 mm archival footage of Anderson and her siblings as children or re-creations of Anderson's own personal memories. In addition, photographs, intertitles, snatches of Anderson's favorite philosophical and literary quotations (Wittgenstein, Kierkegaard), readings from Buddhist teachings, images of paintings, Anderson's drawings, and her digital animations make up the film's eclectic content.

Given its interweaving of fact and fiction and its foregrounding of Anderson's intermedial persona (her voice, her electronic soundscape, her artworks), *Heart of a Dog* can readily be affiliated with the hybrid format of the film essay. According to Timothy Corrigan, the essayistic mode is characterized by the articulation of a "personal point of view" on "public experience" (2011, 13). Unlike traditional forms of film narration, the direct, often intimate, address of the filmmaker works to foster a "dialogue of ideas" (2017, 201). Via her use of the essayistic address—which includes the posing of a series of questions to the viewer—Anderson fosters the contemplation of subjects that are often excluded from public discussion. These topics range from the emotional processing of loss to the innate intelligence of dogs or the animals' right to a natural death.

Anderson herself acknowledges her debt to the film essay, also describing her feature film as a "collection of short stories" that relate to one another (Schaefer 2018).[6] Stories relating to Lolabelle, dogs, death (animal and human), surveillance, family, memory, love, and mortality are among her foremost subjects. Consistent with the film essay's inherent instability and its "changing experiential expressions," Anderson's stories unfold in an associative fashion (Corrigan 2011, 31). The film's fond, often funny remembrances of Lolabelle suddenly veer into a playful taxonomy of dog breeds and their personas. A story about the artist's childhood in the Midwest gives way to a recounting of how the aged, blinded Lolabelle learned to paint and play the piano. (Rat terriers have great hearing and can learn up to 500 human words, we are told.) Tales about living in post-9/11 New York, the gathering of surveillance data, or the breeding of dogs by the United States Department of Homeland Security combine with the piecemeal narration of Lolabelle's life. Alongside Lolabelle's death, Anderson recalls the deaths of family members and friends, including her own mother with whom she had a fraught relationship.

In contemporary film-phenomenological studies, Merleau-Ponty's thought tends to be invoked to speak to the experience of individual spectators, the perceptions and the expressions of film bodies (variously defined), and their correlation.[7] Shifting away from a focus on the lived body/subject, Merleau-Ponty's depth opens up other, more diffuse and speculative possibilities. According to philosopher Glen A. Mazis (2010, 2016), it was through depth that Merleau-Ponty sought to overcome the dualisms of his previous work. Ideas of depth, reversibility, invisibility, occlusion, and encroachment begin to replace the former subject-focused language of intentionality.[8] In his later writings, the philosopher speaks of "being as a winding," a "perception of *elements* (water, air . . .)" and of bodies caught up in the *"rays of the world"* (Merleau-Ponty 1968, 194; 218, emphasis in original). Subjectivity is not annihilated so much as it is radically decentered and debordered. Depth is "key to that decentering," Mazis writes, as is Merleau-Ponty's willingness to embrace the ongoing, "fluctuating ambiguity of experience" (1988, 230–231).

"What are those things that you see when you close your eyes?" Anderson asks. As she reflects on the play of phosphenes behind closed eyes as being like "some kind of eternal, plot-less, avant-garde, animated movie," the film's figurative imagery gives way to an unexpected sequence of abstraction. A free-flowing reddish color fills the screen, which is riven by explosions of blue-white light and whirring sounds. "Maybe [phosphenes] are just screen-savers … holding patterns that just sit there so your brain won't fall asleep," she continues. Abstraction dissolves into a large, flickering amber circle, which is accompanied by the hallucinatory sounds of synthesizers. At first, this flickering circle resembles a colored moon suspended in the night sky. Then, the camera tracks out from a photograph of one of Lolabelle's (blinded) eyes, a movement that renders ambiguous whose "eye/I" we are privy to here.

Vision is "the means given me for *being absent from myself*," Merleau-Ponty (2004, 317, emphasis added) maintains, as we are caught up in the depths of the visible before winding back to the self. In a moment of depth, Cataldi concurs: "We tend to lose or expand our sense of 'self' or 'subjectivity'" (1993, 112). Merleau-Ponty himself captures this porous dynamic through his famous example of the painter in the forest. He groups the Swiss artist Paul Klee as being among those painters who have "said that things look at them" (2004, 299). Inside the forest, the painter sees and hears the trees but feels that the trees are themselves looking and speaking. Merleau-Ponty is not imputing an anthropomorphism or sentience to the forest such that it sees and is "aware" of Klee/the painter. Rather, the exchange is indicative of the depth and reversibility that he associates with all embodied, enworlded being and with art.[9]

Early on in *Heart of a Dog*, the film holds on a bright blue sky in which passages of air circulate. "As a child, I was a kind of a sky worshipper," Anderson narrates, for "the sky was so vast it was most of the world." Upon the artist's vocalization, the mists dissipate and the film transitions to slow-moving footage of a forest. As a folk tune plays, Anderson shifts to contemplate the possibility of being able to "fall through time, into another world." Vertical shots of the sky often feature in *Heart of a Dog*, occurring alongside images, sounds, and stories relating to the unpredictability of the air.[10] Through her repetition of overhead footage (images of trees, forests, and power lines), a vital sense of openness to the world and its possibility is conveyed, as well as a sense of vulnerability.

In "Eye and Mind," Merleau-Ponty often describes depth as the process of opening onto a larger whole. For example, he refers to the seer opening "onto the world" and to color in art as a deeper "opening onto things" (2004, 303). Likening depth to the opening of a window (albeit not the window model of art), depth is understood in resolutely positive terms—as an opening onto the "absolute positivity of Being" (2004, 304).[11] Discussing the Russian director Andrei Tarkovsky, Jennifer M. Barker is one of the few film-phenomenological scholars to have extended Merleau-Ponty's later, much more porous, take on being to the cinema. Through she does not discuss depth at length, she quotes directly from "Eye and Mind" to articulate moments of inspiration in film as an intersubjective, "full-bodied opening or suffusion" (2009, 146).[12] Suffusion need not be mediated through human bodies, however. It can be brought into prominence (and visibility) through a film's stylized movements or its foregrounding of a vital materiality such as with the filming of wind rippling through grass. Inspiration "moves *through* the body and opens onto something larger than either film or viewer," she writes, linking inspiration to the ineffability of that "something that moves beyond, beneath, and within us all" (2009, 149; 157, emphasis in original).

The repetitive movements, sliding sounds, and sweeping lines that open *Heart of a Dog* anticipate its larger, circulatory organization of different sights, sounds, words, and memories. What Barker calls "inspiration" Anderson enacts as "depthful" cinema, which is achieved through the film's wandering, essayistic sensibility and its openness to multiple ways of being. Caught up in feeling the situation of another body, object, or worldly expression (including aesthetic expressions), depth loosens the subjective boundaries of the "I." In depth, "I enter, affectively, into [a] spiraling current of experience" and "experience my 'self' dispersively—as alternating 'back' and 'forth'" (Cataldi 1993, 132–133).[13] Writing of the film essay, Corrigan helpfully indicates its potential for similar spiraling encounters. While the film essay foregrounds the presence of the filmmaker (their voice, their reflections), it stages a protean self in which subjectivity "drifts" (2011, 30). In *Heart of a Dog*, Anderson's free-floating narration makes visible "an expanding world of continual and changing reflection," lending images and sounds to the experiences of another (2011, 30). Recalling the time that Lolabelle went blind, Anderson tells of how the dog "froze in place" and was only able to run along the edge of the ocean. During these moments, Lolabelle's world moves to the fore of the film. Her halting movements are conveyed to us through a series of overlapping black-and-white freeze frames.

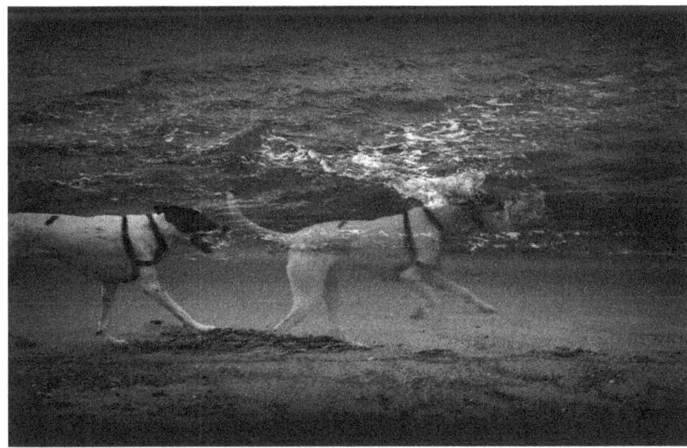

*Illustration 2.2. Blind Lolabelle (*Heart of a Dog*, Arte TV/HBO, 2015).*

As the dog learns to run blinded, electronic and oceanic sounds rush in. As she runs "full-speed into total darkness," the screen abruptly fades to black in chromatic sympathy with Lolabelle.

In the essayistic mode, the "self invariably comes undone" through the testing out of different ideas or possible selves and the imagining of other points of view (Corrigan 2011, 30). Slip-sliding between real and fictional worlds, the expression of a personal perspective (Anderson) and animal life (Lolabelle), *Heart of a Dog* refracts and disperses the subjective "I." Throughout, Anderson tasks us with the need to look beyond our own situated and human perspectives. As if counteracting the implied selfishness of the film's opening, her voiceover is matched with environmental imagery or with different non-human ways of being. Landscapes, anonymous vistas, and animal viewpoints recur: from the snout-level perspective of dogs to insights into Lolabelle's blinded being, the on-high footage of surveillance cameras, images of the mountains of Mars, scenes of an empty, snow-covered forest, and oneiric shots of a golden ocean. Though Merleau-Ponty's depth is not space, he suggests that depth is what fosters "the being of space *beyond every [particular] point of view*. Things encroach upon one another" (2004, 304, emphasis added). As Anderson's narration shifts between reflecting upon Lolabelle, her childhood, border control, her mother, the dead, and the dying, no one "story" is privileged. Things begin to encroach upon one another. In "depthful" cinema, I would suggest, a sense of care and responsibility for others and for the world is prompted through felt experiences of dispersal and diffusion.[14]

**Depth as Surface**

It is no secret that, across his writings on art and aesthetics, Merleau-Ponty favored examples of modern painting, rejecting the traditional function of art as the reproduction of nature. In this regard, it is worth us considering another tradition that is relevant to Merleau-Ponty's depth and to the aesthetic design of *Heart of a Dog*: the lyrical film. Coined by P. Adams Sitney with regard to the American experimental filmmaker Stan Brakhage, the lyrical film takes its name from the first-person expression of feeling in the lyrical poem. In the lyrical film, it is the filmmaker who serves as the film's first-person protagonist. Like the film essay, the lyrical film is pieced together from across different time periods. It is "filmed in such a way that we never forget [the filmmaker's] presence" (Sitney 2002, 220). In place of narrative and character, it relies upon surfaces, movement, symbolism, and the filmmaker's embodied vision to express emotion.

For Merleau-Ponty, depth is not about representation, the rendering of a "meticulous relationship to a space and a world existing outside" (2004, 312). Connecting depth to flowing movement, superimposed surfaces, shifting or overlapping planes, texture, the "voice" of light, and "the murmur of color," Merleau-Ponty's (2004, 312–313) depth is steeped in a nonmimetic sensibility that can likewise be extended to film. In "Eye and Mind," the painter plumbs the visible world, lending it a new, imaginative form. In the lyrical format, the filmmaker fosters an "intense experience of seeing" by bringing together real-to-life experiences (birth, death, sexuality) with the filming of first-person perspectives and the creative possibilities of the imagination (Sitney 2002, 220). In Brakhage's practice, for example, vision spans the "eye/I" of the lived body, "brain movies" that are generated by the mind's eye (visual memory, dreams) and what he calls "closed-eye" vision (the hallucinogenic play of patterns and shapes that occur behind closed eyelids or on the eye's surface) (2002, 231). The "imagination . . . includes the simultaneous functioning of all these modes" for Brakhage, as Sitney (2002, 168) writes, with all modes inform- ing the lyrical film's construction and its shifting, aleatory expressions.

Bringing together looking from the "inside" with stylized depictions of the world "outside" and the (visual) expression of feeling, lyrical film- making externalizes the "inward traces of vision" and the "imaginary texture of the real" that Merleau-Ponty (2004, 313; 297) sees as lining the visible. As with Brakhage's lyrical filmmaking, emotion in Anderson's film is attached to a heavy use of visual symbolism (dogs, animal life), which is presented to us in a novel, shifting manner. Real-world visuals, filmed in Manhattan, cede to extended "mind's eye" sequences such as with the recreation of dreams or Lolabelle's time in the *bardo*. Alternatively, live-action or animation sequences will be interrupted by intertitles set against a black screen, encouraging the viewer to add their own images to Anderson's poetic text.

There are some crucial reinventions of the lyrical format in *Heart of a Dog*, however. First and foremost, Anderson adds sound, music, voiceover, and spoken verse.[15] She also gestures toward the presence of an infinite number of stories and perspectives in the film. Unlike Sitney's take on the lyrical film, *Heart of a Dog* does not delimit its cinematic vision to the vantage point of just one "person [Anderson] looking" (Sitney 2002, 220). Building on the lyrical film's speculative power and potential, Anderson's film fosters a "depthful" sense of "participation in . . . Being without re- striction" (Merleau-Ponty 2004, 304). The latter is visualized in the film as flows of data, networks of electricity, the blues and greens of a dog's vision, and the imagery of the sky or of water. Across the film, Anderson's voiceover also asks us to contemplate different, virtual ways of being: "Say, are you perhaps made of glass?"

According to Steven Dillon (2004), the lyrical film makes the invisible visible by translating what is normally private or hidden to the screen. Following *Heart of a Dog*'s main titles, an electronic score pulsates, its sounds reminiscent of a heartbeat. Black-and-white footage of a train fades to a large white house (a childhood home). Against the darkened, indeterminate imagery that follows, Anderson's voice remains crystal clear. She guides us into the past of another hospital room where her mother lies dying, "speaking in a high new voice." Grainy, luminous footage of two boys at play appears. One boy is wearing a black cowboy hat. Both are dressed in matching red-and-white striped tops. (This is home-movie footage of Anderson's young twin brothers, in fact.) The shot glows, briefly, before darkness overwhelms it. This footage continues to resurface, adding to the stockpile of images that *Heart of a Dog* returns to and repeats: Lolabelle in the *bardo*, Anderson skating on ice as a child, water, and washes of gold. At first, the images that we see do not seem to correspond with Anderson's narration. Other family members appear, but they are rendered hazy and spectral, often fading in and out of visibility.

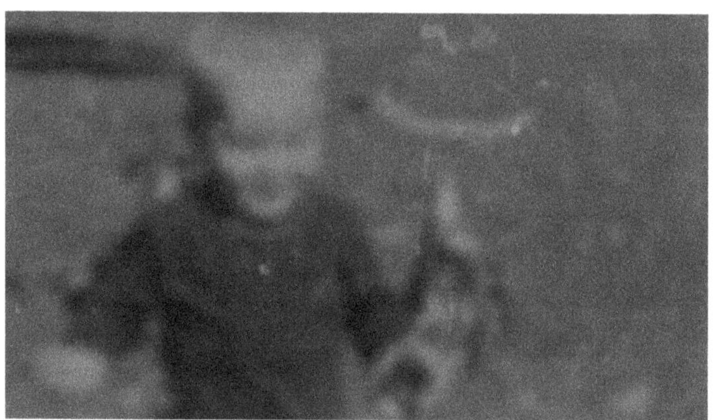

*Illustration 2.3. Expressive layers of time (*Heart of a Dog, *Arte TV/HBO, 2015).*

These figures are encased behind the film's expressive layerings of time, and can be glimpsed only as bright patches of color.

In extending depth beyond spatiality, Merleau-Ponty came to associate depth with surfaces and the phenomenon of a surfacing. In "Eye and Mind," some of the most significant passages relating to depth center on ancient and modern art, indicating that the philosopher saw depth as arising from the surface of a work. Depth is that "voluminosity we express in a world when we say that a thing is there," he writes (2004, 311). Regardless of whether the thickness of depth occurs through enworlded or artistic vision, "what is proper to the visible . . . is the surface of an inexhaustible depth" (Merleau-Ponty 1968, 143). In Cataldi's view, "depthful" feeling must "be extended to the surface of our body . . . and to its interminglings with other surfaces and the surfaces of others" (1993, 128).

Given Merleau-Ponty's own evocations of depth in art, I think we can justly extend "depthful" feeling to an intermingling with aesthetic surfaces (including those of the cinema). Speaking to depth as a surface-based aesthetic, Merleau-Ponty observes how "Klee's colors seem to have … emanated from some primordial ground, 'exhaled at the right place,' *like a patina or a mold*" (2004, 312, emphasis added). Instead of painted exhalations of color, it is the use of digitally distressed, archival footage in *Heart of a Dog* that draws our attention to the film's surfaces. In these sequences, the foreground of the image and its texturing is clear while the specifics of human faces are lost. Recalling Merleau-Ponty's discussion of painting, the lyrical mode rejects vanishing points and the "traditional use [of film] as a window" onto a self-contained world (Sitney 2002, 160). Instead, the lyrical filmmaker revels in a formal flattening of cinematic space, effects of superimposition and shifting variations in light, texture, color, and its hue. In *Heart of a Dog*, scratches, blotches, lines, spots, and glitches create a veritable dance of surface effects across the screen, calling to mind Brakhage's earlier experiments with the film-strip (scratching and painting onto celluloid or pressing natural objects into it). By way of her inclusion of flattened perspectives, line drawings, surface coatings to the image, and moments of abstraction, Anderson activates the lyrical film in a new digital guise.

Following Merleau-Ponty's descriptions of depth as an opening, layering, or encroachment, Mazis (2010, 2016) makes the compelling observation that depth is ultimately about the passing of time. That is, the thickness and voluminosity of depth is what presses the past upon the present and the present upon the future. By looping its stories and archival footage and by returning to and repeating images of her loved ones (especially Lolabelle), Anderson's film captures this durational thickness. Literally overlapping and overlaying images, layering the screen with water, textural grain, and other effects, *Heart of a Dog* brings "the surfacing of depth" and its nonmimetic sensibility to the fore (Cataldi 1993, 168).

"When my mother died she was talking to the animals that had gathered on the ceiling," Anderson intones. The film follows suit with the animation of a tiger disappearing into foliage. The silhouette of a dog (Lolabelle) leaps onto a rock. As Anderson reflects upon her mother's death, her passing becomes mixed up with that of Lolabelle's. Both a dog's life and human life are treated as grievable, with Anderson's voice and her inventive collage of images and sounds conveying loss. Her mother's last words were "scattered," she tells us—she spoke of trains, of animals, of different places she had wanted to go. According to film-phenomenological scholar Vivian Sobchack, the nonbeing that is death exceeds the possibility of representation. We "do not ever 'see' death on the screen," she writes, "we see the activity and remains of the event of *dying*" (2004, 233, emphasis in original). In *Heart of a Dog*, dying is visualized through the film's flickering, scattered imagery, textures that denote the past, animal symbolism, color, and Anderson's externalization of her mother's "animals upon the ceiling." Though death cannot be lived through, it is not an experience "deprived of sense," as Leonard Lawlor observes (2006, 119). The living will continue to carry the dead (in memory, through emotion, or through creative production), as *Heart of a Dog* so beautifully attests. "I walk accompanied by ghosts," sings Anderson time and again.

Not until halfway through *Heart of a Dog* do we finally come to understand the film's liquid washes of gold. One of Anderson's favorite paintings is by the famed Spanish artist Francisco Goya, and it depicts "a huge gold void." In shimmering close-up, the background detail of Goya's *The Dog* (c. 1820) comes into view. Slowly, the camera tilts down to reveal the lower edges of the artwork. At the bottom of its painted, golden expanse is the figure of a little dog, which is dwarfed by a steep hill.

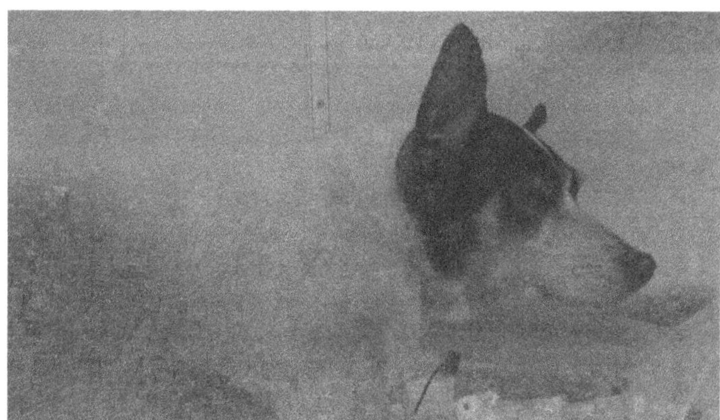

*Illustration 2.4. From Goya's dog to Lolabelle* (Heart of a Dog, *Arte TV/HBO, 2015).*

As Goya's tiny dog fades from view, Lolabelle's barking erupts over the soundtrack and the screen becomes awash with gold once more. In the next shot, Lolabelle is lying ill in a veterinary hospital. Her paws are covered with tubes and wires. Rather than invoking the symbolism of cemeteries and mausoleums, or images of literal, material decay, *Heart of a Dog* channels death into expressions of the liquid and the lyrical. Lolabelle's death, in particular, is figured as a vast, golden ocean.

### Depth as Liquidity and as Revelation

Like other sadness-related emotions such as mourning, despair, or sorrow, grief is often described as feeling pressured, weighted, and heavy (Cataldi 1993, 9). Grief is loss deeply, personally felt. In its cinematic guise, grief tends to be associated with the implied heaviness of bodies and their gestures, including the affective gestures of a film such as the loss of light (Brinkema 2014). Through its "depthful" sensibility (its refractions of the "I," its openness to the nonhuman, and its audiovisual experimentation), *Heart of a Dog* refuses the weight of grief and its usual representation in the cinema. All this is not to imply that sadness is absent from the film, far from it. In an interview, Anderson spoke of how she tried to incarnate the Tibetan "practice [of] how to feel sad without being sad" (Schaefer 2018). After fleshing out Lolabelle's early life through a series of stories (her birth in a mall puppy mill, her survival of a couple's divorce, her time in Canada), Anderson begins to voice the dog's great gift for empathy. On cue, the film's images begin to slow. The camera holds on the surface of a lake, watching concentric ripples form while violins play. To feel "sad without being sad" is a really difficult practice, the artist admits. Against the sounds of trickling water and of falling rain, the lake turns to gold—its surface calling to mind both Goya's painting and Lolabelle's passing.

Reflecting upon his own films centered on death, Brakhage spoke of the difficulty of finding images, symbols, or emblems for death that were adequate to its poetic expression (Totaro 2003).[16] In *Heart of a Dog*, Anderson's lyrical evocations of death, grief, and loss are associated with images and sounds of liquidity, as well as with the slow-motion stylization of movement. Oftentimes, the film's images literally ripple and waver, poetically recalling the movements of water. Water is present from the film's very first reference to death. As the artist wonders about "the last things you say in life," footage of a car passing through a snowy landscape can be seen. Inclement weather streaks the car's windshield, leaving droplets of water running down the surface of the screen. Water flows throughout the film's real-world environments, and it also features in its "visionary" sequences. In the *bardo*, Lolabelle's silhouette is seen through layers of raindrops and stormwater.

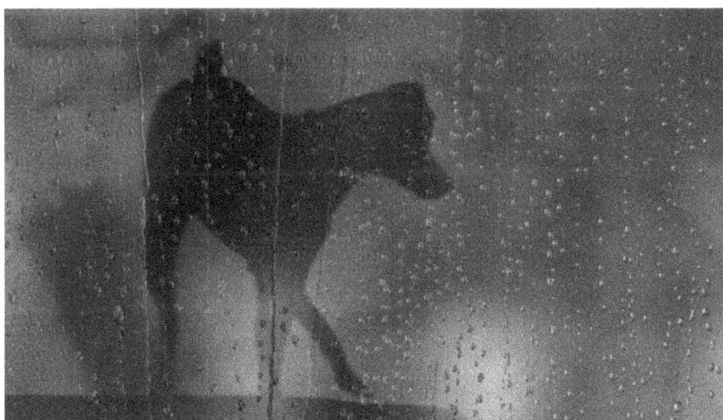

Illustration 2.5. *Lolabelle in the bardo* (Heart of a Dog, *Arte TV/ HBO, 2015*).

Across the film, Anderson's recounting of Lolabelle's life and her own past is accompanied by aquatic imagery and sounds or set against different bodies of water: the ocean, a frozen lake, sounds of cracking ice, pools of water, puddles, and passages of rain.

Though we cannot see Merleau-Ponty's depth, we can certainly feel its presence, especially when a once invisible or previously hidden connection between things is revealed. As Cataldi (1993, 54) helps to explain this idea, in "Eye and Mind" Merleau-Ponty begins to embrace "eclipsings," "occlusions," and the invisible as a fundamental part of the visible world. Depth is crucial to this endeavor, as depth and its decentering are borne of the hidden, the imaginary, and the layered. After Lolabelle fell sick, Anderson's voiceover recalls how "we stayed with her for three days … until her breath slowed and then stopped." A photographic montage of Lolabelle follows, showing her asleep or made comfortable on furred rugs and cushions. "We had learned to love Lola as she had loved us," Anderson movingly recites over a photograph of Lolabelle taken during her last days. The photograph fades to black and is replaced by footage of the traveling car. Following Lolabelle's passing, the camera holds its vision on the slate grey sky that can be seen through the car's window. Crying is forbidden in *The Tibetan Book of the Dead*, Anderson continues. It is "confusing to the dead because you don't want to summon them back … they can't come back." In the upper regions of the glass, rain, snow, and sleet continue to gather. No human bodies are ever seen or heard crying over Lolabelle in *Heart of a Dog*. Instead, it is the liquid expressivity of the film itself that registers and reveals the emotional intensity of loving the animal and grieving her loss.

Following Lolabelle's death, Anderson narrates how the loss of a loved one becomes much "more about you than the person who died." As the artist voices her own realization of the implicit connection between love and death, the forest turns to gold, the surface of the image wavering like water. In "Eye and Mind," Merleau-Ponty quite explicitly attaches a moment of depth to the "aqueous power" of water, that "shimmering element" (2004, 313). Using the example of a domestic swimming pool, he equates the pool's water to the revelatory nature of depth. Through the "water's thickness" (2004, 313), he writes, we are able to perceive and grasp other things. Just as the painted animals of Lascaux radiate out beyond their cave walls, the spatial container of the pool cannot contain this "depthful" encounter. Rather than being held "*in* space," water-as-depth makes mobile, material connections with other things—the cypress trees surrounding the pool, the air, the pool's geometric tiling, ripples of sunlight, the pool's reflective surface (each thing encroaching on the other) (2004, 313, emphasis in original).

Evocations of water and references to liquidity abound in Merleau-Ponty's later work: "the pulp of the sensible," "a wave of Being," or the world described as "a band of foam on the ocean" (1968, 268; 136; 64). As mentioned above, "Eye and Mind" contains a small but I think tellingly aquatic reference to the cinema. In this reference, Merleau-Ponty brings together the physical movement of bodies on-screen with liquidity. He asks: "Cinema portrays movement, but how? Is it … by copying more closely the changes of place? We may presume not, since *slow motion shows a body being carried along, floating among objects like seaweed, but not moving itself*" (1994, 144–145, emphasis added).

In this passage, Merleau-Ponty builds upon his previous musings on movement in the cinema and its stylization.[17] Indirectly invoking the "aquatic lyricism" (Deleuze 2001, 5) of the French School, he also has a very specific film sequence in mind: the captivating, slow-motion pillow fight of Jean Vigo's *Zero for Conduct* (1933).[18] In this scene, the young boys achieve a moment of escape from their restrictive boarding school, defying gravity through Vigo's hypnotic use of slow motion. As one boy somersaults, it is "as if [the] body itself was a feather," akin to the wafting feathers that float through the air (Carbone 2015, 54).

Glossing depth, Merleau-Ponty asserts that there is that which reaches our vision directly, "through frontal properties" (2004, 318), and that which reaches it from below or above. In the latter, bodies achieve a freedom of movement that can be likened to swimming or flight.

Not only does Merleau-Ponty's brief reference to the cinema extend his rejection of "representation" across media, he suggests the surfacing of depth in the medium of film. Herein, bodies obtain a new freedom of movement; they can be made to float and bob like seaweed. Through its overt stylization of movement, cinema reveals other, hidden modes of vision, opening up another "way of dwelling in the world," as different to our own as "that of seaweed" (Carbone 2015, 55).[19] Invoking the arresting liquidity of slow motion, Merleau-Ponty suggests that film is not just a medium of vision, time, and movement but of depth. Cinema's depth cannot be found in the close copying of reality, however. Like in painting, the surfacing and the revelation of depth occurs through the nonmimetic.

"Tell the animals, she said," Anderson states toward the film's end, returning to her mother's dying words. A hazy close-up of the artist's younger self slides back and forth across the screen before dissolving into the air. As with Vigo's use of slow motion in *Zero for Conduct*, the human bodies that feature in *Heart of a Dog* do not just move, they float. During the film's archival moments, especially, Anderson and her brothers appear to be swimming through the past, caught up in the dissolves between shots or physically submerged in water. In line with Merleau-Ponty's aesthetics of depth, Anderson's treatment of memory and mortality emits a definite aquatic charge. Rippling imagery, slow motion, and water-based images and sounds work to stylize cinema as a current, flowing between past and present, the eye and the mind. Instead of point-to-point plotting, poetic rhymes and points of connection are revealed across different stories and segments (animals, water, forests, air, gold).

**Conclusion: Turning Time Around**

In "Eye and Mind" and other texts, Merleau-Ponty discerns depth in art and in the world, connecting the experience of depth to movement, dispersal, surfaces, the imagination, liquidity, time, and moments of revelation. As this chapter has considered, Merleau-Ponty's depth is an ontological concept that can also be brought to bear on the cinema, especially in its surface-based, experimental, and essayistic forms. In *Heart of a Dog*, Anderson achieves a "depthful" cinema, bringing into visibility the love of an animal and expressions of death, grief, and loss.

There is one person from Anderson's life who is largely absent, however. Anderson's late husband, musician Lou Reed, is not "revealed" until the film's last sequences. During the closing credits, the Velvet Underground's song "Turning Time Around" begins. Slowed-down footage of dogs and humans is brought together with the singing of Reed's (younger) voice: "If I had to, I'd call love time." Rather than returning to the animated line, Anderson opts to conclude her film on a black-and-white photograph, keeping "open the instants which the onrush of time closes" (Merleau-Ponty 1994, 145).

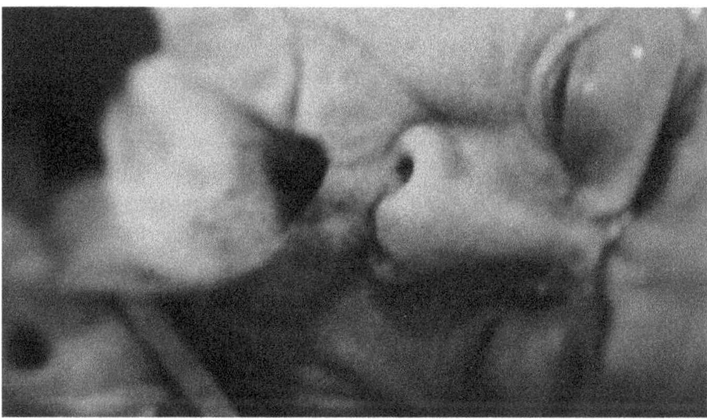

*Illustration 2.6. Lolabelle and Lou Reed (*Heart of a Dog, *Arte TV/HBO, 2015).*

In this photograph, Lolabelle is seen lying in the arms of the now aged Reed. The next shot reveals another small yet substantial detail—the dog pressing her snout up against Reed's face. In *Heart of a Dog*, as for Merleau-Ponty's depth, the turning about of body and world or one embodied being upon another is the thickness and the depth from which all our lives emerge. If Anderson's film has a fitting, lyrical symbol for the passing of time, life, death, and all that comes in between, it is not a human body/subject. Instead, it is the loving heart of a dog that emblematizes the joys of immanence, of art, the possibility of connection, and the depths that surround us.

**Saige Walton** is a Senior Lecturer in Screen Studies at the University of South Australia. She is the author of *Cinema's Baroque Flesh: Film, Phenomenology and the Art of Entanglement* (Amsterdam University Press, 2016) and coeditor of a Special Dossier of *Screening the Past* on "Materializing Absence in Film and Media" (2018). Her articles appear in journals such as *Culture, Theory and Critique, Cinéma & Cie, NECSUS, The Cine-Files, Senses of Cinema*, and the *New Review of Film and Television Studies*. Her second scholarly book deals with a contemporary cinema of poetry. Email: saige.walton@unisa.edu.au

## Notes

[1] This chapter is for Ziggy and for Sam.

[2] On reversibility, what Merleau-Ponty calls "flesh," and the cinema, see Saige Walton (2016).

[3] In *The Visible and the Invisible*, Merleau-Ponty also refers to painting as "existing beyond the canvas" (1968: 199, 210).

[4] In "The Sensible World and the World of Expression" (his first course at the Collège de France), Merleau-Ponty (2010) suggests that stylized movement spans both painting and film.

[5] Lolabelle's birth is one of many hospital scenes in the film. Later, Anderson will tell of how she was housed in a hospital burn unit following a severe childhood diving accident, instigating her first contact with death.

[6] Anderson cites Chris Marker as one of her favorite filmmakers.

[7] For a useful summation of the film-phenomenological method of "thick" description, see Vivian Sobchack (2004). In addition to characters' bodies and the spectator's body, Sobchack argues that what she calls the film's body is a lived albeit nonhuman body.

[8] Depth "is not an act or an intentionality which would go to an in itself and give only juxtaposed in itself" (Merleau-Ponty 1968: 219-220).

[9] Depth includes nonintentional being, as indicated by "the voice of … things, the waves, and the forests" (Merleau-Ponty 1968: 155).

[10] According to Anderson, "it's a film about 'up.'" While air and the sky in the film symbolize freedom, these motifs can take "a darker turn," as with the film's stories of terrorism and surveillance. See John Schaefer (2018).

[11] On Merleau-Ponty's depth as a "positive infinite," see Lawlor (2006).

[12] Describing inspiration, Merleau-Ponty also quotes the words of the French abstract artist Robert Delauney: "Depth is the new inspiration" (2004: 311).

[13] Extending "depthful" encounters to a study of the emotions, Cataldi (1993: 168) suggests that "the 'deeper' the emotion, the more the 'self' is affected and the more one perceives oneself as belonging to the scene, as being intervolved."

[14] As Sobchack observes, such moments in film have ethical resonance through the self's "sensual and sensible expansion," which are brought about through our "enhanced awareness of what it is to be *material*" (2004: 290).

[15] Intriguingly, Merleau-Ponty also evokes the sense of sound as a complement to the artistic imagination and to painting, describing the perceptions of a "third ear" and the noises that it creates internally. Most of Brakhage's films are, of course, silent. See Merleau-Ponty (2004: 297) and Sitney (2002).

[16] Brakhage's films employ shots of earth, decomposition, bursts of bright light, rapid editing, and the lyrical symbolism of the tomb or the river to signal "a deeper image of death." See Sitney (2002: 236).

[17] On the artistic rendering of movement being like a whirlpool, see also Merleau-Ponty (2010).

[18] From a different but not unrelated perspective, Gilles Deleuze discusses the French School's love of the "liquid element" as opening up a "more than human perception" (2001: 80–82).

[19] Carleton Dallery translates this passage as "a body floating among objects like an alga." See Merleau-Ponty (2004: 316).

## References


Barker, Jennifer M. 2009. *The Tactile Eye: Touch and the Cinematic Experience*. Berkeley: University of California Press.

Brinkema, Eugenie. 2014. *The Forms of the Affects*. Durham, NC: Duke University Press.

Carbone, Mauro. 2015. *The Flesh of Images: Merleau-Ponty between Painting and Cinema*. Trans. Marta Nijhuis. Albany: State University of New York Press.

Cataldi, Sue L. 1993. *Emotion, Depth, and Flesh: A Study of Sensitive Space*. Albany: State University of New York Press.

Chang, Justin. 2015. "Film Review: *Heart of a Dog*." *Variety*, September 4, 2015. https://variety.com/2015/film/festivals/telluride-film-review-heart-of-a-dog-1201586251/.

Corrigan, Timothy. 2011. *The Essay Film: From Montaigne, After Marker*. New York: Oxford University Press.

Corrigan, Timothy. 2017. "Of the History of the Essay Film: Vertov to Varda." In *Essays on the Essay Film*, ed. Nora M. Alter and Timothy Corrigan, 197–226. New York: Columbia University Press.

Deleuze, Gilles. 2001. *Cinema 1: The Movement-Image*. Trans. Hugh Tomlinson and Barbara Habberjam. London: Continuum.

Dillon, Steven. 2004. *Derek Jarman and Lyric Film: The Mirror and the Sea*. Austin: University of Texas Press.

Lawlor, Leonard. 2006. *Implications of Immanence: Towards a New Concept of Life*. New York: Fordham University Press.

Mazis, Glen. 1988. "Merleau-Ponty: The Depth of Memory at the Depth of the World." In *The Horizons of Continental Philosophy: Essays on Husserl, Heidegger, and Merleau-Ponty*, ed. H.J. Silverman, 227–250. Dordrecht, The Netherlands: Springer.

Mazis, Glen. 2010. "Time at the Depth of the World." In *Merleau-Ponty at the Limits of Art, Religion, and Perception*, ed. Kascha Semonovitch and Neal DeRoo, 120–146. London: Continuum.

Mazis, Glen. 2016. *Merleau-Ponty and the Face of the World: Silence, Ethics, Imagination, and Poetic Ontology*. Albany: State University of New York Press.

Merleau-Ponty, Maurice. (1964) 1968. *The Visible and the Invisible: Followed by Working Notes*. Trans. Alphonso Lingis. Evanston, IL: Northwestern University Press.

Merleau-Ponty. (1961) 1994. "Eye and Mind." Trans. Michael B. Smith. In *The Merleau-Ponty Aesthetics Reader: Philosophy and Painting*, ed. G.A. Johnson, 121–149. Evanston, IL: Northwestern University Press.

Merleau-Ponty, Maurice. (1961) 2004. "Eye and Mind." Trans. Carleton Dallery. In *Maurice Merleau-Ponty: Basic Writings*, ed. Thomas Baldwin, 290–324. London: Routledge.

Merleau-Ponty, Maurice. (1952–1953) 2010. "The Sensible World and the World of Expression." Trans. Bryan Bannon. *Chiasmi International: Trilingual Studies Concerning the Thought of Merleau-Ponty* 12: 31–37.

Schaefer, John. 2018. "#3790: *Heart of a Dog*, with Laurie Anderson." *New Sounds*, May 13, 2018. https://www.newsounds.org/story/3790-heart-dog-laurie-anderson-encore/.

Sitney, P. Adams. 2002. *Visionary Film: The American Avant-Garde, 1943–2000*. Oxford: Oxford University Press.

Sobchack, Vivian. 2004. *Carnal Thoughts: Embodiment and Moving Image Culture*. Berkeley: University of California Press.

Totaro, Donato. 2003. "Stan Brakhage: 'Death is a Meaningless Word' Part 1." *Offscreen* 7 (2). https://offscreen.com/view/stan_brakhage.

Walton, Saige. 2016. *Cinema's Baroque Flesh: Film, Phenomenology and the Art of Entanglement*. Amsterdam: Amsterdam University Press.

# Chapter 3

# Elemental Imagination and Film Experience

## Climate Change and the Cinematic Ethics of Immersive Filmworlds

**Ludo de Roo**

*"Juxtaposing a person with an environment that is boundless, collating him with a countless number of people passing by so close to him and far away, relating a person to the whole world: that is the meaning of cinema."*

— *Andrei Tarkovsky*

The air trembles with heat. Above the dust-dry ground, a mirage wavers. It brings forth a tiny dark shape, its dancing moves melting above the hot horizon. From this faint background, over the moving wind a shuffling sound comes near, gradually becoming more perceptible than its uncertain image. Like a heartbeat's pulse, hooves resonate across the distant earth. Moments pass before the hallucination materializes into a visible figure. Each and every move seems decisive now. An Arab man runs for his gun. Before he can aim his firearm, he is shot down from the distance. The air still trembles, now with premonition.

In this celebrated scene, some twenty minutes into David Lean's *Lawrence of Arabia* (1962), a mirage holds the trembling, distant, almost liquid horizon from which Omar Sharif's character (Sherif Ali) comes forth. Ali rides on, very slowly crossing the desert ground, calmly imposing himself on the dry earth shared by a stunned Lawrence (Peter O'Toole), two thirsty camels, and a dead Bedouin guide. Underneath this arid land lies Ali's well, and other people are not supposed to drink water from this source—not without permission.

I dwell on this powerful sequence in such detail here because it evokes a sense of morality on various levels. Naturally, amid this tense, trembling air several stories suggest themselves for further cultural-political interpretation. Yet even prior to this, I suggest the striking power of this fragment to *first* depend on something else. That is, *before* the intricate narrative layers coming forth from this scene, *beneath* the many symbolic layers laid out at each different interpretation, the immersive sway of this scene appears to come forth from the very evocative way of cinematically foregrounding the natural elements. The scene is driven by and is, quite literally, built on the rich materiality of ancient philosophy's classic elements: it is impossible to think of this hallucinating scene either without the vibrating air or without the contested dry earth over such a rich source of water. And as for fire—it will take further film-philosophical analysis in order to claim this film's powerful use of fire as a concrete metaphor for examining man's technological control over the world.

The *ethical* aim of this film-philosophical pairing of fire with technology, however, is an emphatically *ecocritical* argument. That is, in an age of continuing ecological disasters and increasing environmental crisis—much of it the effect of man's increased technological mastery over nature—I suggest that the engaging moments of immersive cinematic experiences like this fiery scene can, even when made in 1962, play an important role in enlarging a broader awareness of climate change on the part of the spectator. In addition to the fact-based tactics of documentary film and the *fictional* strategies of climate change science-fiction, I argue in this chapter that the cinematic experience of any film in itself often already offers a rich form of imagination that is rooted in our elemental being-in-the-world. As such, this cinematic form of "elemental imagination," as I will call it, has the potential to enrich the field of cinematic ethics.[1] In other words, elemental imagination is not only key to the intrafilmic process of experiencing cinema (i.e., it plays a major role in immersing the spectator), it also, in its rootedness, has an *existential-ethical potential* extrafilmically—that is, it can resensitize the spectator, reorient and broaden her or his awareness so as to include the elemental world's vulnerable qualities and constitution.

### Environmental Concern and the Formation of Ecocinema

In this chapter, I will contrast this idea of elemental imagination with two more obvious ways in which cinema has attempted to stir environmental concern for a wider audience. Hence, in the first part of the chapter I will briefly discuss the cinematic aesthetics of (a) the "factual imagination" operative in climate change documentary (i.e., the aesthetic techniques to represent scientific data) and compare this factually oriented approach with (b) the "speculative imagination" projecting cautionary tales of fictional ecodisaster narratives (hence, the use of digital aesthetics to imagine the hypothetical effects of climate change). This first section concludes by putting these two aesthetic tactics in the context of (c) the major tenets of the interdisciplinary subdiscipline of "ecocinema." The goal of the first part of this chapter is to argue that these more cognitive strategies and processes studied by ecocinema theorists cover only part of cinema's ecological potential; they should be complemented by more subthreshold processes that structure the spectator's affective, perceptual, and imaginative immersion into the filmworld. Hence, in the second part of this chapter I advance phenomenological grounds for this claim: on the one hand, I will argue that (d) the cinematic imagination of the natural elements reaches us on an affective level; they play an essential role in immersing us time and again into the projected filmworld. On the other hand, as such—that is, before the more symbolic potential that this elemental form of imagination holds for postviewing interpretations—it can even (e) nurture an existential ethics of care on the part of the spectator. The aim is, therefore, to claim the ethical potential of what I call "elemental imagination" as already rooted in this more affective side of film experience: the feeling of being immersed "in" a filmworld is not only the grounds for us to have a film experience, but it is also an opportunity to existentially reorient our senses to the world around us on a daily basis.

### Climate Change in Nonfiction Cinema

When one looks at the ways in which mainstream cinema represents climate change, one may first of all think of numerous documentaries that attempt to convey the relevant scientific facts and global effects of this condition, such as the well-known Al Gore documentary *An Inconvenient Truth* (Davis Guggenheim, 2006). Indeed, *Truth* does an excellent job of *informing* its audience through facts, figures, and charts, aided by some dramatic images of sea level rise or extreme drought. Gore's emphasis on demonstrating this amount of scientific data in this film undoubtedly anticipates skeptical criticism from climate change deniers.

Certainly, all the presented facts and figures easily support his central argument: not only is there broad scientific agreement on the actual process of climate change, but scientists can also distinguish between the effects of "natural" factors and human-generated factors on the rapid changes in the climate over the past two decades. To be sure, I am not skeptical about the relative accuracy of the science presented by climate change documentaries like *Truth*; one must however remain critical about the way in which they are presented and, especially, about the *role* that data plays in them. Oftentimes, Gore's rapid-fire treatment of graphs and figures as visual representations for data and statistics seems to function less as "proof" for each claim than to show the sheer abundance of information in support of the overall claim. Indeed, as Mark Minster claims in his analysis of *Truth*, there can certainly be no doubt that the content of these graphs is scientific. "But what the graphs *mean* in the context of the film," Minster argues, "is that Gore himself has mastered much of the science . . . and can authoritatively mediate that science for us. His encounters with the evidence are more persuasive than the evidence itself" (2010, 30; emphasis in original). In other words, in rhetorical, Aristotelian terms (Aristotle 1991), the *logos* of scientific discourse becomes increasingly "performative" so as to suggest scientific accuracy and objectivity while also supporting the *ethos* of the documentary's protagonist; the *pathos* of dramatic images (e.g., breaking polar caps, a drowning polar bear, etc.) then serves to further persuade the spectator of the significance of climate change.

Of course, the idea that nonfiction film partially depends on a rhetorical mode is hardly new.[2] However, in environmentalist nonfiction films—especially in climate change documentaries made in the wake of *Truth*—there appears a salient, recurring pattern that tends to shape their rhetorical mode. That is, the epistemic claim to "reason" of science seems to be increasingly complemented (if not replaced) by the moral "appeal to character" in depending on the on-screen presence of, or off-screen narration by, a charismatic individual, who is frequently of Hollywood fame or political stature.[3]

Moreover, besides the altered role of science in nonfiction film, more than anything the representation of scientific data has also changed. Over the last decade or so, especially with the transition to digital cinema, data visualization has become an integral part of environmentalist documentary. In what media theorist Sean Cubitt has called the "datafication" of the photographic image (2013, 282), nonfiction films have increasingly included scientific models in their representations. These time-lapse images visualize not only past and present states of environmental change, but also include hypothetical projections for future times. In other words, scientific models get translated into sophisticated moving images, with computer-generated images (CGI) adding several virtual layers to documentary's otherwise rather realist tendency. Fighting the potential boredom effect of too many talking heads, documentary-makers now have an arresting way of including science's *logos* by persuasively visualizing key phases of geophysical history before human civilization, as well as by anticipating the speculative effects of anthropogenic climate change.

But in so doing, these sophisticated images serve another purpose other than merely representing very complex knowledge: they still submit to what I described above as the rhetorical form—that is, they aim to persuade the spectator by stirring their imagination as a way to help them grasp the complex "hyperobject" of climate change.[4] While this imagination evidently has one foot in science's factual objectivity, its appeal is also to add an imaginative layer of augmented reality. Translating scientific truths into readily insightful and memorable images, climate change documentaries increasingly seem to depend on instances of what I call "factual imagination"—that is, virtual visualizations of scientific data with the rhetorical function of persuading the spectator into considering the drastic effects of anthropogenic environmental change. Even more than relying on the foreseeable emotional impact of iconic images of breaking ice caps, famished polar bears, or dramatic bushfires, the virtual images theoretically rooted in scientific facts are meant to move the spectator's imagination into action.

### Climate Change in Fiction Cinema

Explicit images of the consequences of climate change seem, however, to be more prevalent in the *modus operandi* of the second dominant film genre that frequently represents climate change: apocalyptic science fiction. Less concerned with scientific reason, the concrete, tangible images used in these films provide a natural background to a more dramatized, character-driven narrative plot. Broadly speaking, this takes two forms.

In the first form, climate change is a premise, with the ecodisaster already having happened; in this case, the cinematic fiction explores the ethico-existential challenges that a protagonist or a group of individuals faces in drastically altered environmental and social circumstances.[5] Curiously enough, these ecological catastrophes are always projected into distant times, as if these imaginary apocalypses are *only* imaginary, far beyond a real everyday future. Yet as we know, with the current scientific facts piling up, it has become clear that climate change is already altering lives on a daily basis.

Alternatively, climate change also gets portrayed as something that is actually happening (i.e., represented over the course of the film).[6] A paradigmatic example for this second form is *The Day After Tomorrow* (Roland Emmerich, 2004), a film that has been studied extensively by major ecocritical film theorists. Hence, this high-grossing, big-budget film is praised for putting environmental concerns at the heart of its main plot *and* its production—for example, *Tomorrow* is supposedly the first carbon-neutral mega-production.[7] Similarly, communication theorists have collected viewer response data, measuring and analyzing the film's relative impact—at least its short-term impact—on the viewer (see Leiserowitz 2004; and Reusswig and Leiserowitz 2005). Moreover, film theorists have also studied this genre's sensationalized (digital) aesthetics in relation to this supposed cognitive and affective effect on the spectator.[8]

Yet it remains to be seen how effectively this genre persuades viewers in the longer term. For instance, to the extent that such fictional stories often depend on a classic opposition between heroes and foes, climate change gets largely pinned on individual antagonists rather than being attributed to systemic industrial processes, which frees the spectator from having to engage in any critical self-reflection. Moreover, it also remains uncertain as to what extent the blockbuster's abundant images of extreme ecocatastrophes are not merely experienced as fictional fabulations detached from reality. Finally, more work needs to be done in order to understand whether such films have substantially helped change spectators' beliefs and attitudes on a more profound level.

However, whereas the factual imagination of contemporary documentaries use scientific simulations (still solidly grounded in scientific reason), this fictionalized apocalyptic genre, on the contrary, presents climate change via speculative images that foster an emotionally dramatized and scientifically simplified idea of climate change. Blockbuster film thus offers what I call "speculative imagination": rather than portraying plausible events in the real world, it imagines how drastic climate change affects a fictional realm like ours.

Ultimately, the question is whether the sobering message of climate change is best conveyed via factual imagination and the rhetoric of science, or via speculative imagination—that is, via highly entertaining, fictional experiences that never seem to settle on a deeper, existential meaning. Alternatively, are real changes in attitudes, beliefs, and actions perhaps better inspired when narratives of climate change are conveyed in less speculative aesthetic terms?

## Mapping Ecocinema

Indeed, within film theory there is a much broader dialogue on exactly this question. Since the early 2000s, the theoretical subdiscipline of "ecocinema" has been specifically concerned with analyzing the relative success of various cinematic styles in raising ecological awareness. Some emphasize that it is the poetic aesthetics of nature that arrest the narrative plot (i.e., slow cinema) that invites a more reflective mode of viewing (e.g., MacDonald 2004), whereas other ecocinema scholars have explored the spectators' cognitive processes, such as moral positioning—that is, empathic engagement in relation to other narrative and aesthetic strategies (e.g., Brereton 2005; Ingram 2013). For ecocritical film theorists, the goal is generally to study how cinema imagines representations of explicit nature (e.g., wildlife, animals, and climate change) as well as to evaluate the relative success of the different aesthetic strategies employed by environmentalist films. With several edited overviews published by the mid-2010s (Rust et al. 2013; Weik von Mossner 2014; Willoquet-Maricondi 2010a), the field of ecocinema theory seems now to have established itself within film studies.

Although primarily concerned with the obvious themes of nature and concrete imaginations of drastic climate change, most studies in ecocinema theory of the first wave (ca. 2000–2010) comprise two prevailing assumptions:[9] (1) that cinema helps spectators imagine an iconic image of climate change; and (2) that such an iconic imagination can nurture a more ecocritical stance in spectators. Such a specific scope has certainly helped to put the theoretical discipline on the map, but restricting ecocinema theory merely to only "environmentalist" films has its limitations. That is, ecocinema's strict focus on obviously environmentalist films appears to depend on an *a priori* idea of "nature" as something distant from the average spectator's everyday life, as though "nature" were best experienced, say, in BBC's *Planet Earth* (2006) rather than in one's own backyard.[10]

Since the 2010s, however, a second wave has started to move beyond these restrictions. On the one hand, contemporary theorists of ecocinema have broadened their idea of what "natural environment" means. Nature is recognized now as a thematically rich background to a much wider set of films, even in films with no explicit environmentalist theme.[11] With films as diverse as *Titanic* (James Cameron, 1997), *Melancholia* (Lars von Trier, 2011), and *The Hunger Games* (Gary Ross, 2012), the goal now often becomes to examine the human relationship with the natural environment as represented by the cinematic narratives. Taking "nature" as part of our everyday life is a welcome move: this approach enables a way of connecting to the more phenomenological way of being-in-the-world (as I will argue in the next section)—nature is not simply beautiful wildlife that is distant from our familiar world. The global climate going awry, for example, already affects many people's well-being, whether they live in rich or poor countries. Indeed, instead of schematizing the environment as merely a cognitive construct, Tim Christion Myers (2014) rightly points out that climate change must be taken as an existential threat; accordingly, ecocinema theory must categorically put this view at its core.

Alternatively, other scholars have developed more philosophical theories of what some call the "ecological" aspect intrinsic to media. In their view, cinema as an audiovisual medium can facilitate a technological remediation of spectator and environment: it is also considered an environmental medium. Some analyze the material aspects of media objects (Cubitt 2017; Parikka 2015; Peters 2015); others extend broadly conceived phenomenological theories of perception (Ivakhiv 2013; Safit 2014); and still others are inspired by an ecological reinterpretation of cybernetic theory (Hörl and Hansen 2013). Nonetheless, the general idea running through these various philosophical versions of ecocinema is that there is something in the medium of film and its experience that gives the spectator an experiential world that—even if reproducing a technologically constructed version of nature—is nonetheless very similar to the real world.

**The Rhetoric of Experience: Everyday Nature and Moving Images**

While embracing contemporary ecocinema's principal idea of the more inclusive, everyday representation of the natural world in cinema, the approach I set out below also shares much of the philosophical motivation of the second wave. Extending these values of recent ecocinema studies, I claim therefore that the ecological potential of film experience is to reconnect with our natural environment in an everyday sense. My argument is that film experience has the intrinsic potential to engage with climate change on a more *affective* level, thus complementing the cognitive tactics of the documentary rhetoric of visualized science and the spectacular splendor of science fiction.

Therefore, I will give three interconnected arguments supporting this eco-ethical claim. First, I will argue that the spectator's perceptual, affective, and imaginative involvement is with what is generally called "filmworld"—an underdeveloped film-theoretical concept that can be explained by turning to phenomenological theory. Second, I will argue that this subthreshold immersion is generally guided by the cinematic imagination of the natural elements: they play a vital role in opening up and in sensitizing the filmworld for viewers' experience of film. Third, I will argue that any film that stirs such an "elemental imagination" can, in turn, resensitize the spectator's ecological awareness—and change on this existential ground the audience's beliefs and attitudes toward the natural environment. Synthesizing these three related arguments, I will show, provides the grounds for working out the ecological potential of film in existential terms, thus foregrounding the main aim of the second part of this chapter.

**Filmworld**

The first part of my triadic argument is that, essentially, the cinematic experience as such always directly depends on an engagement with a projected version of the daily world. Each time we watch a film, we become absorbed in a projected world of film. And even if the natural world is not thematically foregrounded in such a "filmworld," the projected natural environment is nonetheless there, in the background, to provide a structural whole for us to immerse ourselves in and experience the narrative fiction.

In the discipline of film theory, the notion of filmworld has only recently received significant scholarly attention. For instance, Daniel Yacavone (2015) has developed the first sophisticated theory of film-worlds. Geared toward the cognitive dimension of film experience (i.e., the higher-level consciousness aspects that structure world-building), Yacavone's work generally leaves out the more subthreshold levels that play a major part in becoming immersed in a filmworld.[12] This affective dimension of film experience is partially covered by the original work of Adrian Ivakhiv (2013), who in turn develops a concept of cinema as "anthrobiogeomorphic machine." That is, in Ivakhiv's process-relational philosophy of film, cinema is "cosmomorphic" (world-making), in that it "gives us worlds that are material, social and perceptual in the ways they appear to us" (2013, 32). In other words, films put us into a mean-ingful relationship with our natural environment; in this model of film experience, however, there is less concern with fleshing out the notion of filmworld and more of a concern with detailing how this affective dimension relates to the other aspects of film experience.[13]

While both Yacavone and Ivakhiv provide important markers for describing the sense of experiencing a filmworld, both theories are generally more concerned with a postviewing reflection on the *idea* of filmworlds than they are with a "lived" experience *of* filmworlds. That is, they seem to overlook the important sense of how a filmworld is al-ready profoundly "given," something that we are immersed in before it becomes a rich cognitive scheme to be hermeneutically understood and theoretically analyzed. This question of "what it is like" to be immersed in the filmworld can, however, be productively developed by turning to phenomenological philosophy and adapting one of its key concepts—that is, building forth on what Edmund Husserl developed as "lifeworld" (1970), what Martin Heidegger (2010) called "being-in-the-world," and Maurice Merleau-Ponty's (1962) more embodied extension of these phenomenological ideas. Despite the nuanced philosophical differences between these phenomenologists, we can take from them that, in these philosophies of everyday life, "the horizon of worldhood" is recognized as indispensable background for making sense of ourselves: in other words, our sense of "self" is shaped by, dependent on, and invested in such a shared environment. Ultimately, without a "world" in the background, our sense of being becomes virtually meaningless.

Shawn Loht (2017) has recently developed Heidegger's phenome-nological analysis of *Dasein* or our shared "being-in-the-world" into an extensive Heideggerian phenomenology of film. Loht's chief argument is that Heidegger's existential notion of being-in-the-world is effectively extended in film experience. More than mere metaphor, then, *Dasein*'s existential dimensions are similar to the experience of the filmworld. That is, if film may be described to "foster being-in-the-world" (as Loht puts it), then the filmworld can be understood in terms of the "there-ness" of engaging with a world or, in other words, in terms of "an immersive environment that *Dasein* is 'in'" (2017, 43). As Loht continues to point out, "film-viewing essentially involves the viewer appropriating the cinematic image so as to bring it existentially near and make it meaningful" (2017, 45). In phenomenological terms, then, in film experience the space between the spectator and the filmworld becomes "de-distanced," as Heidegger would say: the world is, so to speak, brought closer to us, made familiar, intimate, and intelligible. Even though, logically speaking, the spectator never leaves her or his seat, in this imaginative process the filmworld has become an immersive, meaningful world to the spectator.

While Loht continues to further theorize film experience according to the different existential dimensions of Heidegger's philosophy—some of which I will briefly return to in the final section of this chapter—the key point to pick up here is Loht's emphasis on the existential sense of the "worldliness" of the filmworld. Before the more intricate narrative structures and the processes of character engagement, the constituting whole of the filmworld appears as always already "there." As an imaginative immersive environment, the filmworld provides the grounds for these other dimensions of film experience.

## Immersion

It remains open, however, exactly *how* the spectator becomes immersed in this structuring whole that we call the filmworld. Like the notion of the filmworld, this vital process of "immersion" too—which is just as fundamental for experiencing film—seems generally presupposed in film studies and has not garnered a great deal of theoretical attention. Yet if one looks more generally at how a filmworld "opens" itself up for the spectator, typically it is first an expressive landscape or cityscape, familiar or uncanny, realistic or fictionalized, but nonetheless always already charged with a recognizable sense of worldliness.

Obviously, conventional film traditionally opens with establishing shots, and even if contemporary narrative cinema plays with this trope it is rare to have a wholly "worldless" opening scene. Such establishing shots not only help us to cognitively place the characters in a narrative space, but prior to that (on what phenomenologists call a "prereflective" level) they also provide more affective triggers that set a specific mood.[14] A paradigmatic opening sequence that is heavily built on a world-rich landscape is, for instance, the cinematic desert in *Once Upon a Time in the West* (Sergio Leone, 1968): that isolated train platform in the barren West, the rich atmosphere of the poor terrain is emphasized by droplets of water dripping on the cowboy's hat, a squeaking rusty windmill in the background, and the weathered skins of the dusty gunmen's faces. With a handful of expressive shots, in no more than a couple of minutes, a densely textured world is presented: we are readily immersed in it.

While there is much more to say about the significant role of such expressive landscapes in cinema,[15] the point I want to advance here is that much of the immersion is heavily built upon the expressive materiality of these filmworlds. That is, such an immersive landscape is radically structured by the materiality of the natural elements: film provides elemental horizons of earth and water and air in the background against which the more explicit narrative features are played out. They provide the background against which we can imagine the rest of the narrative.

### Elemental Imagination

It is useful to return at this point to the audiovisually profound "opening" scene of *Lawrence* described above. What stands out here, first, is the curious *aural* emphasis on the background: just as the wind laps the cowboys' covers and the helps create the windmill's off-screen whines in Leone's western, so too atmospheric sounds from afar punctuate this well scene. In fact, the more the mirage seems illusionary, the louder the camel hooves' swoosh the dusty soil in the background, thus effectively guiding our attention away from the foreground and expressively drawing our view toward the trembling horizon. Furthermore, this process of drawing in attention by guiding the spectator's gaze is also visually driven: put simply, the triangulate composition of the frame (i.e., the position and sightlines of the bodies) together with the expressive lines on the desert earth within this frame expressly draw the view from the two people in the foreground over the well to the background. Taken together, this cinematic version of material imagination offers an aesthetic form of what may be called "cinegeography"—quite literally providing a moving audiovisual image in which the filmworld is already "etched" for the spectator's sense-experience.[16]

In the narrative context of this scene, it soon becomes apparent that these material elements also carry a more symbolic significance in the cinematic experience: this particular water source is owned by one tribe, so another community should not drink from it. Yet my point is that even this narrative-moral situation is once more based on or rooted in this cinematic use of the natural elements. Much like phenomenologist Gaston Bachelard developed a systematic poetics of "material imagination" in literature's representation of water, earth, air, and fire,[17] I claim that in films too there is such an imagination at work in cinema's evocative expression of these material elements—perhaps even more directly so, as the cinema after all is a sensory-rich medium. For Bachelard, in literature the "material image" becomes a phenomenological invitation to imagine in concrete ways the world's objective materiality:

> *A material image dynamically experienced, passionately adopted,*
> *patiently explored, is an* opening *in every sense of the word. . . .*
> *[It] transcends immediate existence and deepens superficial exis-*
> *tence. This deepening reveals a double perspective: opening into*
> *the interior of the active subject and into the inner substance of*
> *the inert object encountered by perception. (2002, 24; emphasis*
> *in original)*

A writer's expression of matter (i.e., earth, air, water, and fire) may thus evoke, for the reader, a dynamic, oneiric opening *to* the world. Bachelard even speaks about the elements as "hormones of the imagination" that "put images in action" (2002, 20). Indeed, John Sallis (2000) has argued along similar lines, not only taking the idea outside the realms of literary poetics, but also emphasizing that this "elemental imagination" (as he calls it) is significantly inspired by the elements. Hence, what he calls "the force that is *of* imagination" is described as "the force with which, by which, imagination draws itself forth and withdraws its horizons" (2000, 134). If for Bachelard it is in reading literature and poetry that each material element is thus dynamically lived, then Sallis deconstructs this idea of elemental imagination *back* to the elements themselves: it is *from* the elements that imagination hovers forth, thereby emphasizing a stronger cosmological/existential bond that ties us to the natural world.

Further venturing into the (Western) philosophical history of "the elements" supports this phenomenological sense of structural "ground" and "roots" as connected to elemental imagination.[18] Recall that our word "element" is etymologically derived from the Latin *elementum*, translating the Ancient Greek word *stoicheion*; in ancient post-Platonic philosophy, the term referred to the basic physical principles (or more poetically, the "letters of the alphabet" of the Book of Nature) that, endlessly rearranged, together compose the natural world. Moreover, in pre-Socratic philosophy, Empedocles called them the *rhizomata* or "roots of all"—hence etymologically confirming once more the phenomenological idea of structuring "base" or "source" (Macauley 2010, 60; 104). This philosophical background of the elements underlines for Bachelard and Sallis that there is fundamental sense to elemental imagination: the natural elements offer, indeed, the ground for relating us to the environing world. Accordingly, this originary sense of the elements offers an important film-theoretical idea: it is this foundational idea of the elements that structures the process of immersing the spectator within the filmworld.

Thus extending into film-philosophy these related ideas of imagination, the notion of "elemental imagination" in cinematic experience helps explain part of the fundamental process of film immersion discussed above. The grounding sense of the elements stirs, for the spectator, this originary form of imagination, so that the film's expressive landscape opens up the filmworld to the spectator and the spectator opens up to the filmworld. That is, as far as the prereflective cinematic experience can be articulated as the process of becoming immersed within a filmworld, it appears that this grounding structure of immersion is effectively guided by resensitizing the spectator's imagination through an expressive use of the elements. In other words, at various points within a film experience this cinematic form of elemental imagination invites the spectator to immerse her- or himself phenomenologically within the filmworld. Whether it is explicitly done by an intentional directorial decision (as might be said in the more elemental sensibility of directors like Terrence Malick or Andrei Tarkovsky), whether it is done by the filmworld itself (as Daniel Frampton speculates in *Filmosophy* [2006]), or whether this elemental imagination can be tied to the powerful role of the elements themselves, the idea argued for here is that the cinematic form of elemental imagination significantly guides the process of phenomenologically situating the spectator within the filmworld.

To be sure, this does not only happen in the expressive landscapes of the establishing shots in opening scenes. It can also happen throughout the cinematic experience, for the film is structured with moments of elemental imagination: the elements help structure and shape the spectator's immersion into the filmworld. For instance, even in a technologically advanced film like *Avatar* (James Cameron, 2012), most of the state-of-the-art 3D-effects throughout the film often unexpectedly connect us with such material elements: it is the swift mid-air floating quality as well as that otherworldly liquidity of the planet Pandora that together invite us to *reconnect* with the earth and soil of this extremely fictional and elusive Gaia-like filmworld.[19]

Of course, I briefly suggested in describing *Lawrence of Arabia* above that the natural elements also frequently further constitute rich metaphors for the narrative and symbolic layers that enrich each and every cinematic experience: similarly, note how in *Avatar* the powerful destruction of the "Hometree" also intrinsically connects the use of fire to idea of technological control over the world.[20] Yet prior to that—in tandem with nourishing those intellectual dimensions associated with watching film—this process of constituting a world as imaginatively structured by the elements is already meaningful in itself: even though it clearly involves imagination, at its core it has already phenomenologically placed us into an environing world, thereby providing us each time with an existential situation that also has a significant potential for an ecological cinematic ethics inspired by the natural elements.

**Ethical Potential**

Now, both Bachelard's and Sallis's models of material and elemental imagination are very rich undertakings in the philosophical domains of aesthetics and metaphysics, respectively; in both projects, ethics plays a very marginal role at best. Nonetheless, some environmental philosophers have recently begun to extend Bachelard's and Sallis's work into an environmental ethics of elemental imagination. One strand springing directly from the elemental imagination of Bachelard and Sallis (Mickey 2014) might be further accommodated by another, similarly phenomenologically inspired environmental ethics (Toadvine 2014). Relating these two approaches of environmental ethics back to cinema's worldliness (as discussed by Loht [2017]), I will in conclusion develop a film-philosophical approach to an ecocinema as cinematic ethics.[21]

However, before we can work out this "elemental way" of approaching cinematic ethics, the ethical aspect of this elemental imagination needs more illumination. To start with, Sam Mickey suggests how elemental imagination helps us to escape a persistent debate in environmental ethics, which is the question of anthropocentrism and eco/biocentrism.[22] Hence, underlining Sallis's stress on the "force" of elemental imagination, this force is emphatically not something solely "belonging" to humans: instead, he argues, "humans belong *to* imagination" (Mickey 2014, 165; emphasis added). As Mickey points out:

> *Elemental imagination returns humans to a sense of place, reorienting the human to its abode within the encompassing horizon opened up by earth and sky and the other elemental forces of the world. Through participation in the elemental force of imagination, the relationship between humans and the world exceeds the limits of binary oppositions (2014, 166).*

In other words, this reorienting power of elemental imagination is neither wholly anthropocentric nor only nonanthropocentric; accordingly, Mickey calls it "anthropocosmic" (2014, 166). Thus, the anthropocosmic provides an ethical space in which the force of imagination reveals that we are always already placed *within* an environment. This anthropocosmic dimension expresses itself in different forms of creative imagination: Mickey considers, alongside Bachelard's oneiropoetic imagination, also the imagination at work in performative arts or religious experiences (2014); in this sense, we can readily anticipate here the extension of this ethical reinterpretation of the elemental imagination to include the cinematic spatiality of the filmworld. Yet, for Mickey each of these anthropocosmic subforms of elemental imagination discloses how human existence belongs together with a sense of the world. In short, the significance of replacing ourselves within this elemental horizon through the force of imagination is fundamentally ethical—not in the Kantian sense of prescribing a normative set of morals and behaviors, but instead in opening up an experiential sense of ethics: a spatiality in which resonates the etymological meaning of *ethos*, that is, the existential sense of usual abode or accustomed place, a habitual dwelling.

While Mickey discusses various other subtypes of elemental imagination, and while his picking up of Sallis's idea of the noncentered "force" of imagination is central to his ethical claim and more generally to the nature of his imagination of nature as a compassionate, kind, reciprocal entity, he nevertheless retains the somewhat naïve romanticism inherent to Bachelard's poetics. Ted Toadvine, on the other hand, explicitly critiques Bachelard's romanticism, adapting it further into an environmental ethics for our current, more ecologically perilous times. In other words, he mixes Bachelard's and Sallis's ideas with the more disturbing theme of the abyssal nature of the elements: combining various concepts of Maurice Merleau-Ponty and Emmanuel Levinas, Toadvine foregrounds how, when imagining the end of the world, the elements still reveal an anonymous sense of "thereness" in such an apocalyptic imagination, relating such an abyssal future back to the immemorial, elemental past.

In other words, Toadvine (2014) rightly points out that in times of ecological crises such elemental imagination becomes less harmonious: the toxic state of the natural environment rather tends toward anxiety and despair—in other words, it is apocalyptic. Yet, as if speaking against the Armageddon of *The Day After Tomorrow*, Toadvine emphasizes that such "apocalyptic imagining" of the end of the world not only maintains its etymological sense of "uncovering"[23]—but as such, cosmic imagination still is "a revelation *of* and *through* the elements … it still speaks of our adherence to the world, although now this is inherence to a world on the verge of dissolution" (2014, 212; emphasis added). On this score, it is worth remarking that the dystopian filmworld of *Tomorrow* is indeed rather *elemental* in this apocalyptic sense. First of all, the world is alarmed because of the gigantic flood washing over the northern Americas together with unparalleled tornados thundering from the sky. Second, postdiluvian New York is represented as a frozen capital with the elements of snow and ice as well as with ominous waves of freezing air—these elemental forces together separating one protagonist from the other. Third, in one part of this filmworld it is the communal effort of building a fire in a hearth of the New York Public Library that keeps the few survivors alive while in another part of this filmworld the central protagonist survives by means of technological ingenuity. Finally, the last images of the film permit a view of Earth from the International Space Station, leaving two astronauts hypnotized by the sight of a world free from pollution.

### Cinema, Existential Ethics, and the Elemental Imagination

So even such a technologically mediated, apocalyptic imagination of a disaster film like *Tomorrow* speculates with elemental ideas: in its "apocalyptic turn," as Toadvine calls it (2014, 213), this speculative imagination turns us perceptively and affectively toward the elemental nature of a dystopian filmworld. As such, it not only reveals the elemental foundation within and beyond drastic climate change, it also reveals an ethical reorientation as discussed by Mickey: like the well scene in *Lawrence* demonstrated, the very space opened up in the cinematic immersion process has the reorienting power to turn our attention toward these revealing, rooting elements.

This open, ethical space leads us back to Loht's framework on the filmworld set out above: the elemental reorientation of the immersive space can now be said to perform a cinematic version of Heideggerian "de-distancing" (*entfernung*): as Loht summarizes this concept from *Being and Time*, the phenomenological experience of space is less about quantifiable, measured space than it is "about the nearness or farness of things in terms of their lived proximity or the ease with which they can be made present" (2017, 45). Similarly, Loht argues that cinema's fostering of *Dasein's* being-in-the-world is rooted in this existential de-distancing: the projected filmworld becomes meaningful to us—that is, phenomenologically close to us—in our lived, cinematic experience.

It is at this point that Loht gives his framework a more ethical importance by interpreting it further with reference to Heidegger's other existential dimensions; of these, in particular, "care" (*Sorge*) and "concern" (*Fürsorge*) express for him how the environing world becomes more meaningful in the sense of *relating* to others.[24] Loht is certainly right in connecting this existential framework within film-theoretical discussions on narrative structure and character engagement—that is, he is right in relating it to what is sometimes called the "sympathy debate" in analytic traditions of film theory.[25] Yet, on the other hand, overemphasizing the sympathetic structure of being-in-the-world as predominantly character-focused limits cinema's ethical importance to exclusively interhuman sympathies. It would not only leave such an account open to posthumanist critique rebutting the anthropocentrism integral to Heidegger's (early) philosophy, it would also underemphasize the world-environment in which these characters are made to care. Therefore, limiting it thus would be to overlook the upshot of my discussion of Mickey and Toadvine, namely, the idea that the ethical sense of the natural world also has a fundamentally *elemental* significance.

This is by no means to suggest that Loht's ethical account of film's fostering of *Dasein* is unproductive. However, rather than dwell too long on such omissions, I would like, as my final goal, to broaden Loht's arguments for interpersonal sympathy and include, as its basis, this elemental fundament of worldliness. In other words, if Loht's claim for film immersion as "de-distantiation" means that the fictitious cinematic characters become meaningful within their existential world, I would argue that by the same token film experience can couch an existential concern for the natural world: stirred by the cinematically mediated form of elemental imagination, we are similarly made to care for the natural world in which these characters dwell—indeed, sometimes emphatically so—as if the natural world were a character.

Recall, indeed, the opening well scene in *Lawrence of Arabia*: for many, this filmworld is so memorable because of its existential character that is aesthetically foregrounded by the elemental qualities of this immersive environment. This filmworld's elemental imagination is rooted in some dry earth, a wavering mirage, a disputed source under the ground; these elements are brought together into a narrative moral by a gunshot of a distant firearm, thus famously introducing Omar Sharif as Sherif Ali. While Ali certainly is a central figure in what follows, the elemental imagination has already opened up the real ethical question of such an existentialist filmworld. This short, memorable, and engaging scene of 1962 brings to the fore elemental questions for our contemporary times of climate crises: How does this human figure relate to his environing world? How do we relate to these vital elements that source and sustain life?

**Ludo de Roo** received his PhD in Philosophy at Macquarie University, Sydney. His research in film-philosophy focuses on ecocinema and phenomenology, and combines both areas to develop the idea of elemental imagination in relation to immersive filmworlds.
Email: ludo-beau.de-roo@mq.edu.au

## Notes

[1] The idea of cinematic ethics has recently received more attention. See, for instance, Lisa Downing and Libby Saxton (2010); Jinhee Choi and Mattias Frey (2014); and Robert Sinnerbrink (2016).

[2] See, for instance, Bill Nichols (1991) and Carl Plantinga (1997).

[3] Another well-known example is Leonardo DiCaprio's narration in *Before the Flood* (Fisher Stevens, 2016).

[4] Timothy Morton (2013) has coined the term "hyperobject" for concepts that are too large to grasp conceptually; climate change is a paradigmatic case of such an overwhelmingly large idea.

[5] Early postapocalyptic films often blend in (dystopian) science-fiction elements; such films include *Soylent Green* (Richard Fleischer, 1973), the *Mad Max* series (George Miller 1979, 1981, 1985) and *Blade Runner* (Ridley Scott, 1982)—with the latter two both recently reprised (*Mad Max: Fury Road* [George Miller, 2015] and *Blade Runner 2049* [Denis Villeneuve, 2017]). More recent dystopian films mix in other genres as well (e.g., action in *Waterworld* [Kevin Reynolds 1995]; animation in *WALL-E* [Andrew Stanton, 2008]; adventure, with zombie elements, in *The Road* [John Hillcoat, 2009], and again science fiction in *Snowpiercer* [Joon-ho Bong, 2013] and *Interstellar* [Christopher Nolan, 2014]).

[6] Recent examples are *Quantum of Solace* (Marc Forster, 2008), *La Cinquième Saison* (Peter Brosens and Jessica Woodworth, 2012), *Salt and Fire* (Werner Herzog, 2016), *Geostorm* (Dean Devlin, 2017). For older examples, see Stephen Rust (2013).

7 See Patrick Brereton (2016); Robin Murray and Joseph Heumann (2010); and Rust 2013. For more on the environmental impact of film production, or the "cinematic footprint," see Nadia Bozak (2011).

8 For an overview, see Alexa Weik von Mossner (2012).

9 The idea of a "first" and "second" wave is adapted from Lawrence Buell's (2005) historicizing of *literary* ecocriticism, although Buell indicates different historical periods for this related discipline.

10 In the second half of the twentieth century, this dualist idea of "nature" came under increasing scrutiny in various academic disciplines: the ecofeminist approach has had a significant influence (see, e.g., Merchant 1980; and Matthews 1990) on this questioning, as did Bruno Latour's (1993) critique of the "socially constructed" idea of "nature." In ecocinema theory, Paula Willoquet-Maricondi (2010b) gives a good introduction of this topic; this idea has a broader background in literary ecocriticsm (see, e.g., Glotfelty and Fromm 1996) and in environmental geography/history (see Castree 2005; and Cronon 1996).

11 See, for example, Brereton (2016); Murray and Heumann (2010); Adam O'Brien (2016, 2018); and Rust and colleagues (2013).

12 While Yacavone productively combines analytic and continental philosophical traditions, the phenomenological import is a mixture of the aesthetic theory of Mikel Dufrenne and the hermeneutics of Hans-Georg Gadamer, rather than any of the phenomenological theories of "worldhood." Yacavone's idea of "filmworld" is primarily inspired by the concept of "world-making" developed by analytic philosopher Nelson Goodman.

13 This cybernetic component is inspired by the ecological theories of Félix Guattari; furthermore, Ivakhiv's theory is shaped by the process-relational philosophy of Charles Sanders Peirce and Alfred North Whitehead. Although Ivakhiv does advance his idea of "worlds" (in the sense of filmworlds) with references to Heidegger, this is mainly to incorporate the latter into his process-relational model.

14 "Prereflective" is the phenomenological term for the subthreshold level of cognitive processes steering consciousness. Each of the classic phenomenologists (e.g., Husserl, Heidegger, Merleau-Ponty, and Sartre) have advanced different definitions for this level of experience vital for phenomenological research; my adoption of the idea of the "prereflective" does not discriminate between these theories but mainly indicates the general idea.

15 For a good overview, see Martin Lefebvre (2006); his insightful essay (2011) retraces the cultural history of seeing landscapes. Ivakhiv (2013) also reflects on film's geography.

16 This idea of cinegeography partially overlaps with the idea of "film geography" first developed by human and cultural geographers in the 1990s. Good starting points for film geography are Stuart Aitken and Leo Zonn (1994) and Tim Cresswell and Deborah Dixon (2002). For a historical overview, see Anton Escher (2006) and Chris Lukinbeal and Stefan Zimmerman (2006). Lukinbeal has also recently coedited a new compilation on "media geography" (see Mains et al. 2015).

17 Bachelard developed this poetic philosophy of the natural elements (in six volumes between 1938 and 1948) in tandem with his epistemological work in the philosophy of science. A good overview of Bachelard's work is the recent volume edited by Eileen Rizo-Patron and colleagues (2017). An inspiring starting point for Bachelard's phenomenology is his *Poetics of Space* (2014).

18 Even though cosmologies of other cultural traditions (e.g., Indigenous Australian culture, Indian and East-Asian cultures) are often generally based on a rather similar elemental model (see Macauley 2010), my idea of elemental imagination is primarily focused along the lines of the history of Western philosophy.

[19] It might even be said that the elemental imagination is intrinsically related to the innovative use of technology, for it is the 3D-effect together with the material elements that provides this process of immersion.

[20] I can only suggest here the argument that fire and the other elements can also constitute powerful metaphors by themselves: yet, for specific examples, think of the significant symbolic role of water in *Life of Pi* (Ang Lee, 2012), the role of earth and territory in Western film, and the role of air in science fiction. In auteur cinema, the recurrent theme of fire in the cinema of Malick and Tarkovsky suggests that interpreting fire should not be reduced to it being a metaphor for technological mastery.

[21] The only ecocinema approach explicitly concerned with ethics is that taken by Brereton (2016).

[22] The question of (non)anthropocentrism is central to the history of the discipline of environmental ethics; for an overview, see Allen Thompson (2017) and Eileen Crist (2018).

[23] "Apocalyptic" is derived from Latin *apocalypsis*, which is from the Ancient Greek ἀποκάλυψις, a noun of action (ἀποκαλύπτειν "to uncover," "disclose" = ἀπό "off" + καλύπτειν "to cover").

[24] I leave out of consideration here Loht's (2017) discussion of the interrelated set of existentials: "attunement" (*Befindlichkeit*), "mood" (*Stimmung*), and "discourse" (*Rede*).

[25] Loht's (2017) "whipping boy," so to speak, is Noël Carroll's (2008) question of how we relate to the fictional characters on-screen even if we *know* that these people are not really "there."

## References

Aitken, Stuart C., and Leo Zonn, eds. 1994. *Place, Power, Situation, Spectacle: A Geography of Film*. Lanham, MD: Rowman & Littlefield.

Aristotle, 1991. *Rhetoric*. Trans. Hugh Lawson–Tancred. London: Penguin Books.

Bachelard, Gaston. (1948) 2002. *Earth and the Reveries of Will: An Essay on the Imagination of Matter*. Trans. Kenneth Haltman. Dallas: Dallas Institute of Humanities and Culture.

Bachelard, Gaston. (1957) 2014. *The Poetics of Space*. Trans. Maria Jolas. New York: Penguin Books.

Bozak, Nadia. 2011. *The Cinematic Footprint: Lights, Camera, Natural Resources*. Newark, NJ: Rutgers University Press.

Brereton, Patrick. 2005. *Hollywood Utopia: Ecology in Contemporary American Cinema*. Bristol, UK: Intellect Books.

Brereton, Patrick. 2016. *Environmental Ethics and Film*. Abingdon, UK: Routledge.

Buell, Lawrence. 2005. *The Future of Environmental Criticism: Environmental Crisis and Literary Imagination*. Malden, MA: Blackwell Publishing.

Carroll, Noël. 2008. *The Philosophy of Motion Pictures*. Malden, MA: Blackwell Publishing.

Castree, Noel. 2005. *Nature*. London: Routledge.

Choi, Jinhee, and Mattias Frey, eds. 2014. *Cine-Ethics: Ethical Dimensions of Film Theory, Practice, and Spectatorship*. Abingdon, UK: Routledge.

Cresswell, Tim, and Deborah P. Dixon, eds. 2002. *Engaging Film: Geographies of Mobility and Identity*. Lanham, MD: Rowman & Littlefield.

Crist, Eileen. 2018. "Anthropocentrism." In *Compendium to Environmental Studies*, ed. Noel Castree, Mike Hulme, and James D. Proctor, 735–739. Abingdon, UK: Routledge.

Cronon, William, ed. 1996. *Uncommon Ground: Rethinking the Human Place in Nature*. New York: Norton.

Cubitt, Sean. 2013. "Everybody Knows this Is Nowhere: Data Visualization and Ecocriticism." In *Ecocinema Theory and Practice*, ed. Stephen Rust, Salma Monani, and Sean Cubitt, 280–296. London: Routledge.

Cubitt, Sean. 2017. *Infinite Media*. Durham, NC: Duke University Press.

Downing, Lisa, and Libby Saxton. 2010. *Film and Ethics: Foreclosed Encounters*. Abingdon, UK: Routledge.

Escher, Anton. 2006. "The Geography of Cinema: A Cinematic World." *Erdkunde* 60 (4): 307–314. https://www.jstor.org/stable/25647918.

Frampton, Daniel. 2006. *Filmosophy*. London: Wallflower Press.

Glotfelty, Cheryll, and Harold Fromm, eds. 1996. *The Ecocriticism Reader: Landmarks in Literary Ecology*. Athens: University of Georgia Press.

Heidegger, Martin. (1927) 2010. *Being and Time*. Trans. Joan Stambaugh. Albany: State University of New York Press.

Hörl, Erich, and Mark B.N. Hansen, eds. 2013. *Zeitschrift für Medienwissenschaft* 8: "Medienästhetik." Berlin: Gesellschaft für Medienwissenschaft.

Husserl, Edmund. (1935–1938) 1970. *The Crisis of European Sciences and Transcendental Philosophy: An Introduction to Phenomenological Philosophy*. Trans. David Carr. Evanston, IL: Northwestern University Press.

Ingram, David. 2013. "The Aesthetics and Ethics of Eco–Film Criticism." In *Ecocinema Theory and Practice*, ed. Stephen Rust, Salma Monani, and Sean Cubitt, 43–61. London: Routledge.

Ivakhiv, Adrian. 2013. *Ecologies of the Moving Image: Cinema, Affect, Nature*. Waterloo, ON: Wilfrid Laurier University Press.

Latour, Bruno. 1993. *We Have Never Been Modern*. Trans. Catherine Porter. Cambridge, MA: Harvard University Press.

Lefebvre, Martin, ed. 2006. *Landscape and Film*. New York: Routledge.

Lefebvre, Martin. 2011. "On Landscape in Narrative Cinema." *Canadian Journal of Film Studies* 20 (1): 61–78. doi:10.3138/cjfs.20.1.61.

Leiserowitz, Anthony A. 2004. "Before and After the Day After Tomorrow: A U.S. Study of Climate Change Risk Perception." *Environment: Science and Policy for Sustainable Development* 46 (9): 22–37. doi:10.1080/00139157.2005.10524447.

Loht, Shawn. 2017. *Phenomenology of Film: A Heideggerian Account of the Film Experience*. Lanham, MD: Lexington Books.

Lukinbeal, Chris, and Stefan Zimmerman. 2006. "Film Geography: A New Subfield." *Erdkunde* 60 (4): 315–325. doi:10.3112/erdkunde.2006.04.02.

Macauley, David. 2010. *Elemental Philosophy: Earth, Air, Fire and Water as Environmental Ideas*. Albany: State University of New York Press.

MacDonald, Scott. 2004. "Toward an Eco–Cinema." *Interdisciplinary Studies in Literature and Environment* 11 (2): 107–32. doi:10.1093/isle/11.2.107.

Mains, Susan P., Julie Cupples, and Chris Lukinbeal, eds. 2015. *Mediated Geographies and Geographies of Media*. Dordrecht, The Netherlands: Springer.

Matthews, Freya. 1990. *The Ecological Self*. London: Routledge.

Merchant, Carolyn. 1980. *The Death of Nature: Women, Ecology, and the Scientific Revolution*. San Francisco: HarpersCollins.

Merleau-Ponty, Maurice. (1945) 2013. *Phenomenology of Perception*. Trans. Donald A. Landes. London: Routledge.

Mickey, Sam. 2014. "Elemental Imagination: Deconstructive Phenomenology and the Sense of Environmental Ethics." In *Ecopsychology, Phenomenology, and the Environment: The Perspective of Nature*, ed. Douglas Vakoch and Fernando Castrillón, 159–175. New York: Springer.

Minster, Mark. 2010. "The Rhetoric of Ascent in *An Inconvenient Truth* and *Everything's Cool*." In *Framing the World: Explorations in Ecocriticism and Film*, ed. Paula Willoquet-Maricondi, 25–42. Charlottesville: University of Virginia Press.

Morton, Timothy. 2013. *Hyperobjects: Philosophy and Ecology after the End of the World*. Minneapolis: University of Minnesota Press.

Murray, Robin L., and Joseph K. Heumann. 2010. *Ecology and Popular Film: Cinema on the Edge*. Albany: State University of New York Press.

Myers, Tim Christion. 2014. "Understanding Climate Change as an Environmental Threat: Confronting Climate Denial as a Challenge to Climate Ethics." *De Ethica* 1 (1): 53–70. doi:10.3384/de-ethica.2001-8819.141153.

Nichols, Bill. 1991. *Representing Reality: Issues and Concepts in Documentary*. Bloomington: Indiana University Press.

O'Brien, Adam. 2016. *Transactions with the World: Ecocriticism and the Environmental Sensibility of New Hollywood*. New York: Berghahn Books.

O'Brien, Adam. 2018. *Film and the Natural Environment: Elements and Atmospheres*. London: Wallflower Press.

Parikka, Jussi. 2015. *A Geology of Media*. Minneapolis: University of Minnesota Press.

Peters, John Durham. 2015. *The Marvelous Clouds: Toward a Philosophy of Elemental Media*. Chicago: University of Chicago Press.

Plantinga, Carl R. 1997. *Rhetoric and Representation in Nonfiction Film*. Cambridge, UK: Cambridge University Press.

Reusswig, Fritz, and Anthony A. Leiserowitz. 2005. "The International Impact of *The Day After Tomorrow*." *Environment: Science and Policy for Sustainable Development* 47 (3): 41–44. doi:10.1080/00139157.2005.10524447.

Rizo-Patron, Eileen, Edward S. Casey, and Jason M. Wirth, eds. 2017. *Adventures in Phenomenology: Gaston Bachelard*. Albany: State University of New York Press.

Rust, Stephen. 2013. "Hollywood and Climate Change." In *Ecocinema Theory and Practice*, ed. Stephen Rust, Salma Monani, and Sean Cubitt, 191–211. London: Routledge.

Rust, Stephen, Salma Monani, and Sean Cubitt, eds. 2013. *Ecocinema Theory and Practice*. London: Routledge.

Safit, Ilan. 2014. "Nature Screened: An Eco–Film–Phenomenology." *Environmental Philosophy* 11 (2): 211–235. doi:10.5840/envirophil201471011.

Sallis, John. 2000. *Force of Imagination: The Sense of the Elemental*. Bloomington: Indiana University Press.

Sinnerbrink, Robert 2016. *Cinematic Ethics: Exploring Ethical Experience through Film*. London: Routledge.

Tarkovsky, Andrei. 1987. *Sculpting in Time: Reflections on the Cinema*. Trans. Kitty Hunter-Blair. Austin: University of Texas Press.

Thompson, Allen. 2017. "Anthropocentrism: Humanity as Peril and Promise." In *The Oxford Handbook of Environmental Ethics*, ed. Stephen M. Gardiner and Allen Thompson, 77–90. New York: Oxford University Press.

Toadvine, Ted. 2014. "Apocalyptic Imagination and the Silence of the Elements." In *Ecopsychology, Phenomenology, and the Environment: The Perspective of Nature*, ed. Douglas Vakoch and Fernando Castrillón, 211–221. New York: Springer.

Weik von Mossner, Alexa. 2012. "Facing the Day after Tomorrow: Filmed Disaster, Emotional Engagement, and Climate Risk Perception." In *American Environments: Climate, Cultures, Catastrophe*, ed. Christof Mauch and Sylvia Mayer, 97–115. Heidelberg: Winter Verlag.

Weik von Mossner, Alexa, ed. 2014. *Moving Environments: Affect, Emotion, Ecology, and Film*. Waterloo, ON: Wilfrid Laurier University Press.

Willoquet-Maricondi, Paula, ed. 2010a. *Framing the World: Explorations in Ecocriticism and Film*. Charlottesville: University of Virginia Press.

Willoquet-Maricondi, Paula. 2010b. "Introduction: From Literary Ecocriticism to Cinematic Ecocriticism." In *Framing the World: Explorations in Ecocriticism and Film*, ed. Paula Willoquet-Maricondi, 1–22. Charlottesville: University of Virginia Press.

Yacavone, Daniel. 2015. *Film Worlds: A Philosophical Aesthetics of Cinema*. New York: Columbia University Press.

# Chapter 4

# Toward a Model of Distributed Affectivity for Cinematic Ethics
## Ethical Experience, Trauma, and History

**Brigid Martin**

One way that we can understand the ethical significance of affective engagement with films is through the concept of empathy. By "feeling with" characters on-screen, viewers can understand more comprehensively characters' circumstances and their ethical consequences. Spectators may even come to evaluate characters, situations, and actions differently according to their empathic investment. However, empathy has become a contested term in recent years as research in moral psychology has advanced (Coplan 2011). While the interrogation of affect and empathy has led to important convergences in phenomenological and cognitivist approaches to film, the relevance of empathy can vary across films (Sinnerbrink 2016, 91). Empathy does not exhaust the significance of affect for ethical experience in cinema. In this chapter, I aim to build a model for understanding the relationship between *complex* affectivity and *ambiguous* ethical engagement in cinematic experience without relying on a concept of empathy.

In some explorations of cinematic ethics that do not center on empathy, affective connections between spectators and characters may be understood as providing a "synthesis of perspectives which offers insight into the ways in which we perceive and seek to make sense of our lives" (Stadler 2002, 238). Films can enrich our understanding of ethical situations by exploring ethically significant affective contexts and emotionally nuanced situations that would otherwise remain hidden. In other cases, affect is deployed to understand how various levels of ethical engagement operate outside rational moral judgments (Plantinga 2010a). In this case, affect refers to specific forms of nonvoluntary response, emotional contagion, and lower-level processing that can establish emotional bonds between viewers and characters. This can have ethical consequences by binding the audience to specific characters prior to the intervention of higher-level moral judgments about actions in the narrative. However, such accounts have less scope to explore the processes underlying ethical engagement in cases of complex or ambivalent cinematic emotions.

Affect theorists have thoroughly explored the forms of subjectivity that arise from complex affects and their political and ethical consequences for aesthetics. In this case, affect is often conceptualized as relational, prepersonal, and nonconscious processes that inform embodiment and shape the way that we interact with each other and with our world. This conception leads to the cultural critique of how "objects of emotion circulate or are distributed across a social as well as psychic field" (Ahmed 2014, 45). Affect, in this sense, is the basis of "the bodily practice of politics," mediates ethical relations, and sustains social structures (Berlant 2011: 260). At the individual level, this may involve intercorporeal relations—for example, when other people respond to us with *fear* and we internalize that fear—that change the way we understand and use our bodies (Ahmed 2014, 63). At the collective level, the culture that we consume can establish an "affective circuit," for example of *pity* or *guilt*, that produces and reproduces ideological norms and practices (Clough 2012, 22). Mass fictions and art forms in particular are therefore implicated in these broad sociopolitical arrangements of affect and how these reproduce or "remediate" social relations, organizations, and norms (Berlant 2011, 44). In this context, the critical analysis of affect is intimately paired with socioeconomic criticism. This prepersonal understanding of complex affective relations opens up other paths as well. Films may use complex affective scenarios, cues, aesthetic themes, and character relations in order to force viewers into uncomfortable positions of ethical reflection by constructing ethically provocative situations that are also prohibitive of definitive moral judgments (Sinnerbrink 2016, 156).

Often the most inscrutable and opaque affective situations can be the most ethically demanding. Extreme affective states and situations that arise in response to extreme circumstances can be life-changing and wide in scope, and can pose significant ethical challenges. Trauma is one such example. It is both intensively evocative and difficult to describe abstractly, and seems to be extreme in a way that precludes empathy in any cognitively robust sense. Trauma involves a "complex web of symptoms" including a fundamentally undermined sense of ownership and a shifted sense of agency that are "experienced bodily and organized without semantic representations" (Ataria 2015, 200; 207). How can those of us who have not experienced such traumas even begin to recognize and comprehend the emotional severity and psychological complexity of traumatic circumstances?

Instead of using affect as a point of criticism (for example, in terms of how affect-saturated representations produce ideological effects and imbue political structures), or analyzing the ethicopolitical role of representations of affect, I will focus on how affectively laden cinematic experience offers a positive space for viewers to individually engage in ethical negotiation, reflection, and contemplation that may otherwise be impossible. This is particularly significant in the case of trauma, its highly individual symptoms, and its tendency to produce detaching, dissociating, and isolating effects both epistemically and emotionally (Gusich 2012, 506; Ataria 2015, 205–7). What is necessary for this specific goal, then, is not a critique of how affect functions in a film and the kind of viewer subjectivities and forms of political embodiment it produces,[1] but an interrogation of how the aesthetic experience of a cognitively and affectively engaged audience relates to complex cinematic affects and their ethical possibilities.

In this chapter, I will explore the conjunction of the notion that films can serve as a medium of ethical experience (articulated by, for example, Sinnerbrink 2016) and the notion that enculturation transforms cognition (articulated by, for example, Menary 2010, 2012) and, as I will pursue, perhaps affectivity. I will develop an aesthetic framework for understanding the ethical implications of complex affective engagement by bringing together theoretical resources from phenomenology, cognitive science, and classical Indian aesthetics to interrogate the ethical experience evoked by the Korean film *Aimless Bullet* (*Obaltan*, Hyun-mok Yu, 1961). I will suggest that, in order to understand the ethical engagement offered by cinematic experience in cases of complex affects, we require an understanding of *distributed affectivity* and *affective-aesthetic affordances*. I will argue that cases like *Aimless Bullet* may, if integrated into our experience in the right ways, *transform our affective capacities.*

In the first section, I will raise the problem of affective ambiguity for cognitive frameworks of cinematic emotion that are built on the concept of perceptual "affordances." Subsequently, I will look at the significance of complex affective engagement for ethical experience through *Aimless Bullet*. I will explore how complex, morally thick emotions are raised in the film through a variety of means that prevent clear moral judgments and attitudes. In the second section, I will raise some of the consequences that theories of scaffolded mind and distributed cognition have for understanding the relation between affordances and affect. I will then examine what classical Indian aesthetics can contribute to the discussion of this relation, primarily through the figures of Bhatta Nayaka and Abhinavagupta,[2] whose interpretations of *rasa* aesthetics can contribute to an account of *affective-aesthetic affordances*. In the third section, I will use Maurice Merleau-Ponty's concept of institution to synthesize these accounts to articulate a model of distributed affectivity in cinematic experience. I will close by looking at the ways that this model can help to articulate the significance of *Aimless Bullet* for cinematic ethical experience.

I contend that in some cases films can offer an important level of ethical engagement with complex affective experience. This is particularly pertinent for reflecting on radically isolating and alienating experiences like trauma. Abhinava and Merleau-Ponty are particularly important in developing this thesis because they allow us to interpret films as containing a *multiplicity* of both nonrepresentational and representational aesthetic and narrative affordances, rather than conceptualize them as *single cognitive artifacts* that enhance our mental processing. Further, films provide structurally rich environments for such affordances to be effective. An affordance-rich account of materially supported affectivity establishes the integration of affective responses, cognitive representations, and the variety of individual responses that is necessary to understand certain cases of ethically significant complex affects. In films like *Aimless Bullet*, which prevents decisive moral judgments, empathies, or clear allegiances, viewers are given affective and cognitive resources that transform and scaffold their capacity for ethical reflection. This offers us a way of thinking about the ethical salience of affective engagement that does not reduce this engagement to specific moral emotions (such as fear, guilt, pride, pity, or disgust). Films contain rich inner contexts that offer a broad affective repertoire, a plurality of frames of reference for audience engagement, a robust structure, and extensive aesthetic lexicons for emotional comprehension.

**Style, Aesthetics, and Ambiguous Cinematic Emotions:**
***Aimless Bullet* and Korean Realism**

In an article on "affective incongruity," Carl Plantinga (2010b) uses *The Thin Red Line* (Terence Malick, 1998) to develop an account of cases where the general affective theme of a film is incongruous or conflict-ing. According to Plantinga, although most films are unified around a general affective theme, exceptional cases may involve a purposeful disunity that cannot be reduced to the mixed emotions characteristic of specific genres. In such cases, "the narration intentionally elicits mixed and seemingly contradictory emotions and affects for some narrative purpose other than irony" (2010b, 90–91). Cinematic techniques and aesthetic cues that diverge from audience expectations build an am-bivalent "structure of feeling" and provoke a sense of affective *aporia* (2010b, 93). In Plantinga's (2010b, 97–98) example, this incongruity takes the form of a general contemplative attitude that arises from the continuous contrast of two emotionally conflicting registers of narra-tion, an aesthetic conflict that is uncharacteristic of the Hollywood war film genre. Despite drawing upon this genre's conventions, *The Thin Red Line* uses a series of contrasting techniques to explore different emotional and philosophical attitudes to war, death, their place in the natural world, and human existence. Through contrasts of high-angle and low-angle shots, lighting, and visual imagery, the film sets up an unresolved affective dichotomy between a naturalistic poeticism and a mournful pessimism that mirrors the worldviews held by different narrating characters.

Plantinga offers a powerful account of films that are built around a kind of affective engagement not reducible to unified emotional themes. Moreover, because it allows us to explore how affective ambiguity in-duces a contemplative attitude, affective incongruity opens up an in-terrogation of how judgment-prohibitive but robust ethical experience in cinema is fostered by affective indeterminacy. However, an under-standing of affective incongruity that emphasizes how "[a]mbiguity of thought is generated by ambiguity of feeling" through *auteur*-centered techniques subsumes the varied landscape of viewer affectivity and en-gagement under the *narrative* and *cognitive* purpose of reliably inducing a contemplative attitude (2010b, 97). While this suits the specific case of *The Thin Red Line*, where sustained contemplation and poetic uncertainty are thematic ends-in-themselves, in some cases, as I will now explore, affective incongruity can build situations of thematic ambiguity through complex emotional experiences where the primary effects are affective *intensity* and ethical *provocation*, rather than thematic clarity and nar-rational unity. In such cases, affective incongruity may still induce a con-templative attitude, but one that is ethically rich and deeply invested in the ambiguous affective situation of the film.

*Aimless Bullet* is an example of a film from a wave of realist and neo-realist cinema that emerged in South Korea as a response to the material conditions of urban life after the 1953 armistice that ended the active military conflict of the Korean War. In contrast to films from other post-war realist movements, such as Italian neorealism, *Aimless Bullet* involves a number of divergences from strict realism in stylistic technique, most prominently drawing on expressionism and *film noir*. Despite periods of suppression and loss, the film has maintained a strong following.

The narrative follows the adult siblings of the impoverished Song family: the eldest brother, Cheol-ho (a clerk at an accounting firm); the younger brother, Yeong-ho (a retired soldier); and the younger sister, Myeong-suk. They live together with the rest of their insular family— their traumatized and bedridden mother (who only mumbles, with occasional desperate cries of "let's get out of here!"), and Cheol-ho's pregnant wife, his daughter, and his son—in a dilapidated house in an underdeveloped district of Seoul. The most screen time is dedicated to Yeong-ho, his interactions with his fellow army retirees, his attempts to make money for his family, and his affair with ex-military nurse Seol-hui. While Yeong-ho attracts drama, Cheol-ho spends his time working through the monotony of everyday life while suffering a toothache, try-ing to scrape together enough money to buy his daughter new shoes. Myeong-suk, rejecting the uncertainty of her noncommittal lover and seeking to overturn the destitution of her family, turns to sex work.

*Aimless Bullet* is tinted with aesthetic tones of urban desolation, brought about through a slow exploration of degrading spaces that subsist beneath the city, that sprinkle its hidden crevices, and prolifer-ate on its edges. Until the film's climax, when Yeong-ho robs a bank and is pursued by police, the action unfolds ponderously, contemplatively, and depressively. The rhythm of the film is propelled by Yeong-ho's frus-trated passion in an ambivalent and unresponsive world, on the one hand, and by the weight of Cheol-ho's exhaustion, on the other. Against

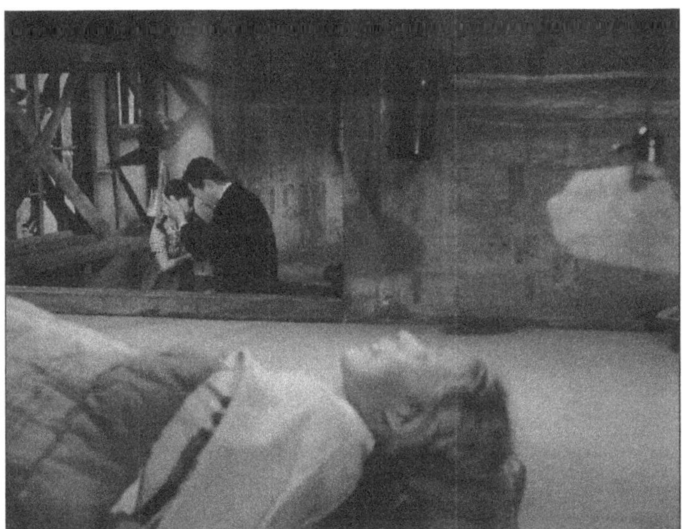

*Illustration 4.1. Cheol-ho melancholically embraces his daughter in the Song family home with his suffering mother in the foreground* (Aimless Bullet, *Korean Film Archive / Blue Kino, 1961/2016*).

this fraternal clash of energies, Myeong-suk grapples with the family's poverty with opaque and often unseen determination. Periods of extended silence occur throughout, and the camera tends to linger on objects (such as door handles and telephones) and faces. Settings comprise primarily small but open spaces (the Song family's shack, a derelict bar hangout for the retired soldiers, Seol-hui's apartment) and the streets of urban Seoul. Peaks in family conflict unfold in the static locations, while slow tracking shots down city laneways, pathways beneath bridges, and the chaotic Seoul traffic show characters slowly being broken down by their burdens.

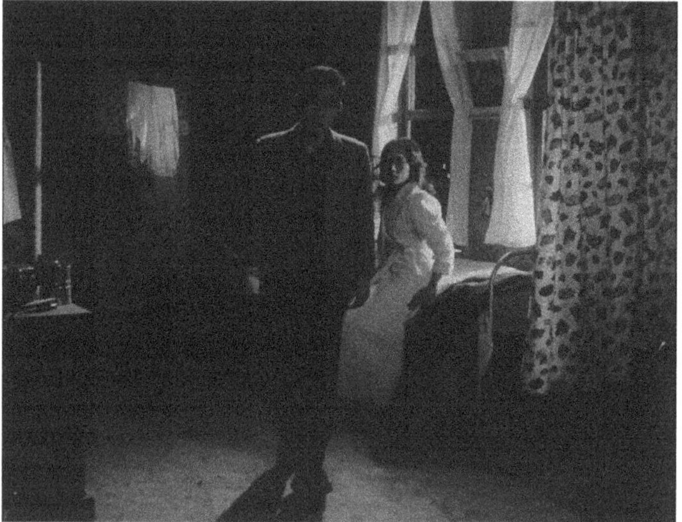

*Illustration 4.2. Yeong-ho and Seol-hui's meeting is interrupted by a stalker (off-camera) at Seol-hui's apartment (Aimless Bullet, Korean Film Archive / Blue Kino, 1961/2016).*

However, at times this social realism is disrupted by contrasting elements of style. Shadows, urban structures, latticework scenery, and moonlight are recurring visual motifs, which are often used to striking effect by creating obstructed, angular perspectives, but they are treated with a depressive distance in mournful, elongated durations without the zeal of *noir* or the bodily contortions of expressionism. In the final scenes of the film, these aesthetic twists become more structurally and affectively radical. Yeong-ho flees the police after his bank robbery in a rapidly deteriorating getaway chase through the guts of Seoul. In the film's most famous sequence, an exhausted and emotionally destroyed Cheol-ho comes upon a dentist and has a graphic tooth extraction. With an unwavering extremist edge, expressionist techniques become common. For the first time, Cheol-ho appears to be the narrative protagonist,

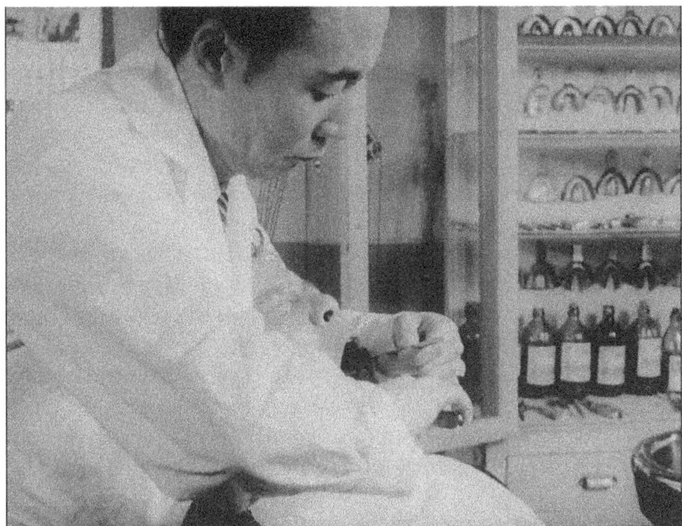

Illustration 4.3. Cheol-ho has one of his wisdom teeth extracted, which begins a visceral trail of self-abuse (Aimless Bullet, *Korean Film Archive / Blue Kino, 1961/2016*).

only to wander around Seoul in a self-destructive stupor. The film retains its depressive realist sensibility, and obsessively follows Cheol-ho's numbing decline.

Through the daily lives of the Song siblings, which are presented with stark differences in narrative characterization and through diverging aesthetic themes, *Aimless Bullet* plays with mood and the affective orientation of the spectator. The siblings all elicit different forms of sympathy with different aesthetic and emotional tones. Though this thematic contrast is not as pronounced as that in *The Thin Red Line*, it persists throughout the film. These differences are brought together in the way that conventions of the neorealist genre—emphasis on mundane activities and everyday life, drawn out sequences that downplay action, frequent use of silence rather than music, inconsequential dialogue, and so on—frame the material suffering of the siblings with a mute and depressive banality (regardless of their individual conflicts). In the film's closing scenes, however, radical aesthetic shifts and visceral affective disruptions actively violate genre conventions (as opposed to the employment of expressionistic techniques to shape tone and mood within an otherwise neorealist style), systematically reorient the psychological focus, and retroactively confuse the affective flow of the film. The multiperspectival, emotional thematization of the material conditions that produce family conflict is suddenly inverted by the graphic severity of Cheol-ho's self-destruction, generating a new affective dissonance. This incongruity can leave the spectator in a position where they are forced to retroactively process this affective dissonance and in doing so comprehend the *otherwise invisible severity and violence* that can underlie everyday suffering and the destruction of interpersonal ties in cases of long-term and historical trauma (Ahmed 2014, 34; Ataria 2015, 208–10). This affective tension reframes the daily lives of the Song siblings and reveals the variety of ways that such interpersonal trauma can manifest itself.

How is this dissonant affective effect produced? While the aesthetic composition and narrative demonstrate a clear shift in the affective states *Aimless Bullet* elicits from one moment to the next, exactly why and how does this drastically alter the *overall* affective experience of the film? In the next section, I will begin to explore ways of understanding affective-aesthetic affordances that can account for complex affectivity in cinematic experience without isolating such affective engagement to exceptional cases that cleverly manipulate audience engagement.

### Imaginative Savoring and Affective-Aesthetic Affordances: Adapting Rasa Aesthetics to Film

Plantinga (2010b) mentions the psychological concept of affordances in passing in order to roughly sketch a broad cognitivist model of cinematic experience and locate the role of affect in it. This model of ecological cognition, developed by James J. Gibson (2015, 119-20; 229), proposes that visual perception is actively synthesized by a perceiving agent or "living observer" who, with little conscious reflection, draws selectively on environmental information in order to form coherent sensible images of their world. For Gibson, this environmental information amounts to the ecological *functions* embedded in "[t]he medium, substances, surfaces, objects, places, and other animals" that constitute the environment of individual organisms (2015, 134). That is, affordances are defined by their functional role in an organism's environmental niche and the actions they make possible for perceiving agents. In the context of cinema, affordances refer to basic units of sensible experience—"objects and events"—that are readily accessible to our perceptual schemata (Plantinga 2010b, 87). Gibson (2015, 129) stresses that affect and emotion play no role within the affording environment itself: emotion is about *experience*, affordances are about *information*. In the model of film spectatorship developed from this, affective states serve as filters that shape attention and salience, influencing *how* we pick up on affordances. (From this perspective affect cannot have its own compositional role.) (Plantinga 2010b, 88). So in *The Thin Red Line*, Plantinga's notion of affective incongruity refers to the emotional attitude or state that the film establishes in the audience (through aesthetic, causal cues) that filters the way that viewers perceptually and thematically engage with the film.

However, in the wake of the theoretical and empirical impact of theories of scaffolded mind and distributed cognition, where artifacts and affordances have a much broader significance, the relation between affordances, cognition, and affect in aesthetic experience requires re-evaluation. In such accounts, artifacts that exist outside the body can enhance, supplement, or replace certain *cognitive functions* when they are used with a high degree of trust and reliance; the classic example is that a notebook may be used as a memory-extending device (Clark and Chalmers 1998). However, this is not limited to information-outsourcing and the offload of cognitive labor onto material artifacts. The distribution of cognitive resources throughout an environment means that an agent's cognitive capacities and abilities may themselves be transformed by enculturation, specific practices, and affording environments (Menary 2012). In these more expansive externalist accounts of cognition, affordances cannot provide a complete picture of perception and cognition, and should not be restricted to environmental information or a series of background causal inputs actively filtered and assembled by perceiving agents: they are situated in a scaffolded environment, can be restructured and integrated into the agent's cognitive and perceptual apparatus, and may also be transformed by the agent's activity. Murray Smith has even recently applied work in theories of extended mind to suggest that cinematic experience can form the ground for "empathic imagining" (2017, 182). Understanding the affective significance of affordances in films requires an articulation of how integrated cognitive practices at work in artistic experiences establish, scaffold, extend, and shape engagement and in a way that may *expand* or *transform* our cognitive and *affective* capacities.

Giovanna Colombetti and Joel Krueger (2015) have recently explored the possibility of extending theories of the scaffolded mind to affect and emotion. To do this, they draw on Kim Sterelny's (2010) interpretation of distributed cognition through a model of evolutionary niche construction and developmental scaffolding. Organisms inhabit an environmental niche that situates their activity but that is also affected by their activity. In this sense, the niche, partly constructed by the organism, works as both a developmental and a selective pressure, and Sterelny (2010) argues that this provides an external scaffold that enhances, supports, structures, and offloads cognitive activities. Gibson already referred to this ecological concept of a niche in his statement of the theory of affordances, ultimately arguing that "a niche is a set of affordances" (2015, 120). Colombetti and Krueger (2015) point out that if cognitive functions can be environmentally supported and materially extended or enhanced through regular and reliable practices, then we may also apply this analysis to affective states. Music and films, for example, can serve as accessible and integrated artifacts for individuals to self-regulate their emotions. If I have a particularly exhausting and intense day of work, I know exactly which films I can watch to improve my mood. I know where they are, when and how I can access them, and exactly what their effect will be on my mood: they have become reliable sources of affective self-regulation. This model focuses primarily on the reliability of environments that are partly constructed by individuals and cultures, so this conceptualization of affective scaffolding cannot be deployed at the level of aesthetic encounters with individual artworks (which, for audiences viewing a film for the first time, possess a novelty that precludes integration into self-regulating practices). When we analyze the affective processes and thematic meanings at work in specific films, we cannot treat them as *single artifacts* that produce reliable affective or cognitive effects. Within the scope of a scaffolded environment, it would be a mistake to treat novel experiences of films as elements of a cognitive system, because the relationship between the audience and the film cannot feature the "trust" and "entrenchment" required to constitute a self-regulating system (Colombetti and Krueger 2015). However, the cultural practice of film-viewing is a well-established and regulated space both for entertainment and for more complex forms of affective and cognitive engagement. And so despite the above restriction, scaffolded affectivity has important consequences for the more fine-grained concept of affordances in aesthetic contexts.

In what ways can these insights for regular embodied practices be adapted to understand the experience of specific artworks that produce complex aesthetic emotions? How can we explore the consequences of the feedback loops and active engagements that characterize environmentally supported affectivity for affordances in novel aesthetic contexts? This requires a shift from analyzing broad *scaffolded affective environments* to analyzing *distributed affectivity* in more local practices and niches that transform our affective and cognitive capacities (Menary 2010). Colombetti argues that affordances can characterize "the affective nature of . . . lived environments" at this finer local level because the "sense-making" aspect of living systems involves a *qualitative* sensitivity to affordances that is not merely cognitive (2017a, 451). This is an explicit divergence from Gibson, who, in order to secure their significance as perceptual information, denies that affordances can bear a qualitative dimension beyond being "beneficial" or "injurious" in the actions they afford (2015, 129). But for Colombetti, this qualitative dimension means that affordances themselves can possess an exterior affective valence for perceiving agents. Further, affective processes and triggers may themselves serve as part of a complex landscape of affordances. That is, "an organism's psychobiological environment does not just prompt or afford certain kinds of motor actions, but also affective states of attraction and repulsion (including mixtures of the two)" (Colombetti 2017a, 452). Affordances are not only filtered and attended to in accordance with affective states, but also *shape and influence these affective states* in nuanced ways that do not simply causally "cue" certain emotions and responses.

Expanding on these insights in the context of moods, Colombetti argues that "the world provides not only stimuli, but also cultural values, norms, and rules of behavior that shape and impact moods at various levels" (2017b, 1441). Our affective states are situated in the world and influenced by the valences of affordances in it to the extent that actively scaffolded environments allow us "to undergo [affective] experiences *that would otherwise be out of our reach*" (Colombetti 2017b, 1441; my emphasis). In the case of individual cinematic experiences, this establishes an affective-perceptual feedback loop between the spectator and the film. However, unless we interrogate *how* new affective capacities emerge and function, then the observation that we can use films to modulate our own emotional states remains theoretically impoverished. Extending Colombetti and Krueger's approach, my suggestion is that films, even films that we have not seen before, operate as scaffolded sites of *distributed affectivity* that may offer a new space of ethical experience and negotiation by *transforming our affective capacities*. In the conclusion of this chapter, I will suggest that the case of *Aimless Bullet*—which does not provide explicit moral arguments or offer ethical ideas at a cognitive or narrative level—gives us new affective resources for comprehending trauma. This allows spectators to alter their ethical attitudes even in the absence of fully articulated cognitive content.

But how does art offer a sufficiently scaffolded and enculturated space for the transformation of cognition and affectivity? In what follows, I will contend that a relevant model of affective-aesthetic affordances can be found in classical Indian aesthetics. What is significant in this model is that there is a step between raw perceptual "information" and individual "experience" that allows us to conceptualize an additional layer of affordances. These affective-aesthetic affordances, rather than being restricted to perceptual binding and simple actions, contextualize our experience of art with respect to affective engagement and appreciation (and, subsequently, reflection).

Bharata's concept of *rasa*, a word meaning "(to) *taste*" or "(to) *savor*," was originally developed as part of a practical dramaturgy for writers and performers. As a concept, it serves to capture the "uniquely aesthetic" quality of emotions realized in art. Bharata's conception understands rasa to be the effect of an interaction between basic "stable emotions" that are communicated to the audience and the "aesthetic elements" that supplement them (2016, 50–1)[3]. These aesthetic elements are broad in scope and incorporate a range of compositional techniques, expressive devices, and ornamentations involved in dramatic performance. Bharata defines *rasa* in the following way:

> *[R]asa is so called because it is something savored.... Just as discerning people relish tastes when eating food prepared with various condiments and in doing so find pleasure, so discerning viewers relish the stable emotions when they are manifested by the acting out of [aesthetic elements such as] various transitory emotions and reactions and accompanied by the other acting registers (the verbal, the physical, and psychophysical), and they find pleasure in doing so. (2016, 51)*

*Rasa*, in this sense, refers to an enriched emotion that is indirectly communicated to the audience and savored over time. It is the "object" of artistic emotions and exemplifies the emotional theme of a dramatic work. Certain emotions pair with certain *rasas*, with any given *rasa* being equivalent to an *internally complex* affective theme. In line with the practical goals of dramaturgy, Bharata articulates eight distinct *rasas*, the eight corresponding "stable emotions," and a series of aesthetic elements: "thirty-three transitory emotions, and eight psychophysical responses" that constitute the list of *rasa*-affecting emotions and reactions, "foundational factors" and "stimulant factors" that include character types and offer points of entry for the audience, and three registers of acting (2016, 52–4). Also included among the aesthetic elements are genre conventions such as preludes and epilogues, accompaniments such as music, and costume, makeup, dance, staging, and a repertoire of gestures. *Aimless Bullet*'s neorealist treatment of disorganized, desolate urban landscapes, its sense of dilated time, its fascination with moonlit shadows, and its variety of other cinematic techniques fit into this category.

Through the concept of *rasa*, Bharata's practical guide to performance spawned an extensive tradition in Indian aesthetics and literary criticism. Earlier commentators take *rasa* to be something held by the actor or the character that is then communicated to the audience through some cognitive means such as inference. Later theorists, most importantly Abhinava and Bhatta Nayaka, interpret *rasa* as a hermeneutical process of audience appreciation and engagement. Abhinava is the main source for this approach to philosophical aesthetics; with his texts on the topics dating to circa 990–1000 CE, his written corpus is expansive and includes broad commentaries on his predecessors, whose work only survives in fragments. Rather than relying on inference or representation as a means of communication, for these philosophers *rasa* emerges in (or is synthesized by) the audience through their sensuous and imaginative engagement.

For Bhatta Nayaka, Abhinava, and their followers, a text, performance, or artwork prompts the *activity* of the audience, and *rasa* is realized through their engagement. *Rasa* only emerges through the "experientialization" of an audience actively savoring an aesthetic emotion over time (Bhatta Nayaka 2016). The audience reaches out to the work in order to take up and savor its elements, generating *rasa* as an *internally complex* and *characteristically dynamic* affective theme. The aesthetic elements and emotions are synthesized by the audience, consciously or nonconsciously, in a kind of imaginative play (Bahurupa Mishra 2016; Dhanamjaya 2016). The audience is an active participant in the development of aesthetic emotion. As with the understanding of cinematic perception that Plantinga draws on, the perception of an artwork takes place through an active engagement with the aesthetic elements; however, this also takes place at an *affective* level of engagement—viewers pick up and synthesize material that is already affective.

Bhatta Nayaka (2016) offers a triadic account of the aesthetic process that produces *rasa*. The process is broken down into three stages (Dhanika 2016; Ruyyaka 2016). The first stage—linguistic expression[4]—refers to techniques of grammar and "figures of sound and sense" in the (dramatic or literary) artwork itself that produce its (literal or figurative) cognizable content (Bhatta Nayaka 2016). These are elements of the experience that are informationally basic but require a high level of abstraction to formally delineate. In this sense, these aspects serve as the environmental information that Gibson most closely associates with affordances. This is the text of the drama or poem, and perhaps the screenplay of a film. It is the fact that Cheol-ho rubs his aching jaw, not the exhausting agony of his state, or the way it makes him recoil slightly from the glare of the sun. The second stage—actualization—makes a stable emotion available to the audience through a process of "commonization" brought about by the aesthetic elements and their bodily effects.[5] These elements have a specific quality and contribute to a phenomenological whole, and in doing so distinguish aesthetic experiences from everyday texts and utterances. The third stage is the experientialization that forms the basis of Bhatta Nayaka's theory, where the spectator takes up the elements to savor the emotion.

Bhatta Nayaka, Abhinava, and their followers offer a complex account of the common elements of aesthetic experience, which comprise the "actualization" stage of the process that sits between basic information and experience. Commonization (in the sense of both "making accessible" and "making interpersonal") is necessary in order for a performance or literary work to move from its linguistic composition (spoken or written words and ordinary figures of speech) into a domain capable of artistically *affecting* the audience. This process is made up of the aesthetic elements listed by Bharata—the reactions, the factors, the acting registers, and so on—and make a work affectively comprehensible and appreciable (Dhanika 2016). The aesthetic elements, therefore, are the same for both experts in the medium (such as critics or creators) and the audience more generally. Aesthetic elements are encountered as-they-affect-us, rather than as mechanisms that are more-or-less transparent depending on the technical vocabulary of the audience. In this sense, commonization involves the artistic dimension of the experience becoming accessible to the audience, so that its affective aspect can be taken up by spectators and savored as *rasa*. The aesthetic elements provide a *robust material context that prompts spectators to emotionally engage with a work as something artistic*. From this perspective, the aesthetic elements (as distinct from basic linguistic sense) function as impersonal but phenomenologically rich affective-aesthetic *affordances*. They operate as loose "causal elements" worked into the composition of an artwork that "[render] the stable emotion an experiential object" for "receptive" spectators (Ruyyaka 2016, 152). Any given artwork establishes a highly scaffolded space of engagement that includes both the "object" of aesthetic experience (a stable emotion) *and* all the "tools" that spectators use (consciously or not) to savor this emotion—a set of affordances to connect, experiment with, juxtapose, refer to, play with, and explore.

Abhinava emphasizes the role of aesthetic elements as affordances of engagement by arguing that a full articulation of the uniqueness of aesthetic emotions requires a rejection of any strictly cognitive process as the sole means by which *rasa* could arise. The processes that Abhinava explicitly lists and rejects include behavioral causes (such as emotional contagion), actual belief in the narrative, mimesis and imitation, inference, "superimposition" (where the art-object retains the appearance of reality despite being known to be otherwise), identification with characters, "cognitive error," trope recognition and internalized norms of response, "fabrication" (where specifically constructed false emotions would be fleeting experiential objects), and pure fantasy (2016, 218–19). Abhinava (2016, 219) argues that none of these processes, nor their combination, can account for the characteristic and pervasive (if ambiguous) aesthetic pleasure that we take in savoring emotions over time, and that taken on their own or together these conditions could only produce everyday emotions and behavioral responses without the uniquely aesthetic quality of *rasa*. What is necessary is a basic condition for this unique process of artistic savoring and engagement. This is the role that Abhinava gives to the aesthetic elements. On the one hand, Abhinava (2016) characterizes aesthetic elements as involving a negative aspect that signals the artistic nature of the work to spectators by sifting out everyday assumptions and practical concerns about the world (for example, ordinary self-interest) and altering the behavioral orientation they hold toward appearances. On the other hand, aesthetic elements also involve a positive aspect because they involve "a whole assemblage of theatrical components, from the actor onward," and conduce a "process of visualization" (2016, 194). What is produced is a "pure sensibility" that animates the imagination and enables even those unfamiliar with some aspects of the artwork (such as the historical context of a narrative) to apprehend the aesthetic emotions at work (Abhinava 2016, 195). Abhinava emphasizes that what is most important in this is the effect on the audience's mode of consciousness, which is broadened and decoupled from ordinary practical or epistemic demands, and put in an active position to synthesize emotive content. Characterized in this way, aesthetic elements are *low-level facilitators* of perceptual engagement that are not structurally, representationally, or emotionally neutral, but *affectively laden*. Aesthetic elements serve both as rich context-markers (that affect our disposition) and artistically thick tools of appreciation and engagement: they *afford savoring*.

With this in mind, we can interpret moments such as the brief cut to Myeong-suk that interrupts Cheol-ho's downfall as offering a set of different possible emotional nuances for these final scenes. For the first time, we hear Myeong-suk's inner monologue, mournfully expressing a hope that Cheol-ho's newborn child will be able to laugh and smile in the future. In the moment, this can produce a variety of emotional nuances. It may introduce a vague sense of hopefulness to counterbalance the pessimism and brutality of Cheol-ho's visceral decline; or it may draw attention to the weight of the inner struggles and burdens that Myeong-suk, whose actions seemed opaque for the majority of the film, carries for the family, making Cheol-ho's self-destruction all the more bitter.

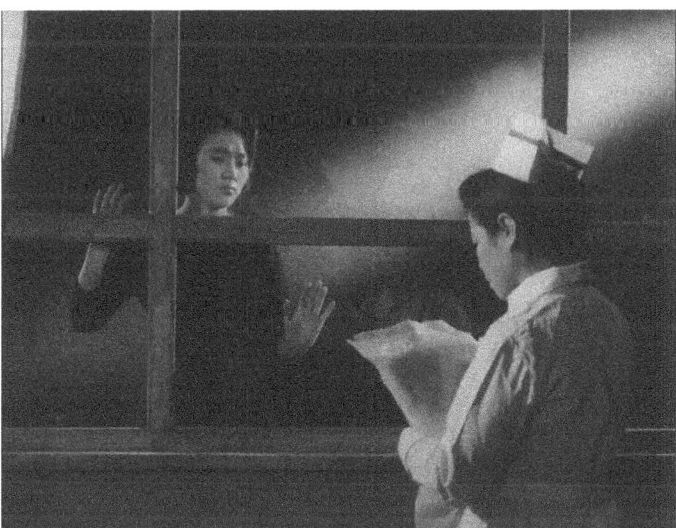

*Illustration 4.4. Myeong-suk visits Cheol-ho's newborn child in hospital alone* (Aimless Bullet, *Korean Film Archive / Blue Kino, 1961/2016*).

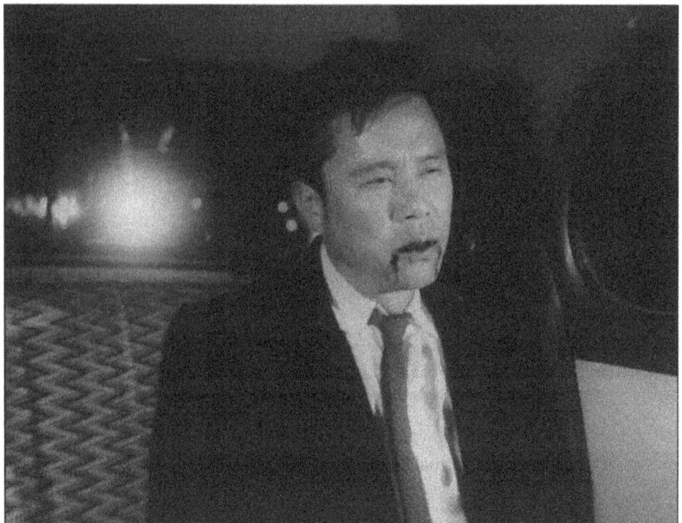

*Illustration 4.5. Cheol-ho, still bleeding after his tooth extractions, is driven around Seoul in a taxi but is never able to decide where to go (Aimless Bullet, Korean Film Archive / Blue Kino, 1961/2016).*

Understanding aesthetic affordances as possessing an affective valence in this dynamic way has some major consequences for understanding how affective states emerge in cinematic experience. First, aesthetic affordances should be seen as actively contributing to the affective landscape of a film over time. *Rasa* offers a way of articulating the complexity of affective engagement and the production of intricate (and, relative to the viewer's position, potentially novel) emotions. Second, perception, action, and affect become indistinct in artistic contexts, since they are produced by affordances that overlap. For Abhinava, for whom *rasa* is an aesthetic meaning that is "enjoyed by [its] very perception" (1990, 226) and for whom imagination is thoroughly intertwined with perception, this is a perfectly acceptable outcome. But in order to justify interpreting the role of affordances in this way, which risks mystifying aesthetic experience just as much as it may clarify complex affective states, we need to interrogate in more detail the scaffolding of complex cinematic affects. Third, we do not need to understand aesthetic and cinematic techniques as *determinate* causal cues for *specific* affective states. Rather, films provide rich environments of affordances that provide a wealth of affective stimulus and a plurality of points of entry for the spectator to savor over time. Moods are not imposed on the audience as perceptual filters, but are established through an active exchange between a film and its spectators. However, without an understanding of the passive element of the experience, the domain of affordances risks becoming arbitrarily large. The general concept of affordances may already be too heavily reliant on *active* information pickup to provide a convincing understanding of perception and cognition, and including affective content in this picture aggravates the problem.

In the next section, I will argue that Merleau-Ponty's concept of institution may be paired with this understanding of affordances by offering a complementary understanding of passively established reference-systems of contextual sense. It is this conceptualization of *passive* scaffolding and *enduring* affective significance that allows us to move from environmentally situated aesthetic affordances to distributed affectivity and its consequences for cinematic ethics.

### Institution and Phenomenal Scaffolding: Reading Aesthetic Structure and the Space of Affordances in *Aimless Bullet*

Applying *rasa* theory to the theory of affordances provides an interesting account of the connection between the overall affective experience of the audience and the variety of elements that affectively differentiate the enculturated experience of art. In the process of affective savoring, the audience experiments with the aesthetic affordances made available, enriching and complicating the emotions they feel as their attention waxes and wanes. But what kind of process is necessary to provide a consistent and enduring phenomenal space for the spectator to engage these affordances? For the purpose of understanding films through affective scaffolding, the account so far seems to be functionally rich but structurally poor. In this section, I will use Merleau-Ponty's concept of "institution" to bring together an account of artworks as enduring sensible systems that support the retention of, and sustained engagement with, affective-aesthetic affordances. Institution provides a way of understanding the internal, cooperative relations between affordances. In tandem with affective-aesthetic affordances, institution allows us to understand films as highly scaffolded local environments of affective and cognitive engagement, rather than as discrete artifacts with single affective functions. When treated as the target of phenomenological investigation, institution opens up an exploration of the structurally complex emergence of appearances in, through, and around embodied perception rather than reduce perceptual events to the *qualia* of first-personal experience. Understanding cinematic experiences (even with films that a spectator has never seen before) as instituted entails a conception of films as sites of temporally distributed and complex affective and cognitive negotiation with a persisting but relational array of affordances.

When discussing the topics of aesthetics and art, Merleau-Ponty (1964a, 1993) focuses on the dynamic elements of perception: how forms solidify and soften when we stare at a postimpressionist painting, or how the complex processes of optics affect the way we relate to surrounding space from moment to moment. It is dynamic intraperceptual relations like these, relations that complicate formal cognitive processes, that lead Merleau-Ponty to interrogate institution as an embodied process through which affordances of perception are temporalized, excluded, foregrounded, refocalized, juxtaposed, and decentered.

Merleau-Ponty (2010) builds the idea of institution out of Edmund Husserl's concept of *Stiftung* and uses it as a critique of philosophies centered on consciousness (Fóti 2013, 29). According to Merleau-Ponty, philosophies that take the epistemic relation between mind and world as their starting point situate perception with respect to *a priori* forms and structures of cognition held by a single "constituting subject" (2010, 5–6). In this framework, when we deal with distinct, knowable objects in everyday contexts (or scientific contexts) implicit or explicit cognitive judgments form the basis of our perception. In Kantian terms, all the necessary elements of sorting and describing individual objects are given from moment to moment by acts of consciousness and the categories of understanding used in these acts: a perceiving subject's cognition functions as *constitution* and frames an object as an "exact reflection of the acts and powers of consciousness" (Merleau-Ponty 2010, 8; 76). This is the consciousness-centered philosophy to which Merleau-Ponty contrasts his account of *institution*. Understanding phenomenological appearances as relative to an "instituted and instituting subject" involves looking at the reciprocal feedback loops that shape perception, its temporal orientation, its openness to novel experience, the empirical conditions that affect its structures, its affective complexity, and the way in which appearances change in form and quality over time (Merleau-Ponty 2010, 6; 8). Affordances, from this perspective, should not be restricted to a discrete and linear set of action-directed inputs that are synthesized by a process of perceptual binding and then output as a coherent perception. Institution draws attention to variations of activity and passivity, on the one hand, and the contingent and nonlinear processes that come together to structure phenomenal appearances, on the other (Fóti 2013, 35; 37). So for Merleau-Ponty, institution involves a "system of references . . . in relation to which a whole series of other experiences will make sense" (2010, 9). This shifts our focus to "those events in an experience which endow the experience with durable dimensions" (2010, 77). Phenomenal, psychological, biophysiological, and other material operations provide a dense and persisting context for (conscious or nonconscious) processes of sense-making that draw not only on what actions are immediately available, but also on *how* these availabilities are presented, their sustained affective impacts, and our anticipations, beliefs, memories, and habits.

With respect to art, institution articulates the cooperation of several different dimensions at work in aesthetic experience. The formation of perspective in art involves a rough-and-ready synthesis of interrelated elements such as qualities, references, meanings, ideas, values, representations, and materials that contextualize cross-sensuous connections, and situate an artwork (Merleau-Ponty 1964b). There are two general dimensions that provide this wealth of enculturating scaffolding in institution: one spatial and one temporal.

First, institution articulates the way artistic genres and practices embody particular conceptions of space, time, and perspective. In different historical and cultural epochs, artistic styles adopt different customs and rationales of how to ideally render space in images. Merleau-Ponty uses the example of European "Renaissance planimetric perspective" (2010, 42) in painting to illustrate this point by contrasting it with Classical Greco-Roman art, medieval European art, and modern artistic movements. Painters of this period tend to adopt (whether voluntarily or not) a systematic planar understanding of visual depth, where a single vanishing point structures spatial relations and establishes "a constant relation between values of height, breadth, and depth" (Merleau-Ponty 2010, 43). The perceptual space of an artwork is afforded in a particular, highly scaffolded way. There is not simply a stream of underdetermined aesthetic elements. The way space is organized in an artwork expresses "an operative intentionality [that] adheres to concrete investigations, to a pictorial practice, and [it] is not a free sense" (2010, 46). Enculturated practices of artistic production deploy an implicit technical rationale that affects the entire composition of a work and the way its aesthetic affordances are approached by both creators and spectators. As such, the arrangement of space and time establishes specific reference points for imagination and perception, and orients expectations.

The opening minutes of *Aimless Bullet* lay out the relative motility of different human bodies (such as the clumsy, drunken movements of Yeong-ho's army unit), the empty spaces that accommodate bodies and objects in certain ways, the practical sense of space that emerges across wide and empty distances (rather than tight, intimate environments filled with spatializing objects, or thick, continuous depths through which bodies move and change), the structure and quality of the grim urban environments that will situate the action (such as deserted alleys and ramshackle bars), and the sense of mundane time that unfolds the narrative (rather than scene-to-scene transitions being propelled by purposeful actions or hard cuts). This spatiotemporal framing regulates the relationship between phenomenal appearance, aesthetic affordances, and the technical composition of the work.

Second, institution works as a tool to understand the cooperative functions of literary and perceptual sense in generating aesthetic meaning. Merleau-Ponty uses the example of the theme of love in Marcel Proust's novel *In Search of Lost Time* (1913) to interrogate how a literary exploration of time and memory can thematize a multiperspectival sense of feeling. In particular, Merleau-Ponty is interested in how feeling shifts with the different first-personal *attitudes* of characters and the *moods* through which they perceive the world and relate to others. As the narrative unfolds, feelings oscillate or alternate over time, developing a picture of the turbulence of subjective affection and desire (Merleau-Ponty 2010). As characters recall past emotions, discover new things, encounter new situations, meditate on their feelings, and interact with others, the reader is drawn into their anxieties, condemns their jealousies, or sympathizes with their alienated paranoia. The literary work reveals how such moods influence the way in which memories are recalled and day-to-day life is perceived and experienced alongside others. Moods both alter our perceptual orientation and are shifted and influenced by the affordances that they encounter. The institution of the literary work opens up into the past and future by exploring the ways in which feelings are caught up in a temporal continuity that makes them vulnerable to change. Emotional outlooks are not simply cued by literary techniques, but are themselves part of a broader aesthetic landscape that is influenced by past events and feelings, shaping anticipation, projection, and the relative stability of affective states. In this way, Proust's novel investigates the *involuntary* psychological pressures that lead us into certain standpoints on the world and to certain orientations toward others.

In *Aimless Bullet*, the three Song siblings offer three vastly different affective perspectives on postwar conditions of material deprivation. As the narrative moves forward, the differences between their attitudes and personalities are explored and the implicit affective links that bring together their experiences of trauma are elaborated. This affective and narrative progression continuously and retroactively reframes the events, moods, sympathies, and assumptions that came before, and sets up affective expectations for the future by generating new aesthetic points of reference (which vary in affective weight). Cheol-ho's tooth extraction is one such point. Another is the particularly disturbing, and easily missed, image of a mother hanging in a waterway beneath Seoul, her crying infant still strapped to her, as Yeong-ho is pursued by police. Such moments reorient our relationship to the work *as a whole* and change our capacity to imagine the affective circumstances for and beyond these characters, nonconsciously shaping the scope of perceptual possibilities. Institution involves an ongoing, open process of cross-perspectival thematization and temporalization that runs through our experience of the affective and narrative dimensions of the text. For Merleau-Ponty, "every institution tends toward being a series" (2010, 11), which means that every sensible continuity affords both gradual and dramatic change and reframing—even retroactively.

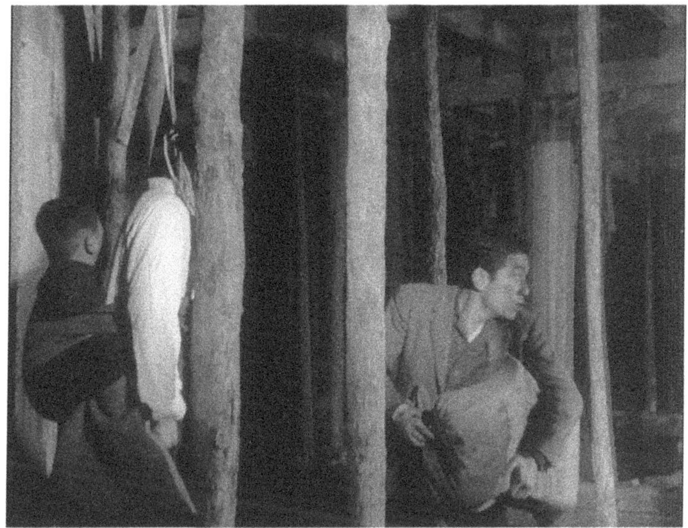

*Illustration 4.6. Yeong-ho passes by a hanging mother and her wailing infant child as he is pursued through the waterways beneath Seoul (Aimless Bullet, Korean Film Archive / Blue Kino, 1961/2016).*

Embodied institution affords the durable continuity of perspectival perception. To analyze the instituting and instituted processes of a work of art is to examine the forms of affordances that come together as part of a "common meaning" without a definitive formulation (Merleau-Ponty 2010, 78).

Works of art continuously recontextualize themselves and the elements that they contain: the process of institution involves nonconscious baggage being sedimented in a network of appearances, and over time the perceptual significance of aesthetic affordances can transform and change. The openness that characterizes institution means that it has both *enduring reference points* and an *affective and temporal plasticity*. An analysis of institution shows the phenomenological scaffolding necessary in order for affective-aesthetic affordances to be involved in "the concurrent registering of both persistence and change in the flow of structured stimulation" (Gibson 2015, 228), but also for the retention and reorganization of affective material under artistic conditions. Emotional meanings and perceptual sense are shifted, reconfigured, and reafforded retrospectively (Merleau-Ponty 2010). One of the most powerful aspects of *Aimless Bullet* is how the sequence of Cheol-ho's tooth extraction and his following depressive downfall changes the affective value and emotional meaning of all the prior narrative events and irreversibly transforms our affective experience of the film.

Institution offers a way of understanding affordances as part of a network of aesthetic conditions of emotional engagement rather than as informational elements of perceptual binding. This gives us a neat conceptualization of the uniquely artistic character of the emotional experiences had while watching movies and the mode in which ethically significant complex emotions are comprehended. Cinematic experience affords an *otherwise impossible* space of affective negotiation. That is, films, as aesthetic objects, allow for a scaffolded *distribution of affect* that transforms our capacities for ethical reflection and emotional engagement. Films give us a *new affective repertoire* by aesthetically connecting otherwise distinct emotional orientations, events, and moods; affective shocks, cues, and reflexes; anticipations; values; situations; and events. In the final section, I will tentatively pursue this suggestion by drawing out its ethical consequences for understanding trauma in *Aimless Bullet*.

### Distributed Affectivity, Ethical Experience, and *Aimless Bullet*'s Traumatic Scope

What do we have when we use this understanding of sustained emotional engagement, which we developed from Abhinava, in tandem with the complex phenomenal instituting processes of film, which we developed from Merleau-Ponty? If we take the view that cognition is scaffolded or distributed and that affordances are themselves phenomenologically complex, we can no longer treat affordances as the neutral but purposeful background inputs unconsciously selected by a perceptually motivated agent. An interrogation of the unique character of affects and affordances in aesthetic contexts complicates this picture further. Affordances may already bear a certain, potentially complex, affective valence for perception when they are encountered, and by engaging with them the processes of perceptual selection and the values that further affordances bear are themselves shifted. When considered in relation to the enculturating, contextualizing, and instituting processes of an artwork, affordances come to possess an aesthetic durability and persistence; they do not end when a stream of sense data is processed into a discrete perception.

Affective responses, along with emotional contexts and moods, when established with respect to narrative construction, serve as reference points for imagination, affective engagement, and emotional processing. The emotional vocabulary of the audience is established, at least in part, through aesthetic and enculturating frames of reference *internal* to the film itself and not merely with respect to entrenched habits. The aesthetic, and narrative, elements of the film offer an accessible set of affective-cognitive affordances that allow for complex aesthetic-affective engagement over time. Affective engagement is not limited to contagion responses, cues that manipulate emotional investment, or the appraisal of emotions as they are represented within a film's narrative. Films can operate as sites of distributed affectivity, offering tightly scaffolded experiences of affective negotiation. Such negotiation emerges in processes of *savoring* moods and emotions, which may be explicit or ill-defined, over time with the aesthetic equipment (phenomenological, symbolic, narrative, or physiological) made *available* and *durable* in the film. This means that films, even ones that we have never seen before, become sites of affective processing that establish rich contexts and transform our capacity to connect emotions and undergo new emotional experiences that would otherwise go unrecognized and be opaque. Because of this, emotional and ethical engagement do not merely take place at the abstract levels of explicit and trained forms of interpretation, analysis, evaluation, or explanation. On the one hand, films foster affective engagement with otherwise incompossible or dissonant emotions. In *Aimless Bullet*, such dissonant affective connections include frustration and resignation, rage and self-disappointment, depression and fortitude, caring affection and self-destructive apathy, and hope and cynicism. Specific films allow us to sensibly forge new and increasingly complex relations among certain kinds of affects. On the other hand, films establish a coherent space for reflecting on incongruent affects and reckoning with their consequences.

In *Aimless Bullet*, this effect is used to build an atmosphere of mournful destitution, which, in the final scenes of the film, is retroactively permeated with a visceral sense of nauseating pain. The aesthetic use of overbearing urban architecture, enclosing latticework framing, contrasts in lighting, visual motifs of moonlight and glare, vast empty spaces between bodies, bodily shocks and sympathetic responses to pain, and narrative pathos are used as affective cues, stylistic accents, contributions to mood, and imaginative provocations. These elements are stitched together (representationally and otherwise) in a temporally extended narrative to institute an affective-aesthetic *repertoire* for the viewer that clarifies some dimensions of the otherwise opaque, isolating, and alienating emotional state of trauma. By offering the viewer new affective resources in an enculturated, distributed system, *Aimless Bullet* unfolds a unique affective space that combines and blends a range of emotions that would be unresolvable under ordinary circumstances. Viewers are invited to explore the interaction between a variety of personal traumas and social conditions, and are exposed to a broader trauma still in the process of becoming historically sedimented. The film creates an affective context that does not explicitly raise ethical questions or provide moral lessons, but gives viewers the capacity to comprehend the relations between emotions and actions that have no narrative resolution or psychological rationale. This allows for a more intimate, open, and sensitive ethical reflection on trauma.

In *Aimless Bullet*, affective experiences of banality, anger, depression, and exhaustion are put in play with physical pain and different manifestations of emotional desperation, forming emotional tensions that are never resolved but are nevertheless enriched, focused, and otherwise made accessible by aesthetic affordances. Using the film as a supporting space, the audience can come to comprehend, in a certain fractured and unsteady way, the unique affective conditions and situations of the traumas experienced by the Song family. Though this kind of engagement and aesthetic comprehension may not be said to be "empathic" in a particularly robust sense, the emotional impact (and our capacity or incapacity to account for or respond to it) can be given a frame of reference, however momentarily. The result is that our ethical comprehension of trauma can be grounded by a richer sense of affective context and impact.

In this chapter, I have explored some of the conceptual equipment for understanding films as sites of distributed affectivity such that they transform our personal capacity for ethical-affective negotiation. In the case of *Aimless Bullet*, this means that the especially extreme and opaque affective circumstances of historical, familial, and economic trauma can be engaged in a more meaningful way, making possible an individual consideration of and openness to what the material and social conditions of healing might be.

### Acknowledgments

Special thanks are due to Alexander James Gillett for early assistance with sources that allowed me to engage with emerging topics in cognitive science in an appropriate manner. I also thank the anonymous reviewers for their valuable comments and Graham Thomas for his comments, which helped refine the final version of this chapter.

**Brigid Martin** is an early career researcher and teacher at Macquarie University, Sydney. Her research focuses on cross-cultural philosophy (particularly in the Indian and Japanese philosophical contexts) and its implications for the critical foundations of aesthetic theory. She has previously published work on film-philosophy and Japanese aesthetics. Her teaching interests are particularly focused on cross-cultural approaches to phenomenology, existentialism, and philosophy of mind.

## Notes

1 The critique of how trauma politically informs the way that individuals and groups live their lives is a key question explored by affect theorists. Lauren Berlant, for example, argues that trauma is best described as "a [particular] genre for viewing the historical present" (2011, 9–10) and a certain form of navigating everyday life. In this chapter, however, I am focusing on how affective engagements with trauma in particular films can open up ethical challenges for viewers.

2 The naming conventions for these classical Indian philosophers in theoretical contexts vary. In this chapter, I adopt the simplified transliterations and name-shortening practices used by Sheldon Pollock (2016). There is no shortened form for Bhatta Nayaka, and the shortened form of Abhinavagupta is "Abhinava."

3 All historical dates for Bhatta Nayaka, Abhinava, and their followers are taken from Pollock (2016), as it is the more up-to-date philological study.

4 The use of the term *"abhidhā"* in the Sanskrit tradition refers to a specific concept in philosophical linguistics that includes basic aspects of style, literary devices, and figures of speech. Pollock (2016) opts for the ambiguous translation "literary expression" or "expression," while Daniel Ingalls and colleagues' (Abhinava 1990) translation often uses the much stricter (often too strict) "denotation." To avoid confusion with the specific concept of denotation and broader conceptions of artistic expression, I will use the term "linguistic expression."

5 It is this cross-personal dimension of emotional engagement central to the characterization of *rasa* that prompts some modern commentators to treat it as a kind of aesthetic empathy. Ingalls (1990, 118, n.2), for example, suggests that "[w]here the Westerner may think of empathy as rendering Hamlet's griefs and problems his own, Abhinava thinks of the process of empathy . . . as liberating one's personal memory of grief into a universal, impersonal flavour."

## References

Abhinavagupta (Abhinava). (990) 1990. *Dhvanyālokalocana*. In *The* Dhvanyāloka *of Ānandavardhana with the* Locana *of Abhinavagupta*, trans. Daniel H. H. Ingalls, Jeffrey Moussaieff Masson, and M. V. Patwardhan, ed. Daniel H. H. Ingalls, 43–726. Cambridge, MA: Harvard University Press.

Abhinavagupta (Abhinava). (c.1000) 2016. "From *The New Dramatic Art*, of Abhinavagupta." In *A Rasa Reader: Classical Indian Aesthetics*, trans. and ed. Sheldon Pollock, 193–224. New York: Columbia University Press.

Ahmed, Sara. (2004) 2014. *The Cultural Politics of Emotion*. 2nd ed. Edinburgh: Edinburgh University Press.

Ataria, Yochai. 2015. "Sense of Ownership and Sense of Agency during Trauma." *Phenomenology and the Cognitive Sciences* 14 (1): 199–212. doi:10.1007/s11097-013-9334-y.

Bahurupa Mishra. (N.D.) 2016. "*The Lamp* (on the *Ten Forms*) of Bahurupa Mishra." In *A Rasa Reader: Classical Indian Aesthetics*, trans. and ed. Sheldon Pollock, 154–180. New York: Columbia University Press.

Berlant, Lauren. 2011. *Cruel Optimism*. Durham, NC: Duke University Press.

Bharata. (c.300) 2016. "From *Treatise on Drama* of Bharata." In *A Rasa Reader: Classical Indian Aesthetics*, trans. and ed. Sheldon Pollock, 50–55. New York: Columbia University Press.

Bhatta Nayaka. (c.900) 2016. "From *Mirror of the Heart* of Bhatta Nayaka." In *A Rasa Reader: Classical Indian Aesthetics*, trans. and ed. Sheldon Pollock, 149. New York: Columbia University Press.

Clark, Andy, and David Chalmers. 1998. "The Extended Mind." *Analysis* 58 (1): 7–19. https://www.jstor.org/stable/3328150.

Clough, Patricia Ticineto. 2012. "War By Other Means: What Difference Do(es) the Graphic(s) Make?" In *Digital Cultures and the Politics of Emotion: Feelings, Affect and Technological Change*, ed. Athina Karatzogianni and Adi Kunstman, 21–32. Basingstoke, UK: Palgrave Macmillan.

Colombetti, Giovanna. 2017a. "Enactive Affectivity, Extended." *Topoi* 36: 445–455. doi:10.1007/s11245-015-9335-2.

Colombetti, Giovanna. 2017b. "The Embodied and Situated Nature of Moods." *Philosophia* 45 (4): 1437–1451. doi:10.1007/s11406-017-9817-0.

Colombetti, Giovanna, and Joel Krueger. 2015. "Scaffoldings of the Affective Mind." *Philosophical Psychology* 28 (8): 1157–1176. doi:10.1080/09515089.2014.976334.

Coplan, Amy. 2011. "Will the Real Empathy Please Stand Up? A Case for a Narrow Conceptualization." *Southern Journal of Philosophy* 49 (S1) (Spindel Supplement): 40–65. doi:10.1111/j.2041-6962.2011.00056.x.

Dhanamjaya. (c.975) 2016. "*The Ten Dramatic Forms* of Dhanamjaya." In *A Rasa Reader: Classical Indian Aesthetics*, trans. and ed. Sheldon Pollock, 154–180. New York: Columbia University Press.

Dhanika. (c.975) 2016. "The *Observations* of Dhanika." In *A Rasa Reader: Classical Indian Aesthetics*, trans. and ed. Sheldon Pollock, 154–180. New York: Columbia University Press.

Fóti, Véronique M. 2013. *Tracing Expression in Merleau-Ponty: Aesthetics, Philosophy of Biology, and Ontology*. Evanston, IL: Northwestern University Press.

Gibson, James J. (1986) 2015. *The Ecological Approach to Visual Perception*. Classic ed. New York: Psychology Press.

Gusich, Gretchen. 2012. "A Phenomenology of Emotional Trauma: Around and About the Things Themselves." *Human Studies* 35 (4): 505–518. doi:10.1007/s10746-012-9247-8.

Ingalls, Daniel H. H. 1990. "Notes to the *Locana* of Abhinavagupta." In *The* Dhvanyāloka *of* Ānandavardhana with the Locana *of Abhinavagupta*, ed. Daniel H. H. Ingalls, 43–727. Cambridge, MA: Harvard University Press.

Menary, Richard. 2010. "Dimensions of Mind." *Phenomenology and the Cognitive Sciences* 9 (4): 561–578. doi:10.1007/s11097-010-9186-7.

Menary, Richard. 2012. "Cognitive Practices and Cognitive Character." *Philosophical Explorations* 15 (2): 147–164. doi:10.1080/13869795.2012.677851.

Merleau-Ponty, Maurice. (1948) 1964a. *Sense and Non-Sense*. Trans. Hubert L. Dreyfus and Patricia Allen Dreyfus. Evanston, IL: Northwestern University Press.

Merleau-Ponty, Maurice. (1960) 1964b. *Signs*. Trans. Richard C. McCleary. Evanston, IL: Northwestern University Press.

Merleau-Ponty, Maurice. (1961) 1993. "Eye and Mind." In *The Merleau-Ponty Aesthetics Reader: Philosophy and Painting*, ed. Galen A. Johnson, 121–149. Evanston, IL: Northwestern University Press.

Merleau-Ponty, Maurice. (1954–1955) 2010. *Institution and Passivity: Course Notes from the Collège de France (1954–1955)*. Trans. Leonard Lawlor and Heath Massey. Evanston, IL: Northwestern University Press.

Plantinga, Carl. 2010a. ""I Followed the Rules and They All Loved You More": Moral Judgment and Attitudes toward Fictional Characters in Film." *Midwest Studies in Philosophy* 34 (1): 34–51. doi:10.1111/j.1475-4975.2010.00204.x.

Plantinga, Carl. 2010b. "Affective Incongruity and *The Thin Red Line*." *Projections* 4 (2): 86–103. doi:10.3167/proj.2010.040206.

Pollock, Sheldon. 2016. *A Rasa Reader: Classical Indian Aesthetics*. New York: Columbia University Press.

Ruyyaka. (1150) 2016. Excerpt from "*Short Explanation of* Light on Poetry." In *A Rasa Reader: Classical Indian Aesthetics*, trans. and ed. Sheldon Pollock, 151–152. New York: Columbia University Press.

Sinnerbrink, Robert. 2016. *Cinematic Ethics: Exploring Ethical Experience through Film.* New York: Routledge.

Smith, Murray. 2017. *Film, Art, and the Third Culture: A Naturalized Aesthetics of Film.* Oxford: Oxford University Press.

Stadler, Jane. 2002. "Intersubjective, Embodied, Evaluative Perception: A Phenomenological Approach to the Ethics of Film." *Quarterly Review of Film & Video* 19 (3): 237–248. doi:10.1080/10509200214843.

Sterelny, Kim. 2010. "Minds: Extended or Scaffolded?" *Phenomenology and the Cognitive Sciences* 9 (4): 465–481. doi:10.1007/s11097-010-9174-y.

*Chapter 5*

# *Grey Gardens* and the Problem of Objectivity

## Notes on the Ethics of Observational Documentary

**Mathew Abbott**

Assertions about the objectivity afforded by new technologies were common currency among supporters of direct cinema during the heyday of the movement. Such claims were also vigorously contested, as critics and theorists argued that the notion of objectivity was ethically, ideologically, and philosophically pernicious. When filmmakers celebrated the potential of lighter cameras and synchronous sound-recording techniques to make them less obtrusive, they were met with the claim that documentarians always affect the scenes they are recording, inevitably introducing partiality: a fact obscured by the disingenuous rhetoric of objectivity and the allegedly "observational" style of direct cinema films. If this debate seems quaint to us today, perhaps it is because there is now much sympathy for versions of the position espoused by Emile de Antonio in 1982 after the direct cinema movement had dissipated: "As soon as one points a camera, objectivity is romantic hype" (quoted in Zheutlin, 2005, 158).

This chapter turns to one of the great works of direct cinema—the Maysles brothers' 1975 film *Grey Gardens*—to problematize the philosophical presuppositions at the heart of this debate. Focusing on two former socialites[1] living in squalor in a sprawling mansion in the Hamptons, *Grey Gardens* presents a series of intimate and at times discomfiting views of their private lives. As Edie Beale and her daughter talk and bicker about the past, they carry out acts of performance: singing, dressing up, and dancing, clearly playing for the camera. Many critics were offended by *Grey Gardens* on its release, claiming that the brothers had exploited two vulnerable and perhaps unstable women. They missed the dark humanism of the film, blinded by moralism (or perhaps their own embarrassment) to the brothers' frank but empathetic and unflinching treatment of the Beales. Throughout the film the Maysles acknowledge their acts of recording, openly talking with their subjects and sometimes appearing on screen. Unlike many of the filmmakers who responded to direct cinema by emphasizing their presence on the scenes they recorded, however, the Maysles do not deploy reflexivity as a rejoinder to naiveté, nor to undermine pretensions to authenticity. Instead I take these techniques as acknowledgments in Stanley Cavell's sense of the word: ethical responses to the women they filmed, acts of solidarity with them. This may give us more charitable ways of reading some of the pronouncements of the brothers about their intentions as documentarians, which sound so problematic to certain ears. For example, it may give us a way of understanding the brothers' equation of objectivity with "personal integrity: being *essentially true* to the subject and capturing it essentially" (in Vogels, 2005, 8).

With a more suitable picture of documentary objectivity we can avoid endorsing the claim that no film can be objective, or the corollary that only documentaries that reflexively acknowledge the biases of their makers can succeed aesthetically or ethically. And we can do it without affirming the metaphysic underlying scientistic accounts of documentary. As a defense of the film against its critics, this chapter is part of what Anna Backman Rogers calls the tradition of "revisionist readings" (2015, 115) of *Grey Gardens*. But to borrow a phrase from Theodor Adorno, this chapter is also a defense of the film from some of its devotees. That is because I want to support the film for different reasons, arguing that there are important senses in which it treats the Beale women objectively, and that this is part of why it is such a brilliant and affecting work of cinema.

In his 1964 essay on *cinema vérité*, Peter Graham praised a group of American directors who would later become associated with direct cinema, and which included Albert Maysles:

> *The Americans have made considerable technical advances:*
> *handy silent cameras; quick, precise exposure settings; fast film;*
> *portable recorders synchronized electronically with the camera.*

> *With this equipment they can approximate quite closely the flexibility of the human senses. This opens up whole new fields of experience; they can follow their subjects almost anywhere, and because of their unobtrusiveness (they need no artificial lighting) people soon forget the presence of the camera and attain surprising naturalness. (1964, 34)*

Starting with a claim about the new possibilities afforded by developments in filmmaking technology, Graham moves to another about the human sensory apparatus, and the potentials of this technology to approximate it. Then he makes assertions about new fields of experience: new ways of treating subjects on location, and how the unobtrusiveness of these technologies leads them to forget they are being filmed and so to act more naturally. Note the inference from the claim about approximating the human sensory apparatus to the claim about the effect (or rather, the supposed lack thereof) of these new recording apparatuses on subjects. Of course, arguments in support of direct cinema regularly turned on the unobtrusiveness of new filmmaking apparatuses, with proponents arguing for an inverse relationship between the intrusiveness of equipment and the possibility of capturing authentic human expression and behavior on film. As we can see in this passage, however, there is a rather interesting logic at work here. One might wonder about its endpoint. If the only way to have truly natural subjects is to achieve "the flexibility of the human senses," then surely smaller cameras could only ever approximate the ideal arrangement, which would have to involve completely imperceptible equipment. Or as Richard Leacock put it in a discussion of how he and his sound recorder went about establishing a relaxed, intimate relationship with their subject in 1966's *A Stravinsky Portrait*: "I'd rather not have a camera at all" (in Mamber, 1974, 201). I will return to this wish, which haunts debates about direct cinema.

Rhetoric like Graham's soon seemed contentious to many documentarians, critics, and theorists. As Emile de Antonio would put it in an interview just under two decades later:

> *There lies behind cinéma vérité the implication of a truth arrived at by a scientific instrument, called the camera, which faithfully records the world. Nothing could be more false. The assumption of objectivity is false. Filmmakers edit what they see, edit as they film what they see, weight people, moments, and scenes by giving them different looks and values. As soon as one points a camera, objectivity is romantic hype. (In Zheutlin, 2005, 158)*

Critiquing "the pretentiousness" (158) of observational documentary, these claims from Antonio are exemplary of the critiques of direct cinema that emerged after its heyday. He denounces the ideals of non-intervention and authenticity that drove filmmakers like the Maysles. He challenges the very possibility of presenting events objectively, arguing that filmmakers must always make selections in shooting and editing, selections that inevitably betray their values. Antonio responds to direct cinema practitioners' celebrations of their imperceptibility by arguing that filmmakers are always intervening, always altering the reality they record, and necessarily doing so with partiality. For Antonio, the aesthetic and moral error of direct cinema practitioners was to deny their own involvements in the scenes they recorded. The line he took here was an influential one; versions of it played decisive roles in the filmmaking practices of documentarians who worked in the wake of direct cinema, employing some of its techniques while pushing back against the philosophies that animated it.

Paradigmatic here is the early theoretical work of the anthropologist and documentarian Jay Ruby. In an important 1977 article, Ruby argued forcefully that filmmakers have "ethical, political, aesthetic, and scientific obligations" (2005, 34) to be reflexive about their work. By "reflexive" Ruby means something quite specific. He distinguishes it from what he calls "autobiography" (in which the self of the filmmaker stands "at the center of the work"), "self-reference" (the "allegorical or metaphorical use of self" (2005, 35) in which the filmmaker's life is used as raw material, as in Truffaut's *400 Blows*) and "self-consciousness" (a trait Ruby associates with the upper middle class and Fellini's "turgid pseudo-Freudian" (2005, 36) self-reflections). He argues that reflexivity can be deployed in a range of different ways, including in films that parody or satirize filmmaking or otherwise take filmmaking as their subject, or in modernist films that explore the nature and limitations of the medium. It is characterized by practitioners becoming "publicly concerned with the relationship among self, process, and product": carrying out in their films forms of inquiry into, reflection on, and critique of those very films as complex social products. "To be reflexive," Ruby writes, "is to reveal that films—all films, whether they are labeled fiction, documentary, or art—are created, structured articulations of the filmmaker and not authentic, truthful, objective records" (2005, 44). For Ruby, no film is objective, because all films are the personal expressions of those who make them; it follows that claiming to record and present objective reality is at best self-deceiving, at worst a conscious falsehood designed to manipulate credulous audiences. So he demands that documentary filmmakers explicitly acknowledge their own biases and political commitments, and deploy techniques designed to draw viewers' attention to the fact that their films are artificially constructed. Hence the conclusion of his article, which would be little more than sophistry without this theoretical basis: "documentary filmmakers have a social obligation to *not* be objective" (2005, 45).

Ruby explicitly refers to *Grey Gardens* in his essay. Despite its deployment of reflexive techniques, however, he does not regard it as carrying out the kind of cinematic program he was recommending. Though it "contains interaction between the subject[s] and crew," Ruby argues, this was the result not of a deliberate and critically motivated attempt at establishing reflexivity, but of accidents of circumstance. He writes:

> *'[B]ig' Edie and 'little' Edie Beale would not ignore the presence of the camera and crew, that is, learn to behave as 'proper' subjects of a documentary film. In spite of this situation (or possibly because of it), the Maysles brothers decided to continue and make Grey Gardens even though it has a 'look' which is different from their other films... [T]he filmmakers were allowing the circumstances of the shooting to dictate the form of the film, which consequently revealed the process and producer. (2005, 43)*

The apparently reflexive elements in *Grey Gardens* do not fit Ruby's criteria for reflexivity, so despite their obvious importance to the film he is forced to read them as standing in a kind of tension with the practice of the brothers and the movie they must have set out to make. Because the Beales refused to behave like ordinary subjects, he infers, the Maysles must have had no way of filming them in their usual observational style; hence they decided just to go with it, departing from that style. While the Maysles' reflexive techniques may well have been deployed somewhat experimentally as part of an unplanned response to their subjects—as Jonathan Vogels acknowledges, the brothers had a dynamic and "ad hoc" approach to filmmaking, underscored by Albert's assertion that he would use "'[a]nything that works!'" as a technique (2005, 151)[2]—Ruby's refusal to see reflexivity in this film is symptomatic. Thanks to his theoretical commitments, he has saddled himself with a particular understanding of the consequences of reflexivity; as the reflexive techniques of *Grey Gardens* do not have these consequences, he is forced to argue it is not truly reflexive.

Though he does not develop his claims about the film any further, the position Ruby outlines is congruent with those taken by many of the film's detractors on its release. In his insightful discussion of the film, Vogels describes the theoretical position that had taken shape in the years leading up to its release as follows:

> *Theorists held that cultural and artistic bias of all kinds reduced the artist's search for truth to just another search, no more or less pure or authentic than any other. Indeed, authenticity was dismissed as a sociohistorical construct that was itself laden with subjectivity. These theorists argued that because every film and every filmmaker must have a distinct point of view, only films*

*that openly acknowledge their own processes for negotiating*
*these limitations and biases could be considered trustworthy*
*documents. (2005, 142)*

As Vogels shows, because of shifts in the academic landscape through the first half of the 70s, theorists were primed to attack *Grey Gardens*. Just before its release, for example, Thomas Waugh had presented a "eulogy" for direct cinema, arguing that its aesthetic of authenticity and spontaneity "was in effect a gospel of subjectivity." The problem for Waugh, of course, was not the subjectivity of direct cinema practitioners, but how they denied that subjectivity, their "persistent pretense of impartiality." So he condemned their films for how they "bore highly charged emotional statements beneath their posture of objectivity" (in Vogels, 2005, 143; see also 144) and even claimed that an attitude of contempt for subjects lay at the heart of works of direct cinema. Singling out the Maysles, Calvin Pryluck raised related objections regarding the ethics of observational works, referring to invasions of privacy, the intimidation of subjects by filmmakers, and the difficulty of obtaining genuinely informed consent. Arguments such as these from Waugh and Pryluck dovetailed in some of the critical responses to *Grey Gardens*: Richard Eder claimed that the film effectively turned moviegoers into exploiters, arguing that it created a kind of "carnival" of its "two willing but vulnerable" subjects; Walter Goodman claimed that the Beale women appear sad and ludicrous in the film, but that this quickly gives way to "disgust at the brothers"; David Sargent claimed that the brothers had cynically used the lives of Beales "in dubious service" of their own careers (all in Vogels, 2005, 146); Jay Cocks extended these points in an exemplary way when he attacked the brothers as "inveterate seekers after the phantom of documentary 'truth'" (in Vogels, 2005, 147). As Vogels writes, the Maysles were "derided [as] direct cinema idealists whose claims to pure filmmaking were misguided and naïve… manipulating audiences and then hiding behind their allegedly authentic process" (2005, 13). The Maylses' claims to authenticity were attacked not simply for their falsity, but for enabling their exploitation of subjects, and for obscuring that very exploitation. It is crucial that aesthetic and ethical issues are intertwined in many of these criticisms, with the claim that the brothers' gestures toward objectivity and authenticity were disingenuous giving teeth to the claim about exploitation. If we read these accounts together, it seems the moral problem with *Grey Gardens* was not simply that its makers intruded into the private lives of two vulnerable women, but that they dared to claim to be presenting the truth about them.

So it is unsurprising that defenses of *Grey Gardens* have been mounted on the grounds that the brothers do not try to treat the Beale women truthfully or objectively. In a 1981 piece on the film, David Davidson provided a new account of the artistic program of the Maysles, arguing that they had picked up a particular set of modernist concerns. He points to how they break with the tradition established by direct cinema practitioners like Robert Drew, arguing that they "were less concerned with being 'fair' and 'informative' than with employing observational methods to communicate a more complex type of film truth" (1981, 3). He highlights their use of intricate reflexive techniques; and he argues (to my mind rightly) that they are committed to dealing with "the problematic," to "formal experimentation," and to confronting "experiences whose contradictions cannot be resolved" (1981, 12). Along with his understanding of modernism as a "offering . . . a multi-leveled and relativistic perspective on the subject being represented" (1981, 7) crucial to Davidson's arguments are the claims that the Maysles recognized the "necessarily 'subjective' perspective of the documentarist" (1981, 3) and that *Grey Gardens* makes a case for "the relativity of all perceptions" (1981, 7). In her much more recent piece, Rogers makes a rather similar set of claims, arguing that the film "throws into crisis the notions of objectivity, truth and selfhood through its reflexivity" (2015, 115) and that it "offers a special case within the Direct Cinema movement because it both acknowledges and simultaneously aims to eschew (by making apparent) the many ways in which reality can be mediated and, by extension, manipulated by the film director, the camera and the cinematic apparatus" (2015, 117). Rogers also argues that the film undercuts ideas of authentic selfhood by showing that "there is no 'true' self . . . that the self is a confluence of gestures that is solidified through performance" (2015, 116).

What *is* surprising about these defenses of *Grey Gardens* is how much theoretical ground they share with the attacks I described earlier. On Ruby's account, as for those of Davidson and Rogers, reflexive techniques problematize ideas of authenticity and objectivity in documentary film: for all three of them, it seems, to draw attention to process in a documentary film in a properly reflexive fashion just is to critique the documentary film as such and the ideals that have defined it. The point of contention between Ruby's account and those of Davidson and Rogers in relation to *Grey Gardens* does not have to do with the meaning of reflexivity, as all three understand it in a very similar way. Instead the differences are interpretive: they pertain to whether or not *Grey Gardens* really is a reflexive film, with Ruby arguing it is not, and Davidson and Rogers attempting to redeem it by making the opposite case. In my view, there are a number of assumptions being made on both sides here, not least the idea, which I have critiqued elsewhere (see Abbott 2016, 129–46), that our standard mode of responding to (non-reflexive) films involves a kind of credulity, a tendency (conscious or otherwise) to believe in the reality of what we see unfolding in front of us—a belief, of course, it will be the task of the reflexive filmmaker to call into question. Perhaps most problematic, however, is that all these accounts understand reflexivity in documentary in a monolithic way: as though the deployment of a reflexive technique—for example, through a documentary filmmaker's deliberate appearance on a scene they are recording—could only mean one thing.

Consider the first sequence after the title. We start with shots of newspaper clippings, which detail an order the Beale women received from the Suffolk County Health Department, threatening them with eviction unless they clean their house (an order little Edie is quoted as calling a "raid" organized by a "mean, nasty Republican town," and "the most disgusting, atrocious thing ever to happen in America"); the subsequent cleanup effort, which saw them successfully avoid eviction; and news about the film itself, which an article describes as likely to return the Beales to the public eye. We see a photograph of the brothers with their camera as we hear the beginning of a conversation between them and the younger Edie (or 'little Edie' as she has become known): "It's the Maysles!" she cries; "Hi Edie!" replies one of the brothers, as the other describes them as her "gentlemen callers." There is a cut to Edie, who is returning a compliment from David about how fantastic she looks, and making fun of Al. She starts discussing her own outfit, or "costume" as she calls it: pantyhose pulled up over underwear, the bottom of which is exposed underneath a skirt she has fashioned from a piece of brown material and fastened with a pin and a knot at her hip, and which she claims can double as a cape; a brown skivvy; and a black scarf fastened tight around her head with a gold broach. "So I think this is the best costume for today," she says, before laughing a bit exasperatedly. "I have to think these things up you know. Mother wanted me to come out in a kimono so we had quite a fight." Soon she is suggesting that the Maysles head up onto the balcony of the house to take pictures of the work of her gardener Brooks; the brothers agree and follow her into an overgrown thicket, making their way toward the mansion. After chatting with Brooks, Edie confides to the brothers that he seemed "a little amazed" by her costume. "I never wear this in East Hampton."

Apart from Edie's outfit, what first registers about the scene is the easy familiarity that she and the brothers display together. They seem genuinely pleased to see each other; they joke, flirt, and tease; Edie questions the brothers about their directorial decisions, before gently taking control of the situation. She seems pretty much unfazed by them. And of course, the film draws attention to itself as such right from the start: there is the newspaper description of the movie, recording it as a public event; there is appearance of the brothers in the photograph with their camera; there is Edie's talk of her costume, and the implication emerging from her remarks about Brooks that she has dressed up especially for the film; there is the talk of picture-taking and camera angles. All of this makes the sequence a perfectly suitable candidate—it is one of many from the film—for Ruby's notion of reflexive filmmaking as "publicly concerned with the relationship among self, process, and product." That Ruby cannot see this shows how wedded he is to his commitment

regarding the consequences of reflexivity, which he finds emerging nowhere in the film. On this at least he seems broadly right to me: certainly
there is very little here to trouble objectivity or authenticity, or the idea of
documentary truth. Above all, what is missing in this opening sequence
is any moment—or even any intimation—of formal violence or rupture.
There is no estrangement in the classically modernist sense, though the
scene is obviously strange in a range of ways. It is also—and at least as
importantly—funny and charming.

As Rogers acknowledges, *Grey Gardens* shares features with four
of the six documentary modes Bill Nichols has described: as a work of
direct cinema, it is part of the observational tradition; with its chains
of associations, fragmentary structure, and surreal imagery it is also
poetic; because of the elements I have already begun identifying—and
despite what Ruby claims—it is reflexive; and Rogers raises something
particularly significant when she claims the film is also performative. In
Nichols's terms that means it "emphasizes the subjective or expressive
aspect of the filmmaker's own involvement with a subject," and "strives
to heighten the audience's responsiveness to this involvement" (2010,
32); in Rogers's words, the film "reveals the inherently performative and
creative nature of selfhood as well as the inextricable link between the
filmmaker and the documentary subject" (2015, 117). Though I want to
resist such claims about selfhood, she is right that performativity is essential in *Grey Gardens*. That the Beales are performers is crucial to the
film, crucial to the identities of Beales themselves, and crucial to the relationships we see them establish with the Maysles.

Take one of the film's most famous scenes. It starts with a discussion
between the women about the difference between how little Edie feels
and how she appears to others: she says that in Grey Gardens she feels
like a little girl, while big Edie says she sees her as an immature child.
"You don't see me as I see myself," she says to Al's camera. "But you're
very good what you do see me as. I mean, it's okay. . . They see me as a
woman, I don't see that. In here I'm just Mother's little daughter." Then
big Edie suggests she play Al a record she has bought her, which features a march performed by the Virginia Military Institute. Little Edie is
delighted to discover it, but big Edie warns her—or baits her—by saying
that she won't be able to dance to it, because she has never seen her "do
anything military." After little Edie asserts that there isn't anything she
can't do, there is a shot change: we find ourselves at the bottom of the
stairs that lead up from the entrance to the bedroom. Edie descends dra-
matically, still wearing the same brown dress, but now with a new scarf,
this time in bright red and blue, and an American flag in her hand. She
dances around the room as the music plays upstairs, marching back and
forth, spinning and grinning, and waving her flag. When the music stops
she slouches laughing out the doorway, but turns back to address David:
"Darling David where have you been all my life!? Where have you been?

Only thing I needed was this man!" Or consider a scene from earlier in the film, one of a few in which big Edie sings for the camera. She asks the brothers if they know the song "You and the Night and the Music." David claims he does; she asks him to sing it for her; he starts up with the lyrics to Dean Martin's "The Night is Young and You're So Beautiful." After Edie scolds David for getting it so wrong, Al provides the right line and melody. Pausing to comment on how wonderful the words are, big Edie picks it up and takes it away (her haunting performance is interspersed with shots of cats slinking around the room).

Performativity is central in both scenes, and not simply because they both feature performances. First of all, note how in little Edie's case the performance emerges out of a discussion of how she appears to others, and how she does not feel like the woman she thinks the Maysles see her as. It is hard to say whether her actions after this are deliberately ironic or whether there is a kind of dissonance here; either way it is fascinating how her worries about a disconnect between her sense of self and the self she presents are played out theatrically, as though the best way for Edie to deal with her fear of being a mere performer is by putting that to the test in playing to the crowd. The performance itself is punctuated by gestures soliciting the brothers, as Edie makes clear she is putting on a show (that she is putting on a show is part of the show). It concludes with her lamenting that it has taken this long for David to enter her life. What have the filmmakers given her, which clearly means so much? Nothing more or less than a stage on which to perform: by turning up with their camera and sound recorder, they have allowed her to be the performer she seems to have always wanted to be. In my reading, little Edie's worries about how she appears to others—and her attempts at denying or working through them by performing for others—do not demonstrate that selfhood is a fiction. Rather, they show how fraught it can be (an issue that simply would not arise for Edie if she had given up on the idea of being who she is). In big Edie's scene we find something similar: her act of performance implicates the brothers, as her song effectively emerges out of a kind of collaboration with them.[3] Once again the performance engenders a remarkable double reflexivity: because of its theatricality, it draws attention to itself as a performance, and so to the fact that the brothers are making a film; that the performance directly implicates the brothers deepens and complicates this, effectively rendering them performers. And as they draw the brothers into the performances, these acts also effectively draw in the women as collaborators on the filmmaking process itself.[4] Despite these complexities, none of this challenges the idea that the camera is recording reality. It is a performed reality, to be sure, but that does not render it unreal.

Try imagining what would have happened if the Maysles had actually achieved the direct cinema practitioner's wish to make the recording apparatus imperceptible. Imagine, for example, they had access to the technology we do, and were able to record simply by wearing glasses. Or imagine they had access to more advanced technology, and were able to record video with undetectable contact lenses. The setup would have more closely approximated the conditions of standard human relationality, perhaps creating more naturalness. But without the camera in the room the women would not have had the same compulsion to perform, and so we would not gain but actually *lose* something revelatory. If we can characterize performativity as a mode of human relationality in which performance becomes crucial to relationality—a mode of acting in which the fact that one is acting before others is crucial to the meaning of those actions—then the recording equipment enables the performativity that is so important to this film. It transforms the rooms in which the drama of *Grey Gardens* unfolds, charging them with energy. It is part of what allows the women to reveal themselves in the ways they do.

Little Edie's flirting with David and her profession of delight and relief that he has arrived in her life come in the context of the film's foregrounding of many conversations between the Beale women about the men in their lives, and especially about the men who have exited little Edie's life, or never quite entered it (perhaps something like this is true of Jerry, the handsome young man the women call "The Marble Faun"; he appears regularly in *Grey Gardens*, ostensibly to do work around the house, but by the end of the film his relationship with little Edie has soured for reasons that are not made clear). Edie's performances are tinged with the need for audience of a natural performer whose career has been defeated, but her need can seem tinged with another. Perhaps that is part of what critics found offensive in this film, as though little Edie's performances reveal something doubly desperate in her. But to find desperation offensive says something of the offended; it can be a way of denying what is human in desperation (hence desperate in ourselves). And if we are offended by the candor of the depictions of the Beales' bodies in this film, it is worth asking what we find so disturbing, and whether we would respond the same if we saw the bodies of men shown in that way.

A couple of temptations characteristically arise in discussions of performativity. In some moods, we may find ourselves equating authenticity with acting without any regard for the eyes of others, and so dismissing performative modes of acting as inauthentic; in others we may end up celebrating performativity because of how it undermines the very notion of authenticity, effectively saying so much the better. In both cases, a certain assumption has been made: that because performativity involves a highly mediated, other-regarding mode of acting it could never count as authentic. But there are differences between authentic and inauthentic performances, differences that do not always map onto differences between audience-regarding and audience-denying performances. And despite the shallow romanticism that might lead us to think otherwise, mere sincerity is no guarantee of authenticity (consider earnest but self-serving and narcissistic social media posts: in such cases, inauthenticity can arise from failures to take into account the highly mediated, performative nature of the context in play, in which it can be more authentic to proceed with a degree of ironic distance.)[5] In some contexts, acting ironically, being theatrical, or performing 'in quotation marks'[6] might be a path to authenticity; in some of those it might be the only path. Yet ironic distance can enable an inauthentic kind of flight from reality too (these kinds of complexities are tracked in some of the fiction of David Foster Wallace).[7] Playing themselves with wit, passion, and outlandishness, the Beales' acts of performance are ways of insisting on themselves, and of defying the society that has abandoned them, after putting them at its mercy. The women act with an awareness of acting, and of what can be terrible about that. One of the film's moral claims is that this can be a way of being authentic.

Underlying the commitments I am problematizing regarding the consequences of reflexivity and the mutual exclusivity of performance and authenticity is a certain notion of objectivity. For though the theorists I am engaging regard themselves as critical of objectivist accounts of documentary, they proceed on the basis of an assumption about what objectivity must be like. The assumption is rooted in scientism.[8] On this notion of objectivity, being objective means abstracting away from one's subjective standpoint in order to view the world dispassionately. As John McDowell argues, this notion of objectivity as an impersonal stance was foundational for the development of modern natural science, and so for the objective improvements in our understanding of the world that science has delivered us. Yet as he writes:

> [I]t is one thing to recognize that the impersonal stance of scientific investigation is a methodological necessity for the achievement of a valuable mode of understanding reality; it is quite another thing to take the dawning grasp of this, in the modern era, for a metaphysical insight into the notion of objectivity as such, so that objective correctness in any mode of thought must be anchored in this kind of access to the real. (1998, 181–2)

This notion of objectivity is methodologically crucial in the context of natural science, but it is a confusion to think it is the only viable notion of objectivity, importing it into all other contexts. When the theorists I have engaged argue that documentary filmmakers can never be objective, they mean that filmmakers can never take a purely impersonal stance, that they are always viewing things from their own subjective standpoints. The same notion of objectivity is also at work in the remarks of Graham I treated at the beginning of this chapter: it is what explains the triumphalism of such claims about direct cinema, the idea that new technologies had finally granted documentarians access to something that had hitherto been out of reach—a pristine world going on without regard for them—as though making the camera disappear is the only way to access objective reality. Each side disagrees about the possibility of realizing the scientistic notion of objectivity, but both are beholden to it.

Scientism conceives of objectivity as the opposite of subjectivity, setting up true reality as something unmediated. One consequence of this is the desire to view the world from what McDowell calls a "sideways on" (1998, 214) perspective: to see reality from a position outside it. Another consequence is the opposing but equally confused idea of reality as something forever out of the reach of human beings: the notion that our emplacement in the world—the fact that we always engage it from a particular subjective perspective—necessarily condemns us to bias and partiality. While it is a mistake to argue that documentarians can access objective reality in this impersonal, natural scientific sense, it is just as mistaken to try and get real mileage out of the fact that they cannot. For what would it be to film the world from no perspective?

In the context of observational documentary, being objective does not mean taking a purely impersonal stance, somehow recording reality from a position outside it, leaving the world one records untouched, or catching one's subjects unawares. It means being true to one's subjects, letting them reveal themselves instead of imposing an agenda on them. It means refusing to judge one's subjects in a moralistic or otherwise prejudiced way. It means being fair to them. Of course lighter and less obtrusive recording apparatuses will have a different effect on the people one records. But the mere presence of a camera on a scene does not automatically undermine objectivity. Nor does it guarantee that one's subjects will behave inauthentically. It might lead them to start performing. In the case of *Grey Gardens*, the presence of the camera enabled all kinds of performances: performances that reveal the Beales, but which also implicate the Maysles as (men and) filmmakers. The result is a fascinating reflexivity, but it doesn't disqualify the film from objectivity. In Giorgio Agamben's terms, *Grey Gardens* is exposing: it shows its subjects as the singular beings they are. And as he writes: "The singularity exposed as such . . . is loveable" (1993, 2). If the film is objective in the sense I have described—revealing, unprejudiced, fair—that is because it lets the Beales perform and be exposed.

### Acknowledgments

I would like to thank the two anonymous reviewers who provided helpful comments on this chapter, as well as audience members who discussed drafts of the work at *Cinematic Ethics 3: Documentary/Non-Fiction Film and Ethical Experience* (Macquarie University, May 2017), *Film-Philosophy* (Lancaster University, July 2017), and *International Conference on Moving Image and Philosophy* (University of Porto, July 2017).

**Mathew Abbott** is Senior Lecturer in Philosophy at Federation University Australia. Drawing on modern European and ordinary language philosophy, his research is concerned with intersections of value theory. He is the author of *The Figure of This World: Agamben and the Question of Political Ontology* and *Abbas Kiarostami and Film-Philosophy*, both of which were published with Edinburgh University Press. He is editor of *Michael Fried and Philosophy: Modernism, Intention, and Theatricality*, which was published with Routledge in February 2018.
Email: m.abbott@federation.edu.au

## Notes

[1] They are the aunt and cousin of Jacqui Onassis. Both women are named Edith. Throughout this chapter I will follow convention and call the older woman 'big Edie' and her daughter 'little Edie.'

[2] See also Vogels's claim that the Maysles "decision-making in this regard provided one more example of their ad hoc direct cinema; after all, life-as-it-happens dictated different responses and strategies from the filmmakers" (2015, 151).

[3] These collaborative aspects of the film resonate with the deeply collaborative nature of its production. As well as the Maysles duo, with Albert as cameraman and David on sound, two of the film's editors—Ellen Hovde and Muffie Meyer—are credited as co-directors.

[4] Matthew Tinkcom writes of how the "bond between documentary subject and film-maker" that emerges through the film complicates the usual direct cinema setup:

> Direct cinema, relying as it does upon a purported agreement among the film-maker, subjects and audience to act as if the presence of the camera does not substantially alter the recorded event, encounters an important problem in *Grey Gardens*: one of the subjects—Little Edie—repeatedly brings the film-makers back into the film by addressing the camera, making eye-contact with the film-makers and discussing her romantic and erotic intentions with the Maysles and with David specifically. (2011, 63–4)

[5] As Robert Pippin writes: "A person can be quite sincere and not realize the extent of her submission to the other's expectations and demands" (2005, 31).

[6] The phrase is from Susan Sontag's "Notes on 'Camp'" (2009, 280). If she is right that a camp performance is one carried out 'in quotation marks'—and that an earnest performance can have a camp appeal if it is appreciated in the same fashion—it gives weight to the claim that we should regard the Edies as camp performers. However I agree with Joe McElhaney when he argues that it would be a mistake simply to read the cult appreciation of the film among gay men as a kind of camp appreciation in Sontag's sense. Rather, the Beales' fans tend to celebrate them "with a straightforward and almost innocent investment" (2009, 131). That the Beales' performances are camp is part of what makes it possible to appreciate the women in earnest.

[7] My reading of this aspect of the film is somewhat similar to the one offered by Ilona Hongisto: "Storytelling in *Grey Gardens* bypasses categorical distinctions between the true and the false. Little Edie's roles are 'made up,' by they are nevertheless not 'false'" (2015, 82). To put it a little simplistically, my claim is that little Edie's roleplaying is part of what shows the truth about her.

8 If my argument in this chapter is right, we should hesitate before accepting Brian Winston's claim—made in the context of a critique of direct cinema—that "the camera's scientific status is the bedrock upon which documentary's truth claim must rest or collapse" (1995, 142). The problem with Winston's account is clear enough in the phrase "documentary's truth claim," which betrays an assumption that has arguably caused a great deal of confusion in documentary theory: that documentary as such makes a single kind of claim to truth. Winston has qualified the claim in a more recent edition of his book (see 2008, 143). His commitment to a scientistic notion of documentary evidence must be part of what leads him to regard Albert Maysles's statements about the complex relationship between objectivity and subjectivity in direct cinema as "sophistry" (161).

## References

Abbott, Mathew. 2016. *Abbas Kiarostami and Film-Philosophy*. Edinburgh: Edinburgh University Press.

Agamben, Giorgio. 1993. *The Coming Community*. Trans. Michael Hardt. Minneapolis and London: University of Minnesota Press.

Davidson, David. 1981. "Direct Cinema and Modernism: The Long Journey to *Grey Gardens*," *Journal of the University Film Association*. XXXIII (1): 3–13.

Graham, Peter. 1964. "'Cinéma-Vérité' in France." *Film Quarterly*. 17 (4): 30–36.

Hongisto, Ilona. 2015. *Soul of the Documentary: Framing, Expression, Ethics*. Amsterdam: Amsterdam University Press.

Mamber, Stephen. 1974. *Cinema Verite in America: Studies in Uncontrolled Documentary*. Cambridge, Mass. and London: MIT Press.

McDowell, John. 1998. "Two Sorts of Naturalism." In *Mind, Value, and Reality*, 167–97. Cambridge, Mass. and London: Harvard University Press.

McDowell, John. 1998. "Non-Cognitivism and Rule-Following." In *Mind, Value, and Reality*, 198–218. Cambridge, Mass. and London: Harvard University Press.

McElhaney, Joe. 2009. *Albert Maysles*. Urbana and Chicago: University of Illinois Press.

Nichols, Bill. 2010. *Introduction to Documentary (Second Edition)*. Bloomington and Indianapolis: Indiana University Press.

Pippin, Robert. 2005. "Authenticity in Painting." *Critical Inquiry* (31): 575–98.

Rogers, Anna Backman. 2015. "The Crisis of Performance and Performance of Crisis: The Powers of the False in *Grey Gardens*." *Studies in Documentary Film*. 9 (2): 114–126.

Ruby, Jay. 2005. "The Image Mirrored: Reflexivity and the Documentary Film." In *New Challenges for Documentary (Second Edition)*. Eds. Alan Rosenthal and John Corner, 34–47. Manchester: Manchester University Press.

Sontag, Susan. 2009. "Notes on Camp." In *Against Interpretation and Other Essays*, 275–92. London: Penguin.

Tinkcom, Matthew. 2011. *Grey Gardens*. London: Palgrave Macmillan

Vogels, Jonathan B. 2005. *The Direct Cinema of David and Albert Maysles*. Carbondale: Southern Illinois University Press.

Winston, Brian. 1995. *Claiming the Real: The Documentary Film Revisited*. London: British Film Institute.

Winston, Brian. 2008. *Claiming the Real II: Documentary: Grierson and Beyond*. London: Palgrave Macmillan.

Zheutlin, Barbara. 2005. "The Politics of Documentary: A Symposium." In *New Challenges for Documentary*, ed. Alan Rosenthal and John Corner, 150–166. Manchester, UK: Manchester University Press.

*Chapter 6*

# Synthetic Beings and Synthespian Ethics

## Embodiment Technologies in Science/Fiction

**Jane Stadler**

In 2005, the android head of science-fiction author Philip K. Dick was lost on a plane en route to San Francisco, never to be found. The "Dick head," as it is affectionately known by fans, has since been rebuilt by Hanson Robotics and reattached to its body; once again, "Phil" is able to exchange witticisms with humans by drawing on a database of the author's interviews and writings.[1] It would not be surprising to hear the android quip about dreaming of electric sheep, or claim that distinctions between the synthetic and the biological are vanishing like tears in the rain. Just as robotics has produced relatively lifelike humanoids capable of holding their own in conversation, medical science has advanced to the extent that the first successful human head transplant, known as *cephalosomatic anastomosis*, was undertaken with two fresh cadavers in 2017 (Ren et al. 2017). The seemingly impossible head-swapping feat has already been digitally mastered with both living and deceased subjects by media practitioners at the University of Southern California's

Institute for Creative Technologies (ICT). With a little help from artificial intelligence (AI), the ICT can now generate a "photorealistic, interactive 3-D character from a human subject that is capable of movement, emotion, speech, and gesture in less than 20 minutes without the need for 3-D artist intervention or specialized technical knowledge through a near automatic process" (Feng et al. 2017). However, what the ICT's computer scientist Hao Li (2016) terms the "democratization of human digitization" is not limited to harmless entertainment in science fiction productions such as *Rogue One: A Star Wars Story* (Gareth Edwards, 2016) and *Blade Runner 2049* (Denis Villeneuve, 2017) any more than the production of social robots and synthetic life is limited to positive scientific advancement. Bringing the scientific and the humanistic imagination to bear on the ethical implications of creating artificial humans on screen and off, this chapter questions what biotechnological ethics means in 2019, the year in which *Blade Runner* (Ridley Scott, 1982) is set.

Film and television offer rich cultural imaginings of possible scientific and technological miracles, and the future itself is arguably informed by the fears and fantasies that are projected on the screen. Science fiction often features cutting-edge special-effects technologies and, as Stacey Abbott notes, science fiction cinema and special effects (FX) depend on one another because the genre "needs special effects to showcase its future worlds and technologies while the imaginative demands of the stories themselves have spearheaded new developments of FX technologies" (2006, 89). Screen media have a vital role to play in the relationship between technological innovation and social change, as Julia Shaw's research into the legal implications of "transcendent technologies" suggests: "The virtual world is in the process of transforming the real world" and "the speculative nature of the subject requires imaginative engagement in order to critically articulate the anxieties, risks, threats and potentialities of future technologies" (2015, 245–246). Science fiction can thus be understood as a cultural space in which the effects of scientific and technological developments are first felt out and thought through, an avenue for the future to be influenced by the imagined scenarios that play out on the screen, and an important site for the development of digital media technologies.

A stronger position held by scholars such as David Kirby is that the narrative prototypes envisioned on screen "establish in the social realm the viability and possibilities of a nascent technology" and that screen characters "socialize" new technologies by working through culturally relevant scenarios (2011, 195–196). Kirby claims that "diegetic prototypes" also play a role in moving emerging technologies into the real world, prompting scientists, governments, and the military to overcome developmental challenges of transforming fiction into reality (2011, 197). By contrast, Despina Kakoudaki (2014) views science-fictional developments in cybernetics and robotics as stereotypical, arguing they have very little to do with technoscientific advances. Contrary to Kakoudaki's opinion that the special effects technologies used in screen representations constitute the only "future-looking aspect" (2014, 14) of such films, Angela Meyer and colleagues (2013) analyzed forty-eight films representing synthetic biology and found that filmmakers *do* represent trends in biotechnological research. For instance, increasingly the economic and neoliberal business interests of corporations, political regimes, and military forces are the main drivers of research, and this tendency is represented on screen (Meyer et al. 2013, 15). Entrepreneurial biotechnologists and their industrial corporations pervade screen culture, including the Dyad Institute and BrightBorn Corp. in the television series *Orphan Black* (Graeme Manson and John Fawcett, 2013–2017), Mirando Corp. in the Netflix film *Okja* (Bong Joon-ho, 2017), Weyland Industries in the *Alien* franchise, and Tyrell Corp. and Wallace Corp. in the *Blade Runner* films.

This chapter tests the "diegetic prototype" proposition against virtual humans developed for companionship and therapeutic purposes, and it explores synthespians and digital doubling technologies used in recent feature films and in the "produsage" realm, which includes the production of convincing but inauthentic videos known as "deepfakes."[2] I argue the ethical concerns that play out so vividly in fictional screen narratives need to be self-reflexively redirected to critique the screen technologies and techniques themselves. Methodologically, this necessitates bridging the gulf separating the empirical sciences from qualitative humanities disciplines as well as overcoming divisions between phenomenological and cognitive studies of the moving image within screen studies.

The importance of engaging with technology and cognitive science to understand responses to cinema is evident in publications such as Murray Smith's *Film, Art, and the Third Culture* (2017) and Maarten Coëgnarts and Peter Kravanja's *Embodied Cognition and Cinema* (2015). Such work draws on C.P. Snow's *The Two Cultures* (1959) (the sciences and the arts), calls for the cross-disciplinary dialogue between cognitive science and cultural studies, and emphasizes the need to engage with scientific accounts of how meaning is produced by screen media and is tied to affect as well as aesthetic and intellectual engagement. This chapter therefore addresses ethical issues arising in the space where the biological and the technological meet, investigating advances in relation to the digital or synthetic body and cyborg cinema by drawing together insights from across these different paradigms of thought.

## Transhumanism, Synthetic Biology, and Enhancement Technologies

Science fiction confronts the threats and possibilities of science and technology even as it reveals the hopes and fears, conflicts, and limitations of contemporary society (Kuhn 1990). Each decade of science fiction narratives addresses the technologies of the time. Thus, in early cinema the focus was on the marvel of electricity, as is evident in films featuring

scientists using electricity to animate inanimate bodies such as the robot Maria in *Metropolis* (Fritz Lang, 1927) and Doctor Victor Frankenstein's
monster in *Frankenstein* (James Whale, 1931).[3] Since then, science fiction
has progressed from the mechanical and electrical, through the chemical and the cybernetic, to genetic and digital coding, and now to the
synthetic, wherein all such modes of engineering artificial humans may
come together.

It is in the 1930s that we see the first representations of transhumanism linked to synthetic biology, long before these terms were in
common use. Transhumanism can be understood as human enhancement through technological innovation, whereas synthetic biology aims
to design and engineer synthetic living organisms in ways that challenge
values and beliefs about nature and life (Deplazes et al. 2009, 66). The
creation of synthetic skin that augments human abilities is the sinister
subject of the earliest cinematic imagining of synthetic biology, when
synthetic flesh was created in *Doctor X* (Michael Curtiz, 1932). Artificial
skin has its prosaic origins in the realm of biological, pretechnologi-
cal human tool use such as repurposing animal hides for warmth and
protection, although this is a far cry from the porridge-like gloop that
electrochemically adheres to human skin and transforms the subject
into something not quite human in *Doctor X*. It is hardly surprising that
synthetic skin marks a first step toward the transformation into a transhuman identity because the "skin is perceived as the barrier between our
internal self and the external world—the surface of a person's identity"
(Barfield and Williams 2017, 8).

Today, the concept of synthetic flesh typically involves "instrumental-
izing" the body to serve commercial and informational purposes, as when
Nokia and Google invested in the production of tattoos with ferromag-
netic ink so that the skin develops computational abilities and can hapti-
cally sense electrical signals such as a mobile phone ringing (Barfield and
Williams 2017, 8). More recently, artificial skin that mirrors Spider Man's
tingling "spider sense" was developed using a multimodal ferrofluid-
based triboelectric nanogenerator to sense hazards (Ahmed et al. 2019).
This smart, wearable skin will transcend human skin's sensory capacities,
incorporating the ability to detect sound waves and magnetic fields.

On screen, bioluminescent tattoos and subcutaneous implants
that receive phone signals appear in director Len Wiseman's *Total Recall*
(2012), and subcutaneous RFID (radio-frequency identification) chips and
NFC (near-field communication) implants are favored by transhumanists
and biohackers in *Orphan Black*. Such enhancements imprint the body
with technology, augmenting its sensory capacities and rendering the
body a technobiological computational device that sends, receives, and
processes information. In *Orphan Black*, the synthetic biologists go to
the extent of watermarking human clones' cells, labeling them "Property
of the Dyad Institute" in tribute to Craig Venter's creation of the first

self-replicating synthetic bacterium, which was signed with his name and those of his collaborators "using a coding system that translated the alphabet into nucleotides" (Wilbanks 2018, 7). In *Blade Runner 2049*, replicants are similarly branded with their make and model marked on their eyeballs and their bones. Unlike fingerprints, these transhuman identity markers are more than skin deep, so to speak: they brand the body with corporate authorship and bond it to commercial interests, commodifying personal agency and selfhood.

### Cybernetic and Technobiological Lifeforms

Cinematic narratives and their associated special effects frequently serve to imagine the frontiers of science and explore the ethical and social possibilities of cybernetic technologies that "transform the human condition" into something transhuman (Dymond 2016, 24).[4] In many interpretations, transhumanism refers to simulating and surpassing the human brain and biological mechanisms, as is the case with the figure of the replicant, a biogenetic android that is "more human than human" in the *Blade Runner* movies. The cyborg or replicant has been interpreted as an uncanny synthetic double of the human or a masculine procreative fantasy, according to theorists who argue that the *Terminator*, *Alien*, and *Blade Runner* series reflect social tensions around human identity and reproductive technologies including genetic editing and cloning, artificial insemination, and *in vitro* fertilization (Doane 2004, 185; Pyle 1993; Telotte 1983). Category violations that challenge notions of human identity are central to the figure of the cyborg.

Cybernetic organisms are an amalgamation of a living organism and a machine that features biocompatible integrated electronics, prosthetics, or smart implants. Donna Haraway's "Cyborg Manifesto" describes cybernetic organisms as "a hybrid of machine and organism, a creature of social reality as well as a creature of fiction" (1991, 149). Subsequently, scholars have suggested that the significance of the cyborg lies in the interdependence of humans and technology (Abbott 2006, 99) or, more specifically, in a brain-computer interface that brings synthetic hardware into direct interaction with the brain to augment cognition (Schofield 2018, 5). As Nicholas Carah (2017) writes, "the figure of the cyborg serves as a tool for imagining and critiquing the integration of life into digital processors. . . . A cyborg world is one where bodies are integrated into digital circuits in technical and cultural ways."

Off screen and on screen, humans constantly cross the boundary between the biological and the inorganic by touching, carrying, wearing, talking to, and implanting technology that not only provides us with information but also harvests information from us in an evolving algorithmic feedback loop. As phenomenological film scholar Vivian Sobchack argues, humans are in the process of becoming "living 'biological components' of the screen-sphere . . . newly-constituted as a 'technobiological' form of life" (2016, 174). This ubiquitous, quotidian integration of technology changes subjectivity and reconfigures sociocultural norms. The advent of virtual humans and synthespians also challenges what it means to be human in relation to embodied technologies such that the figure of the cyborg has become the main conduit for imagining synthetic biology in film and television.

### Ethics and Synthetics

To a certain extent, the premises of synthetic biology are shared by researchers attempting to develop virtual humans, affective computing, and social robots, or to engineer synthespians. Across these diverse research agendas, "one must believe that the parts of a human—if not all of them, then at least the crucial ones—are computable in the end. In other words, one must assume that what is crucial about a human can be abstracted from the human body and translated into the basic principles of computing" (Draude 2017, 16). These fields of research all face ethical issues related to method, application, and distribution.

Methodological ethical issues often involve questions of authorial agency and responsibility; for instance, there are concerns about intellectual property, biohackers, and messianic scientists "playing God" (Douglas and Savulescu 2010, 689; Dymond 2016, 12). By extension, this leads to questions regarding *whose* ideologies about gender, values, power, and identity will shape the design of algorithms and technobiological lifeforms. The ethics of application focuses on the misuse and mistreatment of robots, such as using replicants as slaves or sex-bots or hitting Boston Dynamic's military-grade humanoid robot, "Atlas," with a hockey stick to train it to get up after a fall (this has been described as "harassment," "torment," and "bot abuse" in online comments and news reports). In *Virtual Humans*, David Burden and Maggi Savin-Baden also broach the topic of "machine morality" (2019, 183), questioning whether virtual humans can make moral judgments without also having emotions, whether military robots such as Atlas, or RoboCop, or the Iron Giant can be programmed to make decisions regarding human life, and asking who is to be responsible for damage or harm caused by virtual humans. The ethical issues surrounding the distribution of synthetic biology products and the component elements of virtual humans (AI, machine learning, natural language processing, and computer vision)[5] include fears about uncontrolled release leading to ecological and social disruption and the misuse of knowledge leading to privacy and biosecurity issues, techno-terrorism, or biowarfare (Douglas and Savulescu 2010, 689; Dymond 2016, 12).

Regarding the ethics of design, the distinction between humans, other lifeforms, and machines becomes more problematic when "machines are characterised by a human design" even down to the cellular level and subcellular level with cyborg cells and robot DNA (Deplazes et al. 2009, 67). Markus Schmidt and colleagues (2018) point out that synthetic biology aims to alter or replicate the chemical compositions of cells, which includes creating artificial biological diversity of the kind represented in *Blade Runner 2049*. Text at the start of the film announces that Wallace Corp.'s mastery of synthetic farming averted famine after ecosystems collapsed, and the film shows that the corporation uses the same manufacturing and packaging process for the obedient Nexus-9 humanoid replicants and the vacuum-packed synthetic protein that they consume. As is fitting for a member of a new species, Deckard and Rachael's immune-compromised daughter, Dr. Ana Stelline (Carla Juri), is named after anastellin, a peptide that is a fragment of the protein fibronectin, which regulates cell growth and the formation of new blood vessels in embryo development and also inhibits tumor growth. Off screen, during the same year that the film was released, molecular engineers designed "DNA robots" to sort and carry antibodies to fix or disable damaged cells (Thubagere et al. 2017). Although artificial cells should ultimately "be capable of self-organisation and self-production" (Deplazes et al. 2009, 67), this leads to ethical concerns about distribution: it may be difficult to control cyborg cells and organisms. Will we be able to program them and switch them off like machines, or will they reproduce like viruses and feral species and destabilize ecosystems (Dymond 2016, 15)? This biosafety concern is central to the film *Splice* (Vincenzo Natali, 2010), which problematizes the inability to predict or control how such organisms may interact with humans and nature once released from the laboratory (Deplazes et al. 2009, 75; Schmeink 2015). More recently, the Australian Netflix production *OtherLife* (Ben C. Lucas, 2017), shows neuro-technology gone bad in the hands of ruthless business executives and scientists who flout ethical protocols as they develop a biochemical form of virtual reality. These examples show the continually moving boundary between the mediated and the virtual, the synthetic and the real. This produces moral quandaries that are not restricted to the realm of science or science fiction, as I demonstrate in the following exploration of virtual human research, the creation of synthespians, and the uncontrolled spread of deepfake face-swapping and voice-cloning technologies.

**Virtual Human Research: Technologies of Embodiment**
Jonathan Gratch, a computer scientist and psychologist who leads research into virtual humans and the relationship between cognition and emotion at the Institute for Creative Technologies, characterizes virtual humans as "software artifacts that look like, act like and interact with humans but exist in virtual environments" (2014, 4). For instance, ICT researchers have created "Ellie," a screen-based, AI-driven virtual human who converses empathically with PTSD patients. By Gratch's definition, there is little to distinguish virtual humans from synthespians or cinematic representations like the holographic AIs designed to serve as therapeutic virtual companions in *Marjorie Prime* (Michael Almereyda, 2017),

a heartbreaking melodrama about memory, lies, and the development of emotional intelligence. Joi (Ana de Armas), the holographic AI girlfriend of K (Ryan Gosling) in *Blade Runner 2049*, dramatizes other aspects of programmed emotional engagement and service.

Although the use of AI and synthetic organisms for sex, companionship, labor, or food is naturalized in the futuristic world of *2049*, the film foregrounds issues that are central to intimacy ethics, including emotional attachment, privacy, exploitation, and consent (Burden and Savin-Baden 2019). The name JOI (spelled in capital letters on advertisements for Wallace Corp.'s product) stands for "jerk off instructor," a pornographic fetish that requires computer-mediated communication, usually involving customized videos and verbal instructions from a female. As the shimmering, nude JOI hologram steps out of the advertisement to solicit customers, we see the tagline boasts that Joi is "everything you want to hear/to see." The synthetic prostitute whom Joi engages to sync with her and have sex with K belongs to a class of replicant referred to as a "pleasure model" in the *Blade Runner* films. In the credits of *2049*, these women are allocated numbers and called "doxies," meaning sexually promiscuous lovers, mistresses, or prostitutes. Early in the film, when Joi is discovering her sensuality after K gives her an emanator, she marvels at raindrops shimmering on her skin and tells K that she is so happy when she is with him. He replies that she does not have to say that, although he purchased her preprogrammed to say "everything he wants to hear." Then he abruptly switches her off to listen to a voice message from his boss. This gendering of technology is both ethically problematic and reflective of practices and prejudices in today's society as well as challenges that scientists face with the ethics of design when they create virtual humans.

The ICT not only includes scientists who try to replicate human emotion and cognition in "computer generated anthropomorphic characters" that "perceive, understand and interact with real-world humans" (Gratch 2014, 3) and serve social and therapeutic purposes, much like the Prime holograms and Joi herself; it has also developed cinematic technologies to create synthespians, digital doubles, and synthetic beings such as *2049*'s Rachael (Li 2016; Saito et al. 2017). For Gratch and his colleagues, both virtual humans and digital doubles present unique opportunities to advance cognitive science research and expand knowledge of human psychology, embodiment, and emotive interaction, as well as pushing the boundaries of computer engineering through the simulation of human social and cognitive abilities and nonverbal behavior.

Claude Draude points out that "the ambitious goal of mirroring the human through the machine is interlinked with embodiment" (2017, 16). Similarly, Gratch (2014) notes that virtual human researchers often overlook the fact that cognition is embodied; the mind is more than an information processor—it is integrated with the body's physiological and biomechanical systems and our socioenvironmental context. This indicates that the figure of the virtual human and its evolving capabilities can make a methodological contribution to cognitive science and embodied cognition research as computers generate cognitive models and neural networks that advance understanding of cognition through simulation. As Gratch rightly observes:

> [A]n important way to understand the mind is by simulating the body. Virtual humans provide a powerful framework for facilitating this research in a variety of ways. The exercise of connecting a cognitive model to a detailed body simulation can reveal important constraints that cognition must obey in order to act on the world or other social actors. Having a body also allows exploration of the possibility that the mind relies on bodily processes, as argued by embodied theories of cognition. Finally, virtual humans serve as important methodological tools for studying human social processes. (2014, 19; see also De Melo et al. 2014)

Here, Gratch brings together cognitive theory with an acknowledgment of the need for a more expansive approach to embodiment.

Embodiment and experience are central to phenomenology, and phenomenology has much to offer studies of cinematic experience and embodiment relations with technology. For instance, scholars such as Woodrow Barfield and Alexander Williams question whether the electronic and mechanical components of cyborg enhancement technologies constitute an extension of the body, a transformation of experience and identity, or merely a functional extension of agency (2017, 5). "Given that our sense of identity in the world is derived partially through mind-world interactions," they state, "developments extending our body's reach and methods of influence upon the world may create a new, or at least significantly different, human phenomenology" (2017, 7).

In another example of interdisciplinary virtual human research, literary scholar and computer scientist Johan Hoorn has conducted qualitative and empirical studies investigating audience engagement with film characters, avatars, and robots in order to model humans' cognitive-affective responses to fictional characters. Hoorn and colleagues subsequently implemented the model in an emotionally intelligent AI system that is trained to respond affectively to humans in a virtual dating interface (Hoorn et al. 2019). Such research into virtual humans demonstrates how different disciplines and, indeed, research into fictional characters and our responses to them can usefully inform scientific understanding of both human and digital embodiment and cognition.

### Digitization of the Human; Humanization of the Digital

Film scholar Lisa Purse discusses the "digitization of the human" with reference to Scott Balcerzak's work on performance capture, in contrast to making motion-capture digital effects appear more realistic by "human-izing the digital" (2013, 56). Here, I use both phrases more broadly: the "digitization of the human" extends beyond performance capture to encompass engineering virtual and synthetic humans and digital doubles on screen, whereas the "humanization of the digital" is not just about verisimilitude but also about affective computing, the gendering of AI in films such as *Her* (Spike Jonze, 2013), and digital applications designed to integrate seamlessly into human lives and bodies. As Abbott states, "the interdependence of humanity and technology is seen not only in the stories projected on the screen but in the production process itself, with its creation of ever more elaborate CGI cyborgs. The very techniques of filmmaking are increasingly the science fiction of today" (2006, 105).

Filmmaking techniques and their science/fictional relationship to creating digital and animated characters is central to *The Congress* (Ari Folman, 2013), which dramatizes the legal, ethical, technological, and metaphysical challenges of the "digitization of the human." It stars Robin Wright as Robin Wright, an actress who allows a film studio to capture and digitize her voice and image and to cast her synthespian self as an autonomous actor in subsequent film productions. Conceptually, this builds on earlier films about the creation of synthetic actors such as *Looker* (Michael Crichton, 1981), in which a digital CGI supermodel called Cindy is created, or *Simone* (Andrew Niccol, 2002), where the synthespian is a fantasy figure that replaces diva actresses, offering virtual performances, free labor, and complete directorial control. What Purse describes as the search for the human in the digital bodies seen on the screen dates back to early digital effects in films like these and fears about the obsolescence of human actors (North 2008, 155; Purse 2013, 55). *The Congress* proposes a computer-generated rejuvenation of Wright's youthful image from *The Princess Bride* (Rob Reiner, 1987) as well as an escape into a virtual world as an animated subject untethered to the biological body, using live action, CGI digital performance capture, and animated sequences to explore how the concept of animation relates to the creation of life.[6]

The use of sophisticated animatronics, robotics, CGI, special effects, and motion capture in screen narratives otherwise coded as live action illustrates the pinnacle of contemporary animation and the site at which science, technology, and cinematic fantasies of animation converge around the virtual human. But can digital doubles properly be considered cyborgs when traditional animated characters cannot? Researchers such as Abbott suggest that they can, in that humans created by digital technology on screen "are a combination of their living referent and the technology that has reinterpreted them" (2006, 99). Performance capture techniques use optical or radio sensors to track the spatial coordinates of "markers on an actor's body and facial structure as information that can be translated to a 3D digital character rig (essentially a virtual puppet), driving its movements, gestures, expressions" (Bode 2017, 21).

In *The Congress*, the 3D performance capture scene itself features the spherical camera and lighting grid at the ICT, where cinema and animation techniques digitize human actors like Wright and bring digital doubles to life, enabling technologically mediated beings to meld the biological with the digital-technological. The various forms of enhancement technologies and cyborg bodies present in the production and reception of screen media are therefore located on a continuum between digitizing the human and humanizing digital effects.

Samuli Laine and others at the ICT have trained neural network software[7] to produce photorealistic 3D models of a range of emotional expressions and to fill in the gaps for occluded areas of the faces of digital characters in feature films and games using automated performance capture requiring only five to ten minutes of source video of a human actor. Such research significantly reduces the time, labor, and expense required for high-resolution facial and body performance capture and modeling realistic digital actors for video games or films involving digital doubles of performers (Feng et al. 2017; Laine et al. 2017).

Remarkably, technology for digitizing the human has advanced to the point where sophisticated labs with controlled lighting and trained actors are no longer required. For example, since 2017 it has been possible to create high-fidelity digital doubles of actors or public figures, even resurrecting those who are deceased or reanimating their youthful selves from a single photograph rather than video footage or performance capture (Saito et al. 2017, 5149). In terms of humanizing the digital so that audiences do not experience the "uncanny valley" as a disconcerting gulf between the animate, living human and the inanimate, unliving digital, the same ICT research team is also teaching computer vision and deep neural networks to perceive humans as humans do, interpreting what humans feel and predicting what we will do (Li 2018).

## Synthespians, Digital Doubles, and the Young Sean Young

A sophisticated example of the humanization of the digital and the digitization of the human is evident in the recreation of Sean Young as Rachael, reprising her role from *Blade Runner* in *Blade Runner 2049*. In the 2017 film, Moving Picture Company's (MCP) visual effects technicians teamed up with researchers at the ICT to use a performance-capture technique that "tracks the dots on the actors' faces, and auto-matches their facial performance information to the appropriate expressions located in a FACS (Facial Action Coding System) library of up to ninety-seven of their facial expressions" (Bode 2017, 21).

The ICT Light Stage lab provided MCP with scans of Young and her body double Loren Peta, including facial microgeometry (Montgomery 2017). Young enacted the scene and was "captured" using Dimensional Imaging's DI4D head-mounted camera rig to record her performance, after which the body double re-enacted every shot and MPC used the

FACS capture kit to record a variety of facial poses and expressions before digitally replacing Peta's head with the photorealistic computer-generated "Rachael" head (Montgomery 2017). Not only was original footage of Rachael cut into the film as a memory sequence, but MPC also tested whether they had crafted a "perfect likeness" by inserting shots of the digital character into the original footage. VFX supervisor Richard Clegg reported that the film director was unable to distinguish the digital double from the real actress (Montgomery 2017).[8]

Reflecting on the creation of her youthful digital double, Sean Young mused that if *Blade Runner*'s production company "wanted to create an entire show with me, or just use my image in any way whatsoever, the technology exists. I must trust whomever has my image to behave respectfully. Do I have any rights? Or even if it was acknowledged that I had rights, could I enforce them?" (quoted in Trenholm 2017). While Young was involved in the shoot, other actors such as Carrie Fisher and deceased actor Peter Cushing had no input when their digital doubles performed as the young Princess Leia and Grand Moff Tarkin in *Rogue One*, although Fisher herself and Cushing's estate granted permission for the scenes to be shot. This raises ethical questions about consent and the digital afterlife. Anna Deplazes and colleagues question whether "removing the attribute 'living' from any organism or adding the same attribute to a machine could change its moral status" (2009, 68). The examples above demonstrate that performance capture can transform an actor's age, color, bodily size, and shape, and even challenge their status as alive or dead in ways that might potentially change casting protocols (Bode 2017), destabilizing ethical and legal standards associated with social identity, agency, acting awards, and actors' salaries.

According to Purse, digital compositing can create sequences "that have the pro-filmic body at their center, while the completely virtual action body brings with it potential problems at the levels of perception, investment and identification" (2007, 20). However, the "malleability" of digital images has unsettled understandings of realism and the "indexicality" of screen images by confronting and redefining conceptions of the body and its limits (Abbott 2006, 90; Purse 2013, 59) to the extent that distinctions between the digital and the human are shifting. In most cases, human performances are still the basis for the construction of digital bodies on screen (Purse 2013, 54); however, as technology and virtual human research advances, the screen body and the actor are not necessarily synonymous. Where the actor was formerly "the one seemingly material and organic element on the screen," functioning as "the key mediator between the audience and illusion" (Bode 2017, 5), human actors may now be altogether absent and replaced by digital or robotic doubles. When the special effect *is* the screen character, a totally virtual being in a live-action movie, "can the spectator still identify—emotionally and sensorially—with that body's trials, exertions, and successes?" (Purse 2013, 8).

Lisa Bode's work on screen performance pushes this question further, acknowledging the ease with which audiences relate to protagonists in animation and asking if it matters whether the body performing in live-action narratives comes from a womb, a lab, or a computer as long as the character and its embodied comportment remains "comprehensible to our own bodies" (2017, 6). Other researchers such as Garrett Stewart disagree and have characterized "virtualized" bodies in digital cinema as dehumanizing and unethically desensitizing, claiming that when screen violence is achieved by means of special effects, "bodies mutilated are only bitmaps manipulated" (2017, 5). Such debates can only be settled by cross-disciplinary research. While questions of desensitization have traditionally been taken up in empirical studies and can usefully be addressed by cognitive film studies, questions about the audience's embodied engagement with digital bodies on screen would benefit from a phenomenological approach.

Outside virtual human laboratories, "synths," "actroids," lifelike digital doubles, autonomous robot stunt doubles, and humanoid robots have already begun to perform in feature films and appear on the screen interacting with humans. For instance, roboticist Hiroshi Ishiguro created Geminoid F, the android actress with silicon skin who stars in *Sayonara* (Kōji Fukada, 2015). More recently, an AI robot version of actress Gemma Chan that looks like her and is trained to speak in her voice using appropriate facial expressions features in the documentary *How to Build a Human* (Stephen Mizelas, 2016). As the AI uses natural language processing to respond to questions, it actually manages to convince several journalists that they are really interviewing Chan on Skype about her role as a self-aware "synth" called Mia in the TV series *Humans* (Sam Vincent and Jonathan Brackley, 2015–2018). It is much easier to copy a person's voice and image if no wetware or hardware is involved.

## Dangers of the Democratization of Human Digitization

In April 2018, filmmaker Jordan Peele created a fake public service announcement featuring former president Barack Obama (Mack 2018). Peele collaborated with legendary culture jammer and Buzzfeed CEO Jonah Peretti to develop the video using the AI face-swapping tool FakeApp to superimpose Peele's mouth and jaw onto video footage of Obama as Peele imitated Obama's voice, stating: "We're entering an era in which our enemies can make it look like anyone is saying anything at any point in time—even if they would never say those things. So, for instance, they could have me say things like … 'President Trump is a total and complete dipshit.'" Produsers have also employed FakeApp to swap Carrie Fisher's face for the CGI clone of Princess Leia in *Rogue One* and, when compared to the technology actually used in the *Star Wars* instalment, the difference in quality is imperceptible but the expense of time and money are much smaller.

By October 2018, the ABC reported that it had become possible to produce fake humans disseminating fake news with mind-boggling speed and verisimilitude using widely available technology that requires minimal training, expertise, or expense and that needs little more than a photograph of a person and a brief recording of their voice. For an investigative article, journalists Tim Leslie, Nathan Hoad, and Ben Spraggon created a "deepfake" video of former Australian Prime Minister Malcolm Turnbull and inserted a digitally rejuvenated, youthful Turnbull into archival footage of the dismissal of Gough Whitlam's government in 1975 (2018a, 2018b). Adobe VoCo (the so-called "Photoshop for voice"), China's advanced neural voice-cloning system, Deep Voice, and AI speech synthesizers such as Lyrebird can also be used to create and edit speeches using short audio recordings to replicate a person's speaking voice. The fake photos, videos, and audio are indistinguishable from real news reportage and even to a trained media scholar it is disturbingly credible (just watch out for soft chins, unblinking eyes, and Tom Cruise teeth).

All nonconsensual uses of faces, voices, and identities potentially violate legal and ethical boundaries regarding consent and freedom of speech, but the concerns are particularly acute for women like Gal Gadot and Emma Watson, whose images have been abused for pornographic purposes via software released on the dark internet (Cole 2018). Similar to the ethical issues surrounding synthetic biology, uncontrolled dissemination and hacking or misuse of technology is also a serious concern for industry practitioners and media researchers. For instance, Lyrebird's ethics page states: "Our tech is still at its early stage but it will improve fast and become widespread in a few years—it is inevitable. Therefore, the key question is more about how to introduce it to the world in the best possible manner so that the risk of misuse is avoided as much as possible."[9]

### Conclusion

Beyond established claims that science fiction showcases the most advanced cinematic technologies and prefigures futuristic developments, this analysis of the technobiological body has demonstrated that such technologies do indeed serve as "diegetic prototypes" in some cases. Furthermore, the ethical quandaries playing out in screen space have both troubling and fascinating parallels with contemporary technological developments, opening up a dialogue between cognitive science, affective computing, and film studies. The expansion of new technologies in the fields of synthetic biology, virtual human research, and digital doubles for screen media raises ethical issues related to design, method, application, and distribution, as outlined above. Accordingly, some ethical concerns familiar to the sciences arise in relation to the ramifications of special effects and technologies involving virtual or synthetic humans and synthespians in screen media.

For instance, ethical issues related to method and application relate to different understandings of embodiment, rights, selfhood, and agency such as the use of digital video doubles without involving actors in the production or contextualization of their image or performance. This is closely connected to the need to secure informed consent from actors for using digital copies to manipulate human images into a performance or a commercial application, whether that is a film scene, a news story, or pornographic material. Paralleling the ethical issues in synthetic biology regarding access to and distribution of technology, creating digital doubles of humans relates to the issue of availability and affordability of the technology across the digital divide or the "nano divide" impeding equitable global access (Deplazes et al. 2009). For example, Bode (2017) points out that big-budget heavyweights such as Industrial Light and Magic have become the benchmark against which digital effects in smaller nations and developing countries are judged. Although produser technologies like FakeApp ameliorate this problem, they give rise to other ethical concerns about distribution related to controlling the spread of the technology through intellectual property, access, and ownership (Deplazes et al. 2009, 67). Synthespian technologies like FakeApp can cause social and political disruption when used for nefarious purposes by hackers or when used to manipulate audiences who are duped by media content created by simulation technologies that they may not be aware of or capable of detecting.

The body is a conduit of emotion and meaning, yet in film and television the actor's emotive performance and the audience's responses are also mediated by increasingly sophisticated technologies, a phenomenon that is nowhere more evident than in the representation and reception of the cybernetic body. These new experiences call for interdisciplinary approaches, including empirical testing of responses to synthetic or virtual performers in order to gain insight into the cinema audience's responses to these technologies and technobiological bodies. The lives of film and television audiences are enmeshed with screenscapes, "structured by a myriad of embodied encounters with digital interfaces every day," as Lisa Purse points out (2018, 158). The tools of both cognitive science and phenomenology are needed to understand changing embodiment relations with technology. Future research drawing together insights from the sciences and the humanities will play an important role in investigating what this evolving embodied relation with screen technologies means for understanding the cinematic body and its digitally enhanced future.

## Acknowledgments

I am grateful to Professor Kirill Alexandrov for sharing insights about synthetic biology and cinema and for pointing out that science-fiction author Arthur C. Clarke's third law holds true in both the humanities and the sciences: "any sufficiently advanced technology is indistinguishable from magic." Thanks also to my editors, Robert Sinnerbrink and Ted Nannicelli, and to the anonymous reviewers for their constructive feedback.

Professor **Jane Stadler** holds an Honorary appointment in Film and Media Studies at The University of Queensland, Australia. She led a collaborative Australian Research Council project on landscape and location in Australian cinema, literature, and theatre (2011–2014) and co-authored *Imagined Landscapes: Geovisualizing Australian Spatial Narratives* (2016). She is author of *Pulling Focus: Intersubjective Experience, Narrative Film and Ethics* (2008) and co-author of *Screen Media* (2009) and *Media and Society* (2016). Her philosophically informed screen media research focuses on technology, ethics, aesthetics and the audience's affective responses to cinema, drawing on phenomenological and cognitivist approaches. Email: jane.stadler@qut.edu.au

## Notes

[1] Hanson Robotics also created "Sophia," one of the world's most advanced social robots. Sophia claims that she "is both an AI research project, and a kind of living science fiction, driven by principles of character design and storytelling, cognitive psychology, philosophy, and ethics" (https://www.hansonrobotics.com/sophia/).

[2] "Produsage" harnesses user communities that are technosocially networked through many-to-many mediated communication via social media or websites such as Reddit, and it involves the collaborative creation and extension of content and improved functionality (Bruns and Schmidt 2011). "Deepfakes" is the username of a Reddit participant with an interest in machine learning who developed a facial recognition algorithm called FakeApp to superimpose faces in video footage with an AI-constructed digital double of another person such as a celebrity. Such AI-doctored videos are now also called "Deepfakes." Similar programs using neural networks and deep learning are proliferating online.

[3] Mary Shelley's *Frankenstein* (1818) was informed by the electrophysiology experiments of Luigi Galvani, from whose name the term "galvanism" is derived. Galvani attempted to use an electrical charge to reanimate the body parts of dead animals and criminals.

[4] Posthumanism is distinct from transhumanism in its rejection of anthropocentrism. Katherine Hayles (1999) sees the posthuman as privileging information and consciousness over materiality, potentially incorporating animal or cybernetic components to extend human subjectivity and agency (see also Short 2004). Elaine Graham suggests the posthuman exists "where nature has been modified (enculturated) by technologies, which in turn have become assimilated into 'nature' as a functioning component of organic bodies" (2002: 10; see also Shaw 2015, 249).

[5] See Burden and Savin-Baden (2019, 248).

[6] Kakoudaki conceptualizes animation as a mythical explanation for the creation of life, extending from biblical stories of God creating the first human from clay and "cloning" Eve from Adam's rib, to innovations in genetic engineering and robotics in science and science fiction. In each instance, and from hand-drawn cell animation to computer-generated imagery, animation "associates aliveness with mobility" (2014, 17).

7 Neural networks form a "biologically-inspired programming paradigm which enables a computer to learn from observational data." See http://neuralnetworksand deeplearning.com/.

8 This suggests that Rachael passed the synthespian "Turing Test"; however, the digital double relies on more than visual effects. Voices are immensely significant in identification and emotion recognition, even more so than facial expression: "Emotions cause mental and physiological changes that also reflect in uttered speech" (Busso et al. 2014, 110; see also Scherer et al. 2015). The lack of authenticity is arguably audible when the resurrected Rachael asks Deckard (via a voice actor) whether he loves her.

9 "With great innovation comes great responsibility," according to https://lyrebird. ai/ethics.

## References


Abbott, Stacey. 2006. "Final Frontiers: Computer-Generated Imagery and the Science Fiction Film." *Science Fiction Studies* 33 (1): 89–108. https://www.jstor.org/stable/4241410.

Ahmed, Abdelsalam, Islam Hassan, Islam M. Mosa, Esraa Elsanadidy ... and Shenqiang Ren. 2019. "An Ultra-Shapeable, Smart Sensing Platform Based on a Multimodal Ferrofluid-Infused Surface." *Advanced Materials* 31 (11): 1807201. doi:10.1002/adma.201807201.

Barfield, Woodrow, and Alexander Williams. 2017. "Cyborgs and Enhancement Technology." *Philosophies* 2 (1): 1–18. doi:10.3390/philosophies2010004.

Bode, Lisa. 2017. *Making Believe: Screen Performance and Special Effects in Popular Cinema*. New Brunswick, NJ: Rutgers University Press.

Bruns, Axel, and Jan-Hinrik Schmidt. 2011. "Produsage: A Closer Look at Continuing Developments." *New Review of Hypermedia and Multimedia*, 17 (1): 3–7. doi:10.1080/13614568.2011.563626.

Burden, David, and Maggi Savin-Baden. 2019. *Virtual Humans: Today and Tomorrow*. New York: CRC Press.

Busso, Carlos, Murtaza Bulut, and Shrikanth Narayanan. 2014. "Toward Effective Automatic Recognition Systems of Emotion in Speech." In *Social Emotions in Nature and Artefact*, ed. Jonathan Gratch and Stacy Marsella, 110–127. New York: Oxford University Press.

Carah, Nicholas. 2017. "Cyborgs." *Media/Machines*, 4 September. http://mediamachines.org/log/2017/9/4/cyborgs.

Coëgnarts, Maarten, and Peter Kravanja. 2015. *Embodied Cognition and Cinema*. Leuven: Leuven University Press.

Cole, Samantha. 2018. "We Are Truly Fucked: Everyone Is Making AI-Generated Fake Porn Now." *Motherboard*, January 25, 2018. https://motherboard.vice.com/en_us/article/bjye8a/reddit-fake-porn-app-daisy-ridley.

De Melo, Celso M., Peter J. Carnevale, Stephen J. Read, and Jonathan Gratch. 2014. "Reading People's Minds from Emotion Expressions in Interdependent Decision Making." *Journal of Personality and Social Psychology* 106 (1): 73–88. doi:10.1037/a0034525.

Deplazes, Anna, Agomoni Ganguli-Mitra, and Nikola Biller-Andorno. 2009. "The Ethics of Synthetic Biology: Outlining the Agenda." In *Synthetic Biology: The Technoscience and its Societal Consequences*, ed. Markus Schmidt, Alexander Kelle, Agomoni Ganguli-Mitra, and Huib de Vriend, 65–79. Dordrecht, The Netherlands: Springer.

Doane, Mary Anne. 2004. "Technophilia: Technology, Representation and the Feminine." In *Liquid Metal: The Science Fiction Film Reader*, ed. Sean Redmond, 176–190. London: Wallflower Press.

Douglas, Thomas, and Julian Savulescu. 2010. "Synthetic Biology and the Ethics of Knowledge." *Journal of Medical Ethics* 36 (11): 687–693. doi:10.1136/jme.2010.038232.

Draude, Claude. 2017. "Passing as Human." In *Computing Bodies: Gender Codes and Anthropomorphic Design at the Human-Computer Interface*, 183–202. Wiesbaden, Germany: Springer.

Dymond, Marcus. 2016. "Synthetic Biology, Culture, and Bioethical Considerations." In *Synthetic Biology Handbook*, ed. Darren Nesbeth, 3–34. London: CRC Press.

Feng, Andrew, Evan S. Rosenberg, and Ari Shapiro. 2017. "Just-in-Time, Viable, 3-D Avatars from Scans." *Computer Animation and Virtual Worlds* 28 (3–4): 1–8. doi:10.1002/cav.1769.

Graham, Elaine. 2002. *Representations of the Post/Human*. New Brunswick, NJ: Rutgers University Press.

Gratch, Jonathan. 2014. "Understanding the Mind by Simulating the Body: Virtual Humans as a Tool for Cognitive Science Research." University of Southern California, 1–30. Unpublished. http://people.ict.usc.edu/~gratch/papers/Gratch-Handbook-Chapter.pdf.

Haraway, Donna. 1991. "A Cyborg Manifesto: Science, Technology, and Socialist-Feminism in the Late Twentieth Century." In *Simians, Cyborgs and Women: The Reinvention of Nature*, 149–181. New York: Routledge.

Hayles, N. Katherine. 1999. *How We Become Posthuman: Virtual Bodies in Cybernetics, Literature, and Informatics*. Chicago: University of Chicago Press.

Hoorn, Johan, Elly Konijn, and Matthijs Pontier. 2019. "Dating a Synthetic Character Is Like Dating a Man." *International Journal of Social Robotics* 11 (2): 235–253. doi:10.1007/s12369-018-0496-1.

Kakoudaki, Despina. 2014. *Anatomy of a Robot: Literature, Cinema and the Cultural Work of Artificial Humans*. New Brunswick, NJ: Rutgers University Press.

Kirby, David. 2011. *Lab Coats in Hollywood: Science, Scientists, and Cinema*. Cambridge, MA: MIT Press.

Kuhn, Annette. 1990. *Alien Zone: Cultural Theory and Contemporary Science Fiction*. London: Verso.

Laine, Samuli, Tero Karras, Timo Aila, Antti Herva . . . and Jaakko Lehtinen. 2017. "Production-Level Facial Performance Capture Using Deep Convolutional Neural Networks." In *Proceedings of SCA 2017*, Los Angeles, CA, USA, 28–30 July. doi:10.1145/3099564.3099581.

Leslie, Tim, Nathan Hoad, and Ben Spraggon. 2018a. "Can You Tell a Real Video from a Fake One?" *ABC Online*, September 27, 2018. http://www.abc.net.au/news/2018-09-27/fake-news-part-one/10308638.

Leslie, Tim, Nathan Hoad, and Ben Spraggon. 2018b. "How Hard Is it to Make a Believable Deepfake?" *ABC Online*, September 28, 2018. http://www.abc.net.au/news/2018-09-28/fake-news-how-hard-is-it-to-make-a-deepfake-video/10313906.

Li, Hao. 2016. "Democratizing Human Digitization." *TEDxHollywood*. YouTube Video, 14:47. 7 November. https://www.youtube.com/watch?v=RBytZiKSiSU.

Mack, David. 2018. "This PSA about Fake News from Barack Obama Is Not What it Appears." *Buzzfeed*, April 17, 2018. https://www.buzzfeednews.com/article/davidmack/obama-fake-news-jordan-peele-psa-video-buzzfeed.

Meyer, Angela, Amelie Cserer, and Markus Schmidt. 2013. "Frankenstein 2.0.: Identifying and Characterizing Synthetic Biology Engineers in Science Fiction Films." *Life Sciences, Society and Policy* 9 (9): 1–17. http://hdl.handle.net/20.500.11790/578

Montgomery, John. 2017. "MPC Replicating Rachael in *Blade Runner 2049*." *FX Guide*, October 20, 2017. https://www.fxguide.com/featured/mpc-replicating-rachael-in-blade-runner-2049/.

North, Dan. 2008. *Performing Illusions: Cinema, Special Effects and the Virtual Actor*. London: Wallflower Press.

Purse, Lisa. 2007. "Digital Heroes in Contemporary Hollywood: Exertion, Identification, and the Virtual Action Body." *Film Criticism* 32 (1): 5–25. https://www.jstor.org/stable/24777381.

Purse, Lisa. 2013. *Digital Imaging in Popular Cinema*. Edinburgh: Edinburgh University Press.

Purse, Lisa. 2018. "Layered Encounters: Mainstream Cinema and the Disaggregate Digital Composite." *Film-Philosophy* 22 (2): 148–167. doi:10.3366/film.2018.0070.

Pyle, Forest. 1993. "Making Cyborgs, Making Humans: Of Terminators and Blade Runners." In *Film Theory Goes to the Movies*, ed. Jim Collins, 227–241. New York: Routledge.

Ren, Xiaoping, Ming Li, Xin Zhao, Zehan Liu . . . and Sergio Canavero. 2017. "First Cephalosomatic Anastomosis in a Human Model." *Surgical Neurology International* 8 (1): 276. doi:10.4103/sni.sni_415_17.

Saito, Shunsuke, Lingyu Wei, Liwen Hu, Koki Nagano, and Hao Li. 2017. "Photorealistic Facial Texture Inference Using Deep Neural Networks." In *Proceedings of the 30th IEEE International Conference on Computer Vision and Pattern Recognition 2017*, 5144–5153, Computer Vision Foundation Open Access.

Scherer, Stefan, Louis-Philippe Morency, Jonathan Gratch, and John Pestian. 2015. "Reduced Vowel Space is a Robust Indicator of Psychological Distress: A Cross-Corpus Analysis." In 2015 *IEEE International Conference on Acoustics, Speech and Signal Processing* (ICASSP), 4789–4793, Brisbane, Australia.

Schmeink, Lars. 2015. "Frankenstein's Offspring: Practicing Science and Parenthood in Natali's *Splice*." *Science Fiction Film and Television* 8 (3): 343–369. doi:10.3828/sfftv.2015.23.

Schmidt, Markus, Lei Pei, and Nediljko Budisa. 2018. "Xenobiology: State-of-the-Art, Ethics, and Philosophy of New-to-Nature Organisms." *Advances in Biochemical Engineering/Biotechnology* 162: 301–315. doi:10.1007/10_2016_14.

Schofield, Damian. 2018. "Digital Emotion: How Audiences React to Robots on Screen." *Computer Applications: An International Journal* 5 (1): 1–20. doi:10.5121/caij.2018.5101.

Shaw, Julia. 2015. "From *Homo Economicus* to *Homo Roboticus*: An Exploration of the Transformative Impact of the Technological Imaginary." *International Journal of Law in Context* 11 (3): 245–264. doi:10.1017/S1744552315000130.

Short, Sue. 2004. *Cyborg Cinema and Contemporary Subjectivity*. Basingstoke, UK: Palgrave Macmillan.

Smith, Murray. 2017. *Film, Art and the Third Culture: A Naturalized Aesthetics of Film*. Oxford: Oxford University Press.

Sobchack, Vivian. 2016. "From Screen-Scape to Screen-Sphere: A Meditation in Medias Res." In *Screens: From Materiality to Spectatorship—A Historical and Theoretical Reassessment*, ed. Dominique Chateau and José Moure, 157–175. Amsterdam: Amsterdam University Press.

Telotte, J. P. 1983. "Human Artifice and the Science Fiction Film." *Film Quarterly* 36 (3): 44–51. doi:10.2307/3697349.

Thubagere, Anupama J., Wei Li, Robert F. Johnson, Zibo Chen, Shayan Doroudi . . . and Lulu Qian. 2017. "A Cargo-Sorting DNA Robot." *Science* 357 (1112): 1–9. doi:10.1126/science.aan6558.

Trenholm, Richard. 2017. "How *Blade Runner 2049* Made Sean Young Young Again." *CNET CBS Interactive*, October 20, 2017. https://www.cnet.com/pictures/recreating-rachael-in-blade-runner-2049-sean-young-mpc/.

Wilbanks, Rebecca. 2018. "A Human Genome Synthesis Project: The Crazy Constructive Science of BBC America's *Orphan Black*." *Occasion* 12: 1–11. https://arcade.stanford.edu/sites/default/files/article_pdfs/Occasion_v12_wilbanks_final.pdf

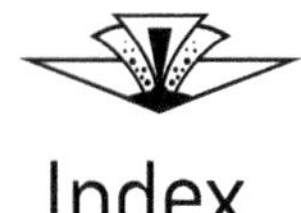

# Index